Perspectives in Jewish Population Research

Westview Replica Editions

The concept of Westview Replica Editions is a response to the continuing crisis in academic and informational publishing. Library budgets for books have been severely curtailed. Ever larger portions of general library budgets are being diverted from the purchase of books and used for data banks, computers, micromedia, and other methods of information retrieval. Interlibrary loan structures further reduce the edition sizes required to satisfy the needs of the scholarly community. Economic pressures on the university presses and the few private scholarly publishing companies have severely limited the capacity of the industry to properly serve the academic and research communities. As a result, many manuscripts dealing with important subjects, often representing the highest level of scholarship, are no longer economically viable publishing projects--or, if accepted for publication, are typically subject to lead times ranging from one to three years.

Westview Replica Editions are our practical solution to the problem. We accept a manuscript in camera-ready form, typed according to our specifications, and move it immediately into the production process. As always, the selection criteria include the importance of the subject, the work's contribution to scholarship, and its insight, originality of thought, and excellence of exposition. The responsibility for editing and proofreading lies with the author or sponsoring institution. We prepare chapter headings and display pages, file for copyright, and obtain Library of Congress Cataloging in Publication Data. A detailed manual contains simple instructions for preparing the final typescript, and our editorial staff is always available to answer questions.

The end result is a book printed on acid-free paper and bound in sturdy library-quality soft covers. We manufacture these books ourselves using equipment that does not require a lengthy make-ready process and that allows us to publish first editions of 300 to 600 copies and to reprint even smaller quantities as needed. Thus, we can produce Replica Editions quickly and can keep even very specialized books in print as long as there is a demand for them.

About the Book and Editors

Perspectives in Jewish Population Research

edited by Steven M. Cohen, Jonathan S. Woocher, and Bruce A. Phillips

Addressing methodological and substantive research problems common to local Jewish population studies, the contributors to this book present the most recent research findings on such problems as how to design studies that will make a contribution to social science knowledge as well as have a strong impact on the planning process; methods of sampling that will optimize the trade-offs between costs and accuracy; how to develop a comparative framework so that results from individual communities may be fruitfully understood in a larger context; and which questions should be asked in surveys and how. Detailed essays discuss every step of the research process. The book includes a compendium of findings from several recent population studies as well as an annotated inventory of questionnaire items, all of which should prove useful to researchers and communities planning to undertake Jewish population studies.

Steven M. Cohen, senior research associate, Center for Modern Jewish Studies, Brandeis University, is also associate professor of sociology at Queens College, CUNY and author of *American Modernity and Jewish Identity* (1983). Bruce A. Phillips is associate professor of Jewish communal studies at the Hebrew Union College-Jewish Institute of Religion, Los Angeles and Jonathan S. Woocher is assistant professor of Jewish communal service at Brandeis University.

Published in cooperation with the
Center for Modern Jewish Studies,
Brandeis University

Perspectives in Jewish Population Research

edited by Steven M. Cohen,
Jonathan S. Woocher, and Bruce A. Phillips

Routledge
Taylor & Francis Group
LONDON AND NEW YORK

First published 1984 by Westview Press

Published 2019 by Routledge
52 Vanderbilt Avenue, New York, NY 10017
2 Park Square, Milton Park, Abingdon, Oxon OX14 4RN

Routledge is an imprint of the Taylor & Francis Group, an informa business

Library of Congress Catalog Card Number: 84-50660

ISBN 13: 978-0-367-28268-4 (hbk)
ISBN 13: 978-0-367-29814-2 (pbk)

Contents

Foreword

The local Jewish population survey is a remarkable phenomenon in American Jewish life, particularly because it constitutes a development brought about by local sentiment rather than mandated by a national Jewish agency. To be sure, a national Jewish agency--the Council of Jewish Federations--serves as a resource for its affiliates, the federations, when they are considering the desirability of conducting a local population survey. However, the Council does not carry out such studies. It confines its efforts to consultation with local leaders and staff members.

The Jewish population survey, then, is the result of local initiative. It demonstrates the desire of local leaders to comprehend the changes occurring in their community. The survey signifies that local leaders are aware of social change and desire to plan for the future. Their hope is that ways to mitigate the effect of developments which could have negative effects on the community's viability and future prospects will emerge from the survey.

The survey is not an entirely new development. Surveys were conducted in the 1930s and 1940s and even earlier. However, only in recent years have Jewish population surveys become commonplace. Almost invariably the Jewish population survey is conducted under the auspices of the local federation, though an outside expert may be retained to design and implement the study plan. The local federation is responsible for financing the survey.

The proliferation of Jewish population surveys indicates that even in a country where individualism is prized, and where individuals are--in theory--free to cast off their inherited religion or ethnic identity, a feeling of community survives. If it did not Jewish population surveys could not be initiated, and if initiated would not be completed. The cooperation of respondents is essential for the success of the survey. Respondents must answer a relatively lengthy questionnaire which may include some rather sensitive items. Furthermore, respondents are not offered money or any material reward for their participation. There is also the fear that since the survey is conducted by a federation--an organization whose task it is to conduct an annual campaign for local, national and international Jewish needs--that the information volunteered by the respondent will be utilized to request a larger gift. Despite these factors a local federation is on solid ground in taking for granted that the cooperation required to complete the survey will be forthcoming.

Although feelings of Jewish identification undergird the population survey, such feelings may be more complicated than appear on the surface.

The preparation of lists for a survey means pinpointing individuals who are Jewish. At various times in the contemporary period this has given rise to feelings of ambivalence and anxiety. Jews have been particularly sensitive to any listing in official sources. Thus the majority of Jewish organizations (and presumably the majority of Jews) have registered strong opposition to the introduction of a question on religion in the Decennial Census. This despite the fact that such a question would be the most economical and scientifically valid way of obtaining national population data about Jews. The vehemence of the objection by Jews to an official question on religion suggests that more is at stake than concern with a possible breach in the wall of separation between church and state.

Sensitivities about possible negative consequences have been demonstrated even when a survey is to be conducted under Jewish auspices. Some individuals become concerned that their name will be included on a list--a list which in their view could be used to their detriment. The most extreme version of this sentiment maintains that if anti-Semitism became rife in American society inclusion on a list could have fatal consequences. The truth of the matter is that the individual's name and identity are already available, particularly if the person has given to a Jewish philanthropy or belongs to a Jewish organization. Furthermore, even if the individual refuses to be interviewed, his name will appear on a list of refusals. Although a fearful potential respondent may have some understanding of the purposes of the survey he focuses only upon what he conceives to be its dangerous aspects. He may view the survey as the one place in a world which is unfriendly to Jews where his identity can be ascertained.

These feelings are a kind of "underground." We do not know what percentage of refusals are traceable to such sentiments. In any case, whatever the nature of an individual's misgivings, the bulk of potential respondents cooperate in the study. As a result the rate of refusal in a properly-conducted Jewish population survey is well within tolerable limits.

As is evident from the contents of this volume the Jewish population survey is not a standardized product. The questionnnaire differs from community to community. The study plan differs from place to place. Given the fact that the population survey is a result of local initiative it could hardly be otherwise. Social scientists would be delighted if all communities utilized the same questionnaire and the identical sampling design. However, each community feels it is special and requires a custom-designed study. In addition the size of the budget differs from city to city.

Localistic orientations have not been countered by pressure coming from national agencies. To be sure, if the study director has conducted several surveys he will draw upon his previous work. Thus there may be some degree of comparability, though it is accidental. The end of the matter is that social scientists encounter considerable difficulty when they seek to integrate the results of several studies and to draw generalizations. Their frustrations do not impress federation leaders. The leaders maintain that while social science has its value, its advancement is not a responsibility of federation. In the view of both lay leaders and staff the contribution of any given study to social-science research is secondary, and in fact serendipitous.

Despite this view of federation leadership population surveys have been of enormous help to students of American Jewish life. While the lack of comparability is frustrating the population surveys are an indispensable source of hard data. The studies contain information on demographic trends as well as issues relating to religious life, philanthropic giving, intermarriage, participation in Jewish organizational life, and a dozen other topics. To be sure the Jewish population surveys are not the exclusive source for such data. It is sometimes possible to utilize research done for other purposes, such as a health survey, where an item on religion was included in the questionnaire. In such a situation one can separate out the Jewish respondents. One can also compare Jewish and non-Jewish respondents. However, this effort is worthwhile only for studies conducted in a handful of metropolitan communities where there are sizeable concentrations of Jewish population. Futhermore, many problems that one would like to inquire into cannot be investigated. For example, the health survey may be utilized to understand the geographic distribution of the Jewish population, but it will not yield data on attitudes toward philanthropic giving.

The importance of the local community survey is magnified by the absence of research on the national level. There is only one national study --the National Jewish Population Study (NJPS) completed in 1971 under the auspices of the Council of Jewish Federations. Since no complete study report was ever issued, the impact of the NJPS was diluted. Furthermore, the Council never conducted a second study. Each year the results of the NJPS become more historical rather than contemporary.

In contrast to inactivity on the national front several new local studies are commissioned each year. Most of them issue their findings in reasonably prompt fashion. Increasingly study reports have become shorter, more heavily illustrated, and designed for easier readability. The obvious purpose is to command the attention of local individuals who would not be attracted to a "heavy" report.

One of the most attractive features of the local Jewish population survey is its dynamic character. This dynamism is frequently traceable to local leadership as much as it is to the study director. Each survey goes through a process whereby the study director solicits the opinions of local leaders regarding what should be included in the study. The dynamic character of the study is traceable--at least in part--to the suggestions of the leadership. While in some cases leaders may confuse their own agenda with that of the community, they generally can report with some degree of accuracy what their fellow Jews are thinking and feeling. Intermarriage is a good example. The studies done some decades ago rarely asked questions about the phenomenon of intermarriage. By way of contrast present-day studies invariably have items on intermarriage. Furthermore, the questions have increased in number and in sophistication. The Jewish population survey, then, is not static. Given the fact that it is sponsored locally and has the input of local leaders, it is frequently an accurate reflection of changing concerns in the Jewish community. Finally, the dynamic character of the population surveys increases their utility for the student of American Jewry.

* * *

Like other significant aspects fo American Jewish life the existence of local Jewish population surveys represents the interaction of Jewish needs and attitudes with the character of the culture-at-large. The United States is singular in its utilization of public opinion polls to measure preferences for political candidates at closely-spaced intervals. Then there are the multitudinous surveys sponsored by large companies as well as by non-profit organizations. These surveys deal with such diverse matters as preferences in alcoholic beverages, automobiles, beauty products, as well as sex habits and the care of elderly parents.

To be sure, urban Americans are increasingly wary of admitting a stranger to their home. The problem of accessibility, as well as that of rising costs, have made it more practical in many surveys to utilize a telephone interview rather than a face-to-face interview. It would seem, however, that the telephone survey would have to neglect the significant group who have unlisted phone numbers. But the use of random numbers makes it possible to contact even the unlisted. Only the telephone answering machine remains a formidable barrier between interviewer and interviewee. Use of such devices is found in a relatively small percentage of households, though the number appears to constantly increase. The final problem is the "refusals." They are encountered in every survey, whatever the content or the auspices. "Refusals" will not respond to even the most persuasive interviewer or supervisor. Despite the national proclivity to participate in surveys these individuals withhold their cooperation. Some do so with pride.

This book, then, is devoted to the subject of the Jewish population survey. It is a unique volume both because of its contents and its contributors--all of them involved in Jewish population surveys in one way or another. Perspectives in Jewish Population Research is at the same time a very Jewish and a very American book. It is Jewish in the sense that it demonstrates how the largest Jewish community on the globe has sought to learn about itself and to use the knowledge gained in a meaningful fashion. It is American in that the enterprise of the Jewish population survey is hardly conceivable in other nations. American openness, American curiosity about oneself and about one's neighbor, and American trust in talking to a stranger, all play their part in the Jewish population survey.

If this volume contributes to the advancement of the field of Jewish population research we at the Center for Modern Jewish Studies of Brandeis University will deem our labor worthwhile.

Marshall Sklare

Introduction

Since 1979, we have witnessed a surge in the number of American Jewish federations sponsoring local Jewish population studies. Significantly, these include some of the largest American Jewish communities: New York, Los Angeles, Chicago, Philadelphia, among others. The simultaneous conduct of so many surveys has helped generate not only a wealth of up-to-date information on American Jews, but also an informal network of researchers and planners in the field of Jewish population research.

The Workshop in Jewish Population Studies at the Center for Modern Jewish Studies, Brandeis University (October 31 through November 2, 1982) drew upon and enhanced that growing network of scholars and practitioners. This conference--the first of its kind--brought together over two dozen leading researchers and professional planners to exchange their insights and experiences in the design, conduct, and utilization of Jewish population studies. Their discussions identified common problems and pitfalls as well as preferred solutions. They also pointed to several gaps in our collective understanding, questions and issues demanding further attention and exploration.

The papers collected in this volume are an outgrowth, and by no means a replication, of the presentations made at that conference. Three of the authors, in fact, were asked to contribute to this collection even though they were unable to attend the conference. Most of the other papers emerged from or followed upon the three days of intense discussion.

If there is a single theme or purpose to the volume it is simply to increase the value of local Jewish population studies while restraining their costs, both financial and human. The authors generally draw upon mistakes they and others have made so that researchers and planners in future studies need not reinvent the wheel (or the questionnaire, sampling procedure, or mode of analysis and interpretation). Not only will attention to the contents of this volume sharply reduce the professional time and scarce money needlessly spent in initially clarifying objective research techniques, social relationships, and design elements, but it will also permit researchers and planners to start their prestudy consultations at much higher levels of sophistication.

The volume is divided into three parts. The first, "Initiating and Utilizing Local Jewish Population Studies," will be of particular interest to planners, lay leaders, and other sponsors or consumers of Jewish population research. The authors elucidate the intimate connection between sound initial design of a population study and its effective utilization months or even years later. The second part, "Issues in Data Collection and Analysis," is written primarily for the researcher with sponsors reading over his or her shoulder. It shares experiences in the conduct of research which could help the researcher avoid some of the common pitfalls in sampling and data collection and in advising the client on alternative or supplementary approaches to the conventional random sample survey. The last part, "Resources for Questionnaire Design and Interpretation of Findings," should assist both sponsors and researchers in deciding what questions to ask in a Jewish population study and how the answers they obtain compare with those obtained in other studies.

The fourteen articles represent what might be called state-of-the-art thinking in a highly fluid field. While they cover many important aspects of Jewish population research, they cannot treat all the crucial questions that researchers, planners, and volunteer leaders typically encounter in conducting a local Jewish population study. While they may represent some of the most advanced thinking in their respective areas, the very dynamism of the field implies that that thinking may soon be surpassed by further refinements and developments. And while they often represent the lessons of experience and the shared insights of several thoughtful individuals, in no sense do they mean to suggest that only one approach is valid or correct.

Thus, while the pooling of information and of experience on this scale may be the most significant endeavor of its kind to date, this volume should be regarded merely as a first step, rather than as the last word; we certainly approach this enterprise with due modesty and tentativeness. That said, we do also believe these papers have much to offer anyone--researchers, planners, and lay leaders--who is seriously involved in Jewish population research, from its early design phases to its eventual utilization.

Steven M. Cohen

Acknowledgments

In the fall of 1982 the Center for Modern Jewish Studies of Brandeis University convened a Workshop in Jewish Population Studies. The Workshop brought together survey researchers, federation planners, and social scientists who had substantial expertise in the conduct of local Jewish population studies. This volume is an outgrowth of that Workshop.

The convening of the Workshop, as well as this publication, owes much to the support of Professor Marshall Sklare, the Director of the Center. For several decades Professor Sklare had utilized the results of Jewish population surveys. In the course of his work he became acutely aware of the limitations of the surveys. Thus he conceived of the Workshop as a first step in the improvement of the surveys so that their utility to the scientific community, as well as to Jewish communal agencies, would be materially increased.

All of us join in thanking Mrs. Abby Shapiro, who served as coordinator of the Workshop. Mrs. Shapiro did her job with a unique mixture of tact and firmness; the result was a meeting in which the arrangements were first-class. We are also grateful to Mrs. Shapiro's husband, Edward Shapiro, for assisting us despite his busy schedule.

The devoted service of Larry Sternberg, Assistant Director of the Center, was crucial in seeing this volume through from conception to completed book. He prodded editors and authors to finish their assignments. He supervised the flow of paper and attended to the multitudinous administrative tasks which inevitably accompany the assembling of an edited volume with a large number of authors.

Sylvia Riese spent many hours typing and copying the papers contained in this volume. She deserves our thanks for her expertise.

Nila Pusin Sklare meticulously copyedited the manuscript. She offered numerous editorial suggestions resulting in revisions which substantially improved the quality of the writing.

We are fortunate to have retained the services of the Word Processing Bureau, Inc. of Boston, headed by Harry Friedmann. Mr. Friedmann's skills and those of his staff are apparent throughout this volume. We are especially grateful to him for his suggestions about layout; they greatly improve the appearance of the volume. We also appreciate his ability to retain a sense of humor even when confronted with material which required special handling and care.

A volume of this type would be impossible were it not for the willingness of numerous federations to share with researchers the results of their studies. While many are cited in the course of the volume, we offer our collective thanks.

Last but not least we wish to record our gratitude to our contributors. To our knowledge this is the first volume of its kind. Our contributors had the courage to join us in an enterprise whose success could not be assured in advance.

This book was made possible by funds granted by the Charles H. Revson Foundation. The statements made and the views expressed, however, are solely the responsibility of the authors.

S.M.C.
J.S.W.
B.A.P.

PART ONE

Initiating and Utilizing Local Jewish Population Studies

Studying the Jewish population is too important an endeavor to be left to demographers. This, in effect, has become the credo of North America's Jewish federations. Over the past several decades, federations have initiated and conducted dozens of local Jewish population studies which have provided a wealth of information for academics, planners, and communal leaders.

Local Jewish population studies are not exercises in pure research. They are undertaken in order to help Jewish federations and other communal organizations better serve and win the support of the Jews who comprise both their clientele and constituency. Because of the unique purposes of these studies, and the unique research environment in which they are conducted, no textbook "recipe" can insure that a population study will in fact justify the cost and effort expended on it. There are a myriad of issues which must be addressed if a local Jewish population study is to be a success not only from a technical standpoint, but as a contribution to communal self-understanding and development.

This section focuses on these issues and on the process of translating a local Jewish population study from an attractive idea to a usable (and used) communal resource. The six papers that follow constitute a clear warning to the sponsors of Jewish population studies: If you fail in the beginning to think through the purposes of your study and how it is to be used, or to establish the appropriate working relationships among all those intimately involved, you court waste, frustration, and ultimately failure.

The first paper in this section, by Jonathan S. Woocher and Steven M. Cohen, offers step-by-step guidelines for conducting a population study geared toward maximal effective use of the results. The authors examine both pre-study and post-study factors that affect such utilization, and outline ways of addressing several primary areas of concern--community preparation, determination of research goals and needs, use of existing data, selection of a consultant, budgeting for the study, activation of a planning process, presenting the results to different audiences, and utilizing the study data for making policy decisions and for other purposes.

Gary A. Tobin, who designed and carried out the recent study of the Jewish population of St. Louis, focuses on the critical process of building communal support for a study from its inception. He illustrates the many ways in which the initiators of a study must work from the outset to create a communal environment in which the study results will be accepted and used. By involving key actors in the process from the beginning, and by being sensitive to the political implications of a population study, it is possible to put together a coalition which will both support the endeavor and promote the utilization of its results.

Facilitating effective utilization involves more, however, than sustaining support for the study. Results must be communicated and interpreted to those who will actually be making and implementing key decisions, as well as to the Jewish population at large. Peter Friedman, Director of Research for the Chicago Jewish Federation, discusses this process, outlining some of the major choices to be made and the techniques available for helping community leaders and members understand the implications of what a study uncovers. Friedman emphasizes as well the vital importance of planning for communicating and interpreting study results long before the data have been compiled. He clarifies the relationships between analysis, interpretation, and dissemination of the results of a population study, and highlights some of the most common types and causes of misinterpretation.

The primary significance of population studies for Jewish federations lies in their contribution to the planning and policy-making process. Jacob B. Ukeles and Steven Huberman, Planning Department Directors for North America's two largest federations, New York and Los Angeles respectively, examine some of the specific ways in which population study data can be brought to bear on communal decision-making. In the first part of his paper, Ukeles reinforces the point made throughout this section: that every aspect of conducting a population study involves political considerations. Even the decision to accept and publicize the estimates of population size and distribution generated by a study must be made in the context of its impact on the position of the federation within the Jewish and general communities.

In light of the substantial financial investment required to conduct a population study, federations naturally wish to get every bit of use possible from the data collected. Both Ukeles and Huberman illustrate that population studies can indeed provide critical information on a variety of issues for community planners. They emphasize as well, however, that maximizing the value of that information requires careful planning. Every phase of the study process, from generation of research hypotheses and questionnaire design to integration of population study data with other types of information and the establishment of mechanisms for ongoing use of the data, affects the extent to which the study will contribute significantly and positively to communal decision-making. As an illustration of how population study data can be brought together with other types of information (in this case, needs assessments involving key informants) to influence policy-making, Huberman presents the experience of Los Angeles, whose community priorities system is one of the most sophisticated in North America.

Federations have not in the past had uniformly positive experiences in conducting population studies. Often the results have been disappointing to community leaders. From his vantage point in the Community Planning Department of the Council of Jewish Federations, Lester I. Levin highlights some of the reasons why local population studies have on occasion not met the expectations of their initiators. He also outlines ways in which federations can secure a greater return on their investment, including alternatives to full-scale population studies.

1
Guidelines for the Design and Use of Jewish Population Studies

Jonathan S. Woocher and Steven M. Cohen

The process of conducting a Jewish population study is deceptively simple: make the decision, hire a consultant (or designate a staff member), write a questionnaire, make the phone calls, compile the results, and write the report. Yet in practice, many pitfalls can make the conduct of a Jewish population study a veritable nightmare. Perhaps the most fearsome spectre is that of a study conducted with great fanfare and at great expense, that in the end produces nothing of value in terms of the goals and needs of the Jewish community itself. Technical pitfalls can be avoided by using competent researchers. But only the federation itself can insure that the study will ultimately be worth its cost by virtue of its contribution to the community's efforts in planning, fund-raising, and service provision.

In this paper we present guidelines to help a sponsoring organization effectively utilize the study in which it has heavily invested. We emphasize avoiding the most common pitfalls which have ensnared federations that have undertaken population studies. We also point to several positive steps that communities have taken to enhance significantly the extent and quality of research utilization. Our purpose is to provide a step-by-step guide for the federation that wants not only to conduct, but to use, a population study in the most effective manner.

FEDERATIONS AND PLANNING

The development of federations into what Daniel Elazar calls the "framing institutions" of the American Jewish polity has been tied to their growing activity and sophistication as planning instruments for the American Jewish community. The initial impulse for the creation of federations was the perceived need not only for more effective fund-raising, but for improving and coordinating services being offered by the charitable agencies of the day. As early as the second decade of this century, Jewish social service workers and organizations were advocating systematic demographic and social research as a vital component of a program of communal planning. In the 1920s, the Bureau of Jewish Social Research (a forerunner of the Council of Jewish Federations) conducted or helped spur communal surveys in New York, Chicago, Cleveland, Boston, Washington, D.C., and a number of other communities, large and small. The post-World War II period saw a new wave of population studies, as federation planning became institutionalized in nearly every community of moderate or larger size.

At least four different types of activities can be placed under the rubric of the federation planning function:

1. Campaign planning: Identifying population segments to be targeted for fund-raising efforts and projecting approaches likely to be effective.
2. Budgeting and allocations: Deciding how the resources available over a given period of time should be allocated among various agencies and programs.
3. Service and program planning: Determining the need for services and programs in the community and assessing the adequacy of current endeavors in these areas.
4. Strategic or long-range planning: Identifying trends in the environment, client population, and organization system that are likely to affect long-term service and program needs, and developing strategic objectives and priorities to guide program and service planning activities.

The information developed in a Jewish population study can be of value to each of these types of planning. However, a population study is not equally useful to all, and the additional information needed for effective planning of each type will vary.

The term "population study" can refer to a variety of surveys differing dramatically in both scope and content. The choice as to what should be included in a population study should be made in light of its intended use. Almost all population studies provide data about the size, composition, and characteristics of the population in a community. A population study can also be useful as part of "needs assessment." For this purpose, however, the study should include appropriate questions beyond those usually associated with pure demographic data. Similarly, a population study can be a tool in campaign planning, provided it is structured appropriately from the outset. In general, population studies will have minimal relevance to immediate budgetary decisions, though the information produced may help to guide long-term shifts in allocations via changes in priorities and identified needs.

In any given instance, the value of a population study for planning purposes will depend on both the context in which it is to be used and the other sources of information currently or prospectively available. Some studies are improperly matched to their context: they fail to reach the right population, or fail to ask the right questions; or they cannot be integrated with existing data. Obviously such studies have greatly reduced value, even though they might be technically sound, and perhaps even useful in other planning contexts. Likewise, other sources of data, either currently or potentially available, may be more valuable and appropriate than population studies for some planning tasks. Since planning is, in addition, always a process involving more than simply assembling and analyzing information--values and political considerations must be factored in as well--the value of a population study will depend on a variety of factors other than its intrinsic merit. Thus the community undertaking or contemplating a population study must always be alert to the ways in which it will want to use the data, and the total context within which it will be utilized, even before the process is initiated.

ALTERNATIVE AND SUPPLEMENTAL DATA SOURCES

Several other sources of data, most of which are low-cost or virtually free, are readily available. These data sources can tell us either about the local Jewish population or about the areas in which Jews live. They can provide valuable information to supplement the population study and, for some purposes, can even totally obviate the need for a costly large-scale Jewish population study.

For example, by using death records available from official sources or funeral homes, researchers can readily establish the size, age structure, residential patterns, and illnesses typifying the local Jewish elderly population (see Ira Rosenwaike's article in this volume). Moreover, these types of information can be similarly derived for the local non-Jewish population, allowing one to determine distinctive characteristics of the Jewish elderly.

Real estate agents and analyses of recent home buyers and sellers from public records of real estate transactions can be useful in identifying new or declining areas of Jewish settlement and in estimating the influx or outflow of Jewish migrants.

Electric and gas utilities maintain detailed and updated information on population movement so as to better plan their facilities. While they will not make their customer records available, their analyses of internal migration trends when coupled with information on neighborhood characteristics can be useful in forecasting Jewish population movement as well.

Telephone directories readily provide reasonably accurate information on the distribution of the local Jewish population, even though by themselves they can offer only limited information as to the size of the population. Clerks can note the distribution of listings with Distinctive Jewish Names (DJNs) classifying them by address or neighborhood. These records may be compiled year by year so as to provide an ongoing indication of the shifting patterns of settlement. The A. B. Data Corporation of Milwaukee regularly applies an ethnication program to a national sample of 55 million telephone listings. The program identifies roughly 40 percent of Jewish households and --due to intermarriage, name-changing, and other historic reasons--includes a small percentage of non-Jews with Jewish names as well. As a result, for each zip code in the country, A. B. Data maintains an annual count of listed DJN households, which can be used as an index of local Jewish population distribution. Comparisons of changes in the index over several years can give a fairly reliable picture of Jewish population movement.

Information on standard sociodemographic characteristics of the Jewish population and its size is often obtainable from local electoral surveys and market research studies. News organizations and academic institutions frequently conduct surveys of the general population and of the electorate. Although the number of Jews in any one study may be too small for reliable analysis, the results of several such studies may be merged to provide a reasonably accurate portrait of local Jewish population characteristics.

Analyses of agency records of client populations can tell much about the changing social service needs of the local Jewish population and the social characteristics of the client populations. The scope and quality of records maintained by service agencies vary dramatically from agency to agency and community to community. The usefulness of these records could be greatly enhanced if every family agency, summer camp, Jewish community center, school, synagogue, or other institution used a standardized form which would supply data to a central data entry and retrieval facility.

Finally, the large amount of data regularly collected by various government agencies and typically assembled at the local planning commission or other such body can be extremely useful in constructing a picture of the residential areas where Jews live. In addition to the U.S. Census, other sources of data include police statistics, school enrollments (size, racial composition), school performance (e.g., achievement tests), housing statistics (building type, ownership, code violations, sales prices), sanitation data (evaluations of street cleanliness), park and recreational evaluations, and a welter of health statistics.

The quality and usefulness of available data will vary by commmunity and by the local research needs. Nevertheless, alternative data sources may dramatically enhance the understanding of population study data, and, in some instances, they may make unnecessary the high-cost conventional Jewish population study using a sample survey design.

ALTERNATIVE AND SUPPLEMENTAL RESEARCH

Ideally, the data from the population study should be interpreted in conjunction with research from other relevant sources. We may divide such research into three areas: other local Jewish population studies, other Jewish social research, and social science research generally. All can offer useful insights and provide crucial background information to the Jewish population study. We may note illustrations from each area.

From other local Jewish population studies we learn that Jewish institutional affiliation rates (synagogue membership, organizational belonging, campaign contributions) vary dramatically from one community to another (see the compendium of studies prepared by Gary A. Tobin and Julie A. Lipsman, elsewhere in this volume). In particular, as professional practitioners well understand, smaller, stable communities tend to have much higher affiliation rates than larger or more residentially mobile areas. This instance is but one example illustrating the need to interpret population study data in the larger context of recent American (if not international) Jewish population research.

From the larger field of Jewish social research we learn several lessons, which can help frame both the design and the interpretation of a local Jewish population study. For example, we have learned that, contrary to recent speculation that many American Jews were translating their discomfort with particular policies of the Likud government into distancing from Israel, recent public opinion surveys show that the familial, personal, and spiritual connections between American Jewry and Israel have remained firm and unshaken, even as some American Jews have become more overtly critical of the Likud and its policies. Such information is useful not only for campaign planning, but also for Jewish educators and those concerned with local programming around Israel.

From general social science research we can cite evidence of drops in institutional affiliation and participation of all sorts in the three to five years following a residential move. Afterwards, participation in formal local institutions (such as houses of worship) recovers to previous or expected levels. The lesson for communal planners is to understand that areas of recent Jewish migration "should" have low rates of affiliation for several years, at least until such time as informal networks emerge and the community can be mobilized to create and participate in Jewish institutions.

Obviously, these examples by no means exhaust the type of information and interpretation that can be gleaned from years of research experience in cognate fields. However, they should serve to demonstrate the usefulness of having a command of allied research and of applying the lessons from that research to the interpretation of local Jewish population studies.

COMMUNITY PREPARATION: INVOLVING FEDERATION, THE AGENCIES, AND LOCAL JEWRY

If a population study is to be used effectively, the groundwork must be laid well in advance of the decision to undertake the study. As the article in this section by Tobin notes, the key elements in the community must be given a vested interest in the study and in its use. The St. Louis experience is a model of how lay and professional leaders in the Jewish community were involved in the following activities:

1. Reaching a consensus that a study was needed.
2. Appreciating the value of a study for the community and its various organizations.
3. Providing input into the research agenda.

All three elements are essential in community preparation. The process itself must operate at several different levels. The first is within the federation--i.e., winning the consent, understanding, and input of federation staff and lay leadership. The decision to undertake a population study should have the broadest possible base of support within the organization. Even those who will not be directly involved in carrying out, supervising, or using the research should be made to feel comfortable with the decision to proceed and should understand the value of the enterprise within the framework of the federation's mission and needs. Failure to secure this support can have several adverse effects:

1. In the worst case, opponents may try to sabotage the study process.
2. Lack of support or understanding at the outset may be translated into lack of willingness to accept (and implement) the results and conclusions of the study. Subsequent decisions in the federation based on the study results will likely require the support of individuals not intimately involved in the study process. If they have been totally excluded from initial decision-making and educational efforts, such support is less likely to be forthcoming.
3. The more federation leaders and staff are involved at the outset, the more likely it is that unanticipated contributions to the study process and unanticipated uses for the information produced will emerge.

The second level of community preparation goes beyond the federation to involve its agencies and other important Jewish organizations. Here again, the rationale for explicit efforts to secure support and input is straightforward: such support and input enhance the likelihood that the study will ask useful questions, and that its results will be accepted and utilized. The same considerations (though with somewhat less immediacy) apply at the final level of preparation as well, that of the Jewish community at large. Here explicit input is less significant, but a willingness on the part of those surveyed to participate is obviously critical.

There is no single correct way to prepare the community for a population study. The methods chosen will depend on several factors: the size of the community; its history and organizational structure; the level of awareness and climate of opinion already existing. Federation processes emphasize consensus-building around every major decision. A broadly representative committee with a strong chair and a senior-level staff member conducting the initial information gathering and transmission will promote acceptance of the project. The committee may be the planning committee itself, or a special subcommittee appointed for the purpose of ascertaining the need for the study and initiating the process.

Depending on the communal environment, federation agencies and other Jewish organizations may be involved at this stage through either formal or informal mechanisms. Personal or telephone consultations with important professionals and lay leaders will often suffice at this point. If more formal approaches seem called for, these may involve a series of meetings between the initiating committee and interested parties, or a questionnaire soliciting views on the proposed study. Whatever the mechanism, the process of preparation at this level is really a combination of "selling" the study concept and securing genuine input into its shape and scope before these are fixed.

For the community at large, direct communication through the Jewish (and general) media can be supplemented by indirect dissemination of information through the organizations and leaders reached directly by the federation.

An important caveat throughout this process of community preparation is to avoid "overselling" the study. Raising unrealistic expectations can complicate the task of interpreting and utilizing the results at later stages. And one should never overlook the possibility that a study simply may not be warranted, either because the need cannot be established or because key actors in the community are unwilling to cooperate.

DETERMINING THE RESEARCH PURPOSE

What can be taken from a study depends on what is put into it. In the simplest terms, no use can be made of data that are never gathered. Thus, in addition to preparing the community to support a population study, the sponsoring organization must, even before a consultant is engaged, determine what it wishes to learn through the study. The range of information which can be gathered is enormous, and the constraints of time and budgetary limitations require that some overall objectives be established for the study at the outset. The task of the study director is to translate these objectives into appropriate questions and, eventually, answers. But the consultant must know what information the community seeks before he or she can frame an approach for getting it.

A federation conducting a population study should be guided by several factors in determining the purposes of the research, including:

1. The state of knowledge already available to it. While there is no point in seeking information about that which one already

knows, acquiring reliable data to confirm or disconfirm what is suspected can be a very legitimate research aim.

2. The uses to which the results of the study will be put. A study designed to support a community-wide strategic planning process will seek information about a much broader range of issues than one which will be used only to guide planning for services to the elderly or to guide the decision whether to build a new facility.
3. The mechanisms and resources available to process the results. Gathering more information than can be effectively used by the consumers of the study data--primarily the federation itself--wastes resources that might more effectively be utilized elsewhere, including in the interpretation of the data.

A federation undertaking a population study should rank its priorities among the major areas in which it would like information. Typically, such lists will include a common core of areas of concern:

1. Population size and distribution.
2. Population characteristics in terms of a number of demographic and socioeconomic variables such as age, household structure, generation, residential history, education, occupation, and income.
3. Jewish identification and affiliation--synagogue membership, denominational preference, ritual observance, philanthropic activity, and Jewish education.

Population studies will also typically be undertaken for other purposes reflecting more idiosyncratic concerns as well. Examples include a desire to gather information about service utilization, or attitudes toward community issues or institutions, or special-needs populations. Such purposes are myriad and diverse. The primary rule in seeking special information is to seek that which is most likely to be used by someone. Much valuable specific information can be "piggy-backed" onto a planned omnibus population study. This should not, however, be done at the expense of more basic data which can feed into many planning contexts. As an example, recent studies in two intermediate cities incorporated extensive research on the elderly and singles, but lacked all but the most rudimentary information on Jewish identification for the population as a whole.

In defining what it wishes to know, the federation should be aware of what other communities have sought to study. Having access to comparative data can be of considerable value in many instances in interpreting local findings.

The process of determining research purposes provides an opportunity for building the base of institutional and communal support and understanding for the study spoken of above. By this point in the overall study process, if not sooner, a special study committee should be appointed and functioning. The committee will have responsibility for overseeing the entire process, and working closely with the study director. Ideally, its membership should include both individuals well situated politically within the organization and community, and persons with some degree of expertise in the social research field. (Too much expertise can sometimes be a problem. One federation found that its committee had so much expertise that it was meeting long into the night reviewing every aspect of the study process.)

The primary responsibility for determining the research purposes of the study should rest with the study committee. Others in the federation and the community, however, can and should be consulted. By inviting input into the process of choosing areas of information to be sought, the sponsor gives those responding a stake in the study. Input from a wide range of sources is valuable at this stage, as long as it is made clear (a) that not everything can be asked, and (b) that the final form in which questions will be posed will be determined by those carrying out the study.

After receiving input from several sources, those charged with setting the research agenda will need to decide among competing research priorities. Their task will be considerably eased if they take the time to think through the specific, detailed information they will ultimately need. Ideally, they will undertake the following steps:

1. Delineate a set of policy questions or issues facing the community. (Example: Is a particular service population large enough to warrant special services? If so, how do we best serve that population?)
2. Specify the information and the level of precision that will be needed to inform the policy formulation process. (Example: We need to know the size of the service population within 10,000; or we need an estimate of the extent to which it belongs to synagogues within a certain percentage.)
3. Define the particular measures or questions that will supply the requisite information. If possible, try to imagine the actual tables that will be run so as to make sure that particular items are included in the questionnaire. (Example: If the respondent or spouse is "Israeli," the birthplace of either or both is relevant to a definition of that term, as is the year of immigration to the U.S.; and the questionnaire should make provision for Israelis who are not native to Israel but lived there for a considerable period of time before coming to the U.S.)

The research committee should, ideally, carry this process as far forward as it can on its own; but, at some point, it will need to obtain the advice of the research consultant with survey research skills. Clearly, the criteria for and process of selection of that consultant are crucial to the successful conduct of the population study.

CHOOSING A CONSULTANT

In addition to the usual criteria by which one engages professional staff, federations will need to consider several criteria peculiar to the research consultant for the local Jewish population study. These include the following:

1. The consultant should be experienced in several aspects of survey research: questionnaire design, quantitative data analysis, and the nontechnical interpretation of research findings through lucid writing and provocative oral presentation.
2. Some aspects of the design and execution of the study can be "farmed out" to subcontractors or benefit from specialists in several areas. Many communities have used consultants who in turn contracted with a local survey or market research firm to conduct

the interviews. The firm administers the questionnaire to the specified sample and provides the researcher with a clean data tape for analysis. Some research consultants have worked with specialists in sampling, questionnaire design, and Jewish population research to provide supplementary expertise in highly technical areas.

3. Ideally, the researcher should have command of the literature in Jewish social research and should also bring to bear skills from a broader discipline such as demography, economics, sociology, or political science. Studies conducted by market researchers or those with little previous experience in Jewish social research or the conduct of Jewish population studies tend to betray a lack of sensitivity to issues important to the Jewish community and the study of Jewish identity.
4. The consultant need not be indigenous to the community. The use of locally based researchers is, of course, advantageous in at least two respects: they are available for consultation in person, and are likely to be familiar with local conditions. However, our sense is that experienced and otherwise capable "outsiders" can usually overcome the drawbacks of not being indigenous. Thus, the criterion of local residence for the consultant represents a desirable but

BUDGETING FOR INTERPRETATION AND ANALYSIS

While there are several issues that could be addressed in a discussion of budgeting for a local Jewish population study, we wish to discuss only one particularly troublesome aspect of the process. Quite obviously, a budget should be properly balanced over different phases of the population study. Our impression is that until recently, many communities budgeted adequately, if not more than adequately, for data collection, but they drastically underbudgeted for subsequent data analysis and interpretation. Thus, the quality of the sampling and the data tapes was unimpeachable; but researchers were given little opportunity to analyze the data and to interpret the findings to key lay and professional groups. Instead, they could produce only population estimates and rudimentary cross-tabulations.

We suggest that if, as is usual, a community can afford a limited budget for research purposes, that it allocate adequate resources for analysis and interpretation even if such a step makes for less than ideal (but still adequate) data collection. Generally, data collection costs are huge and analysis and interpretation expenses are rather modest. Most increases in the budget for analysis and interpretation can usually result in a significantly more extensive and sophisticated research product.

ACTIVATING THE PLANNING PROCESS

Perhaps the single most important key to making successful use of a Jewish population study is activating the planning process in advance of the study itself. As we have demonstrated, it is important to conduct a population study in the context of the larger framework of federation activity, rather than in isolation. This means insuring that the connection between regular social planning activities and the study should be established well before the results are in. That is, the planning/budgeting/allocations committee should be thinking about how the data developed by the study can inform their work as soon as the idea of the study is broached.

These considerations have even stronger force with respect to long-range and campaign planning, where many federations do not maintain permanent structures. The long-range planning committee, which will often be the critical bridge between the study and the federation's programmatic activities, should be operating (even if only in a preliminary fashion) before the study process is fully under way.

A "user education program" to train key staff and leaders in how to make the best use of the study results should not wait until the study is completed. The basic guidelines throughout the study process should be one of holistic planning and anticipation. Although the process will move through distinct stages, each stage must be organized with the eventual end result in mind, and the process as a whole must be integrated as fully as possible into the ongoing work of the federation.

THE OVERALL STUDY REPORT AND BEYOND

A cursory examination of some of the more sophisticated and extensive local population studies reveals a certain uniformity in the topics covered in such reports (see, for example, Gary A. Tobin and Julie A. Lipsman's compendium). The basic report typically includes population estimates (for the entire study area and regions within it); age distributions, household structure and living arrangements, marital status and history; socio-economic status (education, employment status, occupation, income); residential characterics (ownership, dwelling type, migration history, migration plans, neighborhood evaluation); Jewish identification (ritual practice, communal affiliation, campaign and other philanthropic participation); and community service utilization (or needs assessment).

Most federations choose to issue for public distribution a single document summarizing the essential research findings. The report, often replete with graphs and large type, usually serves two useful functions. First, it provides the public with the sense that the federation is the central source of information on the Jewish population in its region. Such a function reinforces the image of the federation as the central framing institution of the Jewish community. Second, the basic report serves the information needs of many Jewish communal institutions.

But ideally, the population study should go beyond the information typically presented in the basic report. The most effectively used studies supply two other sorts of information. First, they can be used to establish an on-line system to provide specific pieces of information to agencies and other users of the study. The agency serving college youth, for example, may need projections of the size of the Jewish college youth population in the next ten years. The unit concerned with planning day care may need to know the number and characteristics of working mothers with preschool children. The agency for the aged may need to know areas where the elderly population is expanding or contracting.

This type of specific information can be provided by a computer programmer with specialized conceptual skills. He or she must be both familiar with the data set and capable of helping professional staff translate their often ambiguously phrased requests for information into specific inquiries. As an example, the unit planning day care facilities may know enough to ask, "How many families need day care?" The programmer may need to help the unit specify its request to arrive at a data-oriented portrait of such families (i.e., those where a mother works at least part-time outside the home and where there is at least one child six years old or under).

In addition to specific requests for data and the basic report, the population study can generate several in-depth topical reports. In the past, federations have requested reports on such topics as campaign planning, the aged, recent immigrants, the impoverished or economically vulnerable, and other service populations; the impact of Jewish education or the intergenerational transmission of Jewish identity; or the patterns and determinants of fertility, divorce, intermarriage, and other demographic phenomena. Once the data are collected, the costs of analyzing and interpreting them are relatively minor.

Communities have utilized the population study data in three major ways: issuing the basic report for the public, supplying answers to specific data requests by agencies and others, and preparing in-depth specialized reports. To the best of our knowledge, few if any communities have utilized the population study data to the fullest extent possible. In part this situation derives from lack of experience of both researchers and clients (federation professional and lay leaders) working together on these studies, and in part it derives from a failure to budget adequately for analysis and interpretation following collection of the data.

The Style of the Report

The utility of the overall study report depends not only on its contents, but also on its style. Lay leaders, and even many professional staff, usually have little experience in reading social research reports. Even sophisticated and intelligent individuals cannot be expected to feel comfortable looking at complex tables or arrays of statistics. On the other hand, they do not want to be presented simply with a set of conclusions without supporting data that they can assess independently.

One way of easing the burden on the report writer is to provide some form of advance training for those who will be receiving the study report. Such skills as reading tables and understanding various statistical measures can be reviewed. Having the study consultant (or other qualified individual) review the report orally, giving special attention to interpreting charts and statistical data, can be similarly helpful. Nevertheless, it is not reasonable to expect that all readers of the report will undergo such training, or that those who do will be able to grapple with regressions, tests of significance, and factor analyses.

This means that the study report must provide enough data to anchor the narrative in numbers, while presenting those data in a form intelligible to the average reader. There are a few relatively simple ways of enhancing readability without sacrificing content:

1. The narrative itself should be clear and simple, without too many numbers embedded in the text. Readers should be able to get the gist of a finding from the narrative, and then be referred to an accompanying chart or table which presents the data in numerical detail.

2. Such charts and tables should be placed as close as possible in the report to the narrative referring to them, so as to minimize the need to jump back and forth.
3. Tables should be clearly labeled. Interpreting cross-tabulation tables can be confusing. Do the numbers shown indicate the percentage of Jews between 18 and 39 years of age who are Orthodox, or the percentage of those who are Orthodox who are between 18 and 39 years of age? The table caption should indicate how the numbers are to be read.
4. Wherever possible, supplement both narrative and numerical tables with bar and circle graphs, maps, and the like. Not only do these graphic presentations make the report more interesting visually and help retain the reader's attention, but they often are the clearest way of presenting data and make it easier for those with numerophobia to understand the findings.
5. Avoid esoteric statistics and statistical procedures. Unless they help make a truly vital point which otherwise would be lost, operations such as regression and factor analyses, and statistics such as correlation coefficients, betas, and levels of significance do not usually belong in the general-consumption study report. A clear statement regarding issues affecting the reliability and validity of data reported should be made at the outset of the report, but except where an adequate number of cases makes a particular finding questionable, the caveats should not be belabored, especially in statistical terms.

An Executive Summary

Not everyone who should be informed of the major findings of the population study needs to receive a copy of the overall study report. Many can make use of an executive summary, which in succinct fashion pulls together the most significant findings, without all of the supporting detail. Not only can the executive summary (a five to ten page document) save printing costs, but it may also induce some who would simply put aside a longer report to read through the major results. In addition, preparing an executive summary gives the federation an opportunity to highlight the areas it believes are most important and to make sure (insofar as this is possible) that these receive adequate attention in the consumer constituencies.

The summary can be a strictly factual document--just reporting findings--or an interpretive one as well. After each set of findings, a section can be included which might be entitled "implications for the community" or "issues for planning." Linking these directly to the major findings of the study establishes a crucial nexus between data and potential utilization. This can provide a further impetus toward insuring that the study findings are in fact used by the appropriate committees and organizations. Naturally, the power to interpret is the power to guide, if not to control, the process of utilization. Thus, those writing the executive summary (who should normally be professional staff of the federation, not the consultant) must be careful to be both fair and accurate in suggesting implications and possible conclusions from the data.

The great virtue of an executive summary lies in its brevity and directness. The results selected for inclusion should be those most significant for planning purposes (with just enough general data to give a sense of the "big picture"). What should be highlighted are trends, findings that suggest a need for action, and data directly related to institutional performance. Attempting to report everything will only vitiate the summary's impact. Stylistically, the executive summary should be "punchy," using underlining, boxing, capitalization, and other devices to make key findings and conclusions stand out. The executive summary should receive wide distribution. Next to the release of information to the media, it provides the federation with its best means of reaching many people and influencing their perception of the study's results and their significance.

INTEGRATING POPULATION STUDIES WITH OTHER DATA SOURCES

As noted earlier, population studies constitute only one of the available sources of data for planners in the Jewish community. In most instances, sound planning requires different types of information, and more of it, than population studies alone can provide. To make the most effective use of the information arising from population studies, one must place it alongside that generated by other sources--needs assessments, service records, program evaluations. A population study can help planners make a reliable estimate of the number of elderly in a community, of their income, and of their living arrangements. If designed to do so, it can also provide indications of how many are receiving various community services and of their perceived service needs. A population study cannot provide an objective assessment of the adequacy of those services, of the cost-effectiveness of various ways of meeting identified needs, or of the alternative organizational arrangements which might be made to provide services. Both types of information are critical for federation planning.

The data from population studies must, therefore, be viewed as only one resource for community planners, but not as a substitute for other types of information. Its value will be enhanced to the extent that it can be integrated with these other data sources.

Maximizing the potential for integration of information from diverse data sources begins when the study is being designed and the survey instrument written. But realizing that potential requires that those who are using the population study be attentive to and creative in extending its "fit" with other data. Focusing on the study alone can result in an unnecessary narrowing of perspective, and a resultant frustration when the study fails to provide the answers to important planning questions. The concept of an integrated management information system, in which the basic demographic and social data provided by the study can be flexibly linked up to other information to provide a total picture of a population segment, its characteristics, needs, and current relationship to communal institutions and programs, is an ideal toward which federation planning structures should be striving.

THE ROLE OF POPULATION STUDIES IN DECISION-MAKING

It follows from this discussion that population studies can play a role in, but do not in themselves dictate, important federation or communal decisions. To invest in a population study and not to utilize its results in informing communal decisions is, to say the least, uneconomical. But it is also unrealistic, as we have emphasized on several occasions, to believe that demographic or even attitudinal data can constitute the only factor in communal decision-making.

Assuming that the study is competently done, the real question is one of how data interact with the many other elements that go into decision-making--notably considerations of values and power relationships--to produce a final outcome. The fact that a new center of Jewish population has emerged within a metropolitan area can be demonstrated by a population study. Whether that population concentration warrants construction of a new community center facility in the area is a question of a different order. Sometimes by pulling together information from the study--by showing that the population exists, that it is underserviced, that it has the potential to contribute more than its share to the community--one can construct a powerful case on behalf of one policy option (in this case, perhaps, building a center). But many other factors, about which a population study will say little or nothing--e.g., the existence of unused capacity in area synagogues, more pressing needs for increasing the salaries of Jewish educators, political tensions within the community--may suggest a very different decision. In sum, objective information about population characteristics can be a tremendous boon to responsible decision-making. However, "facts" do not in and of themselves make such decisions. People do--people equipped with facts, but also with values and political interests. What data from a population study can do is help insure that those who have strong values and interests cannot substitute mere assumptions for solid information as they engage in the decision-making process. And at times, the facts revealed in a study may be so dramatic--a high rate of intermarriage, the existence of large numbers of elderly living at or below subsistence levels--that a lethargic leadership and/or community can be stimulated to take action where otherwise no decisions at all would be made.

USING POPULATION STUDIES TO FOCUS FURTHER RESEARCH

Even with the best of intentions and the most careful planning, population studies may not tell a federation all that it needs or wants to know about a particular topic. This may be due to the inherent limitations in such studies, to inadequacies in budget and/or manpower, or to unexpected findings which demand expansion and clarification.

If a federation views a population study as a one-shot venture, these knowledge gaps may be a source of considerable frustration, sometimes even recriminations. If the federation, on the other hand, sees a population study as one aspect of an ongoing social research program, this liability may be turned into a virtue. In this instance, one deliberate use made of the study is precisely to suggest areas where further research may be called for. Sometimes, if this need is anticipated, the additional studies--of particular population segments, or particular issues--can be linked to the general population study. A portion of the sample may be reinterviewed more intensively, or invited to participate in other forums for ascertaining community attitudes or evaluating services and programs. A segment of the sample can become the subjects for a longitudinal study as a panel to be periodically reinterviewed.

At times, however, the need for additional research--or the area to be studied--may not be anticipated at the outset of the population study process. In such instances, part of the analysis and reporting--usually with the aid of the consultant--should involve identification of subjects for further investigation. If, for example, the population study reveals a concentration of unaffiliated Jews of whom the federation was not previously aware, that may indicate the need for intensive interviewing among that group. The key lies in accepting the fact that no single study can be expected to answer all questions, and that heuristic use may be as important as any other type of utilization for the study results. This demands, of course, that the federation be committed to the concept of research as an ongoing aspect of its planning work, perhaps even to the point, as many larger federations have done, of engaging professional staff specifically for that purpose.

The population study can also be used to establish a system for interpreting available social indicators so as to answer questions planners may have in future years without need to resort to the expense of a new population study. For example, researchers may be asked to investigate the adequacy of triangulating information from the census, local electoral studies, and lists of Distinctive Jewish Names to get a handle on the size, location, and characteristics of the Jewish population. Such information can be used to trace Jewish population movement by annually inspecting telephone directories and analyzing information from publicly available sources.

The experience of the 1965 and 1975 Boston Jewish community studies demonstrates the value of collecting parallel information on the same community ten years apart. As an illustration, side-by-side analyses of the Boston studies, for example, indicated that Jewish commitment had emerged as a powerful predictor of whether one contributed to the campaign in the ten-year period, thereby implying that the federation had a vital stake in nurturing the Jewish commitment of Boston Jewry. Other analyses showed there had been a huge increase in the number of "alternative" households (singles, childless couples, intermarrieds, and the divorced) and that these households had become even more remote from Jewish life than they had been earlier. This finding suggested that the community should expand its efforts to attract "alternative" households to communal institutions and activities. In short, the comparison of studies of the same community ten years apart offers the opportunity to detect dynamic trends and thereby formulate more sophisticated social policy. (For further discussion of methods of updating population studies, see Bruce A. Phillips's "Exploring Possibilities for Followup Studies" in this volume.)

Clearly, every community will develop its own approach to population research suited to its needs and capabilities. We have offered the guidelines above as a way of sharing our collective experience in this still young and developing field of research. Undoubtedly, the thinking of those in the field will be refined and modified as we continue to gather more experience in the conduct and utilization of Jewish population research.

2
Jewish Demographic Studies as a Planning Process: Coalition Formation and Applied Research

Gary A. Tobin

Jewish population studies are proliferating. Since 1970, over thirty communities have undertaken studies. As we write, another dozen communities are in some stage of a study, and at least that many more are contemplating one.

The purpose of these studies has usually been linked to the need for data for planning in two basic areas: fund-raising and human service delivery. The data are supposed to facilitate rational decision-making in budget allocations, goal determination, program innovation, type and size of facility location, and fund-raising strategies and processes. Such a list is extensive, of course, and much to demand from any research endeavor. Yet the success or failure of a Jewish demographic study effort must be evaluated by usage criteria: how is it used, how much is it used, for how long, by whom, and for what range of functions.

Although these are the criteria by which such studies must be judged, little effort has been given in most communities to insure effective usage. Most federations hope that data will be used to guide decision-making within the existing planning structures--including organization committees, informal networks, interagency groups of professional and lay people, and boards of directors. Yet rarely, if ever, are special provisions made to facilitate this goal.

This article discusses the relationship between data collection and planning with respect to Jewish population studies in individual communities. The critical component linking the two functions is the process of building a strong base of constituent support within the Jewish community service delivery system. These constituents include professional staff of the sponsoring agency, usually the Jewish federation, lay leaders, professional staff in other Jewish agencies, the research consultant responsible for conducting the study, and others. The formalization of a working coalition vested in the use of the demographic study can prevent misuse and disuse of the data.

DATA COLLECTION IN JEWISH COMMUNITIES AS A PLANNING PROBLEM

The justification for spending scarce resources in the Jewish community service delivery system for data collection through population studies rests on two basic pillars. The first of these is the more traditional view held by social scientists that data can enlighten and thereby guide decision-making. The subtle effects on perceptions, misconceptions, changing agendas, and so on cannot be measured, but it is assumed that such studies do illuminate and thus affect the quality and direction of decision-making (Boguslaw). However, most federation lay leaders and professionals want a more direct link between data collection and action than the gradual filtering of ideas.

The social science planning paradigm usually can be paralleled by the "business" approach, the second pillar in this research agenda. Its focus is a careful assessment of costs and benefits, aided by available statistics. This view was summarized by the president of the Jewish Community Council in Jacksonville, Florida, in 1947:

> As a business executive, I often have been struck by the lack of intelligent planning in Jewish communal life. No successful person in the world of commerce would enlarge the scope of his enterprise, add new lines of merchandise, or set out to exploit a new territory without first carefully studying the potentials and ascertaining certain fundamental facts.
>
> Essentially, the processes and procedures in community organization should not differ much from sound business. Yet we do see many activities in a community haphazardly planned and loosely conducted, simply because no one has gathered the basic data upon which intelligent decisions can be reached. (Boxerman, Foreword)

Funders often assume that action is a natural outcome of applied research. One system of classifying the nature of these research products is presented by Merton (p. 174) as follows:

1. Diagnostic: Determining whether action is required.
2. Prognostic: Forecasting trends to plan for future needs.
3. Differential Prognosis: Determining choice between alternative policies.
4. Evaluative: Appraising effectiveness of action program.
5. General Background Data: Of general utility or serving diverse purposes.
6. "Educative" Research: Informing publics of pertinent data and particularly countering misconceptions.

All of these functions are often assumed to be key outcomes of the study process. Yet little, if any, provision is made to insure such uses of the data. If the planning process is to move beyond the data collection and processing stage, the action component must be linked through an intentional strategy of information feedback (Bennis). Otherwise, as one analyst notes, plans usually end up on the shelf, or they are used for political purposes that were never intended in the first place (Forester).

Data analysis can be a medium through which knowledge is shared. The filtering of knowledge, information, and ideas can be accomplished in primarily two ways. The first is through informal networks, with no controls exerted on the way information is presented or on the timing of the release of information. Such a method characteristically follows this schema:

1. Assessing need for information.

2. Hiring a consultant to complete a demographic study.
3. Consultant conducting survey with some input from client.
4. Preparation of final report.
5. Report presented either to executive director or board of directors of federation.
6. Copies distributed to interested parties.

The contents of the study are interpreted by individuals; the information might then leak in bits and pieces to individuals or groups; and new conventional wisdoms might even be formed over a period of years. This is especially true for such "facts" as population size. The dissemination of ideas may be limited and torturously slow, and the opportunity for the telephone-game effect--that is, gross distortion in transmission--is enormous. Misinformation is as likely to filter through as accurate information.

The second model calls for managed information use and dissemination. Through committee structures, workshop lectures, media management, and utilization of staff and consultants, information and ideas are released in an orderly, controlled system. Scores of meetings, presentations, written memos, and so on, may be required to accomplish managed information flows. This is not to say, of course, that the telephone-game effect can be eliminated, or that all information should or can be managed. It does suggest, however, that on a continuum from total informality to total control, great efforts are necessary to achieve some measure of the latter.

The specific goal of data usage in the planning process calls for the second model. Given the diversity of the planning network in the Jewish community, and the wide array of institutional and individual actors, careful coordination of information management is essential. Yet this diversity may in itself inhibit the cooperation necessary to manage the information, especially given different agendas, budget competition, and so on. The Jewish community can be characterized by subgroups, institutional conflicts, and competition for scarce resources.

The organized management of information usage and dissemination requires the cooperation, or at least the restraint from sabotage, of all potential users. A coalition of data users (by definition, all planners and subgroups of the community, or their representatives) must be brought into an applied research structure. This coalition will be responsible for management of information. The actual system of information management for Jewish demographic studies is described elsewhere (see Tobin and Boguslaw). We will discuss the steps necessary to achieve an information management system.

Many of these issues have to be worked out in the political process. Agency staff professionals necessarily hold values, which influence their work. The consultant enters with another set of values; no consultant can be described as purely objective (Merton; Gouldner). Some analysts have argued that the planner's values should be made explicit and that the advocacy role be clearly defined (see Davidoff). Staff and consultants have sets of values that they will attempt to achieve in the political structure, as do lay leaders representing personal agendas, various institutions and organizations, and combinations of constituencies. Lay leaders can exert their influence through cash contributions, through persuasive powers that may be linked with the prestige they have built through community service, and through access to individuals with political influence (such as spouses, friends, relatives, or business associates).

Through the use of communicative planning, a coalition may be formed that includes representatives from the professional and lay communities, and, on occasion, the consultant as well. This coalition must develop a vested interest in the demographic study process if the transition is to be made from data collection to data usage. The next section discusses this process in the case of the Jewish population study in St. Louis.

THE STUDY PROCESS IN ST. LOUIS

The Actors

The St. Louis study offers a successful model of incorporating the action component into the study process prior to, during, and after the data collection phase. As the sponsoring agency, the Jewish Federation of St. Louis was responsible for coordinating the study process. Primary responsibility for supervising the study rested with one staff member who carefully and methodically advocated controlled information dissemination and was personally sympathetic to the notion of applied research, facilitating more rational planning. The staff planning director was also committed to this process, and these two individuals formed the staff core of the coalition support that would build around the study process. Futhermore, at no time did either of the individuals become removed from the study process, even though one staff member left the Federation midway through the process.

The composition of the demographic study committee was the second key component in the coalition. The chair was a prominent and innovative businessman who developed a keen interest in the methodological aspects of the research. The committee included two Ph.D.'s, one physician, religious leaders, and business people. All were selected because they were active community participants who would understand and appreciate applied research. This committee was more than a review group. It participated in many aspects of the study process, including questionnaire construction, promotion of the study in the community, acquisition of lists of names used in constructing the sample frame, and so on. As the study progressed, many members, including the chair, became more involved in different phases of the research.

Agency, organization, and institution staff members became the third group of actors to join the study coalition. The study was promoted in such a way as to collect data that would be useful to a wide variety of groups. Many professional staff members developed a vested interest in the study, hoping it would help meet many of their own institutional agendas.

Lay leaders became the fourth part of the coalition. This was especially true of the chair of the Community Planning Committee, as well as the presidents of the Federation. (Because of the length of the process, more than one two-year presidential term was represented.) All were active advocates for the study and exerted critical leadership throughout the process. Some developed personal loyalties to others involved in the process, some represented particular agencies or organizations, and some were philosophically committed to a "better" planning process. As the coalition became more solid, the study process developed its own institutionalization. In a sense, the research collection process evolved into the planning process. The steps in this process are outlined in Table 2.1.

TABLE 2.1
Demographic Study: Time Line of Events (1978-1983)

Date	Events
November 1978	Community Planning Committee of Federation discussed need for demographic study. Task force was approved.
February 1979	Chair appointed. Demographic Study Committee designated to explore need, purpose, scope, costs, and methodology.
March 1979	Letters sent to agencies, synagogues, and organizations inquiring about need for study. Development of subject matter to include in study.
April-August 1979	Demographic Study Committee met to review comments and responses from agencies regarding decision to conduct study and types of information to be included in study.
September-October 1979	Prospective consultants submitted proposals for consideration.
October 1979	Consultant chosen.
November 1979	Demographic Study Committee discussed methodology, sample size, and budget in preparation for Community Planning Committee meeting.
February 1980	Community Planning Committee approved demographic study.
April 1980	Federation board approved study.
August 1980	Mailings to congregations, agencies, and organizations to define areas that study included.
August 1980-March 1981	Collection of lists from organizations, synagogues, agencies, Jewish Light, and "snowball lists." Study promoted in community.
February-May 1981	List collection finalized. Began review of methodologies in other communities. Development of questions with agencies, organizations; consultations with large numbers of groups and community leaders.

TABLE 2.1 (continued)
Demographic Study: Time Line of Events (1978-1983)

Date	Events
May 1981	Finalization of survey instrument. Selection of methodology. Pretest.
June-December 1981	Interviews conducted.
December 1981-November 1982	Data processing. Draft report presented to Federation
January 1983	Presentation to Community Planning Committee.
February 1983	Board presentation. Community presentations by consultant.
February 1983-Present	Data interpretation, planning/action phase.

As can be seen, the process is a lengthy one, with a period of almost two and a half years of planning in the coalition formation stage before the data collection actually began. Even throughout the collection and processing phases, many meetings were held on ways to disseminate and utilize the data and so on. At no time during any phase of the study did the political process surrounding the use of the data become dormant.

The Procedures

The Federation's planning mechanism, the Community Planning Committee, provided an effective forum to discuss the need for a demographic study. The ongoing requirement for critical information, coupled with the continuing requests from congregations, organizations, and Jewish communal service agencies, sparked the demand for the research.

The requests for information were linked to a wide range of community concerns such as change of family patterns, population shifts, intermarriage, increase in one-parent families, and the needs of the elderly and youth populations. These issues were among several areas that fostered the demand for demographic information to assist policy-making. Through the Federation's community planning process, the need for a demographic study was discussed and subsequently supported by the Federation's endowment fund.

The president of the Federation appointed a Demographic Study Committee in 1978, composed of a broad cross-section of the Jewish community. The committee was asked to explore the best way to proceed in conducting the demographic study. At its initial meeting the committee received consultations from the Council of Jewish Federation's staff. The process to determine need and scope was lengthy, but it proved to be prudent in creating a supportive community environment for the study. The potential users of the study were involved very early in the planning process through formal and informal meetings and communiqués. All community organizations were asked to respond to the following questions:

1. Do you feel a demographic study would be of value to your organization?
2. If yes, what areas of information would be helpful to you?
3. How would this information be utilized?

It took several months to get responses; however, it is important to note that these efforts to involve the community users to help define the need and scope of the study proved extremely helpful in gaining cooperation throughout the course of the study.

In addition to the responses from the various Jewish community organizations and institutions, the committee also reviewed the demographic materials of other communities and made selective phone calls to other federations to gain from their experience.

After receiving information from various Jewish community institutions, the committee recognized the importance of going far beyond the scope of most studies. The information requested and interest expressed by the various respondents indicated that both demographic and attitudinal subject areas needed exploration. Requests were noted for information in such areas as perceptions of agencies and organizations, utilization of agency services, and community perception of service needs.

The second phase of the project required extensive interaction among Federation committees, staff, and the consultant. The Demographic Study Committee was actively involved in defining the scope and primary issues of the study and reviewed the survey instrument for clarity, content, and study objectives. The Demographic Planning Committee was also involved in selecting the most suitable methodology to achieve the study objectives.

In addition to asking various Jewish community groups to help shape this study, the committee also asked them to publicize the study through newsletters and announcements at meetings and congregational religious services. Each group was asked to urge its supporters to participate in an interview if they were selected through the sampling procedures. In addition to these efforts, the Federation also utilized the St. Louis Jewish Light to coordinate the publication of articles on the demographic study throughout its various stages. Again, this helped to create a positive community environment to maximize cooperation among Jewish communal organizations and individuals.

Letters were sent out in mid-August 1980 to all organizations, with followup correspondence mailed two weeks later. These letters, written over the signature of the chair of the Demographic Study Committee, served the dual purpose of publicizing the Federation's intent of conducting a demographic study, and enlisting the participation and cooperation of those in receipt of these letters. The letters requested that organizational membership lists and rosters from 1976 through 1981 be made available to the Federation office for compilation of the study's sample frame. Additionally, organizational heads were asked to alert their constituencies to the importance of the study and to invite suggestions for the questionnaire.

The initial letters and followup correspondence were sent to the presidents and directors of all Jewish federation constituent and beneficiary agencies; to the presidents and rabbis of all synagogues and temples; and to all Jewish organizations, including the regional offices of national and overseas beneficiary agencies, Jewish schools and educational institutions, chapter levels of women's and men's organizations, and all other known Jewish organizations.

Charts were developed so that the individual responses of all letter recipients could be cross-checked. Information on these graphs included the name, address, and telephone number of the person to whom the letter was mailed; whether the person planned to promote the study among his or her individual constituency, and whether membership lists were made available. These graphs were grouped according to three categories: synagogues, constituent agencies, all other Jewish organizations.

During the months of September 1980 through March 1981, an intensive telephone followup was directed to all letter recipients. Often, additional information on the study, its purposes and sponsorship was requested. Clarification was also needed regarding the specific uses to which such membership lists would be put. Four types of problems developed over the issue of assembling membership lists. First, there was concern on the part of the organizational leaders that such rosters be used only for study purposes. Second, a number of organizations initially refused to submit rosters, noting that a policy decision had to be made on the national level to release such information. Third, certain smaller organizations felt that, due to insufficient clerical assistance, rosters would be difficult to draw up. Fourth, a few small groups believed that the study would be of no value to them and, therefore, did not want to release their membership lists.

The Demographic Study Committee took an active role during this period with many of the members taking the responsibility for individual organizations. Each member used available contacts to help explain the purpose of the study and obtain membership lists.

The Women's Division of the Federation was helpful in contacting certain women's organizations--for example, B'nai B'rith Women, American Mizrachi Women, and Hadassah--and obtaining mailing lists. In November 1980, as many as 60 of 125 lists had not been obtained. The refusal of various agencies to relinquish their lists accounted for most of the absent lists.

Beginning in March 1981, weekly meetings were held with the people involved in the final stages of the list accumulation. Agenda items included which organizations still had not responded with their lists, as well as the mass retrieval of names through confirmation lists, Jewish Light engagement and marriage announcements, and distinctive Jewish surnames in the telephone directories. A "snowball" collection of unaffiliated individuals was also undertaken at this time. A "snowball list" begins with the identification of the totally unaffiliated, who are in turn asked to provide names of other such individuals.

During the last week in April 1981, a final letter was sent to all synagogues, agencies, and organizations that submitted membership lists and rosters to the Federation. Included in this mass mailing was a cover letter from the demographic study chairman, a copy of the letter prospective survey respondents would receive, a letter of explanation as to the purpose of the study, and a listing of all cooperating organizations as of that date. Finally, over 125 lists were collected, with only two organizations holding back because they could not obtain clearance from their national organizations.

The process of collecting the membership lists was important for a number of reasons. First, the study was publicized to all Jewish organizations and institutions in the area. This would make the field work less difficult since many groups and individuals would have become familiar with the study. Such familiarity could help reduce the refusal rate. Second, the Jewish Federation, as the umbrella organization, was able to foster cooperation among nearly all organizations. This cooperation would later translate into active participation in the information-sharing and analysis process. Finally, high levels of interest were generated because the study would be used as a planning and policy tool, rather than just as a population count.

The process of collecting the lists fostered a cooperative process between the Federation and other organizations. As the purposes of the study were explained and cooperation was solicited, organizations played an active role in promoting the study.

Furthermore, as each organization contributed its list, it was asked to indicate its data needs, issues and concerns for the organization, and its planning needs. The larger organizations each met on at least two occasions to solicit and refine questions for inclusion in the survey instrument. At least forty organizations and institutions submitted data requests, and representatives from twenty organizations met individually or in groups to discuss input into the questionnaire. (This process, of course, could have been accomplished without the list collection procedure. An information usage and dissemination strategy could have been designed employing a different set of mechanisms to spark and nurture interest in the data.)

Caution had to be taken not to solicit more requests for input into the questionnaire than could be reasonably handled. For the most part, data requests fell into broad, common categories. Where this was not the case, efforts were made to accommodate at least some of the data needs of those who requested it. As a result the survey instrument was lengthy, but not unmanageable.

The design of the survey instrument is another means of keeping the coalition strong in the study process. Each section was designed with a particular set of client users in mind. Indeed, each of the institutions or organizations that might use the data for planning purposes was involved in supplying questions and information to help construct the survey instrument. The organizations supplying such information, either through written communication or group discussions, included:

American Jewish Committee
American Jewish Congress
Anti-Defamation League of B'nai B'rith
B'nai B'rith Hillel Foundation
Central Agency for Jewish Education
The Delcrest (housing for the elderly)
H. F. Epstein Hebrew Academy
Jewish Center for the Aged
Jewish Community Centers Association (JCCA)
Jewish Community Relations Council
Jewish Employment and Vocational Service
Jewish Family and Children's Service
Jewish Federation of St. Louis
Jewish Hospital of St. Louis
St. Louis Jewish Light
St. Louis Rabbinical Association
St. Louis Rabbinical Council

In some cases, such as the JCCA, three or four program directors had input, or, as in the case of the Federation, the entire staff was asked to participate in the survey design. Individual temples and synagogues, organization chapters, religious schools, school administrators, and others played a role in the questionnaire construction. In all, over 40 institutions and over 250 individuals actively contributed to the construction of the survey instrument to insure maximum community usage of the data.

Throughout this process, the media were utilized to keep the study on center stage. Public gatherings were held to discuss various stages of development, and meetings were held to enlist participation in the program and the research. At no time did the study process find itself "on the shelf."

CONCLUSIONS

If data are to be utilized after the final report is issued, nothing can be left to chance, nor can anything be assumed. The committee structure, promotion techniques, coalition formation, media coverage, and the involvement of individuals and groups must all be carefully managed. At no time can the planning process be assumed to be divorced from the prevailing political processes. Each phase requires an enormous input of staff and/or consultant hours for the meetings necessary to complete their tasks successfully.

Since the ultimate use of the data in guiding the allocation of resources is either implicit or explicit in the entire process, the study may be an extremely volatile political document. For example, the study may reveal far fewer potential users of a "new" facility for Jewish day campers, and eliminate the need for this budget allocation to the JCC. Only maximum involvement can reduce the risk of any constituent "outside" the process attacking the credibility of the research. Debate will focus upon what the data say as opposed to whether or not the data are reliable or valid. Furthermore, maximum involvement commits the federation to long-range involvement in data interpretation and retrieval. These costs are not small and may create friction if significant staff changes are made or principal actors in the process should cease to be involved--for example, if they retire or move from the community. The coalition (all potential users) must be strong enough to withstand major shifts, and even defections (changing personal agendas, for example).

The study process has political implications for federation relationships in each of the following areas:

1. Within federation staff.
2. Federation to constituent agencies.
3. Federation to temples, synagogues, and other organizations.
4. Federation to Jewish public.
5. Federation to non-Jewish public.
6. Federation to non-Jewish voluntary sector (e.g., United Way).
7. Federation to national Jewish community.
8. Federation to national Jewish communal services structure.

All decisions throughout the study process must be weighed in terms of the possible repercussions and political benefits affecting these different areas.

In the long run, the added costs in time and money are well worth the investment. Accumulation of the lists is very time consuming. In addition, the data utilization system requires additional expenditures for continued data retrieval, community lectures and workshops, additional printed reports, staff time for meetings with agencies and organizations, and much more. The St. Louis example demonstrates that a study can be used to its maximum potential. Even before the study was completed, committees were being structured to utilize the data, a data retrieval system was developed, and the Federation committed itself to future data exploration. The careful contribution of an applied research coalition has provided the link between data collection and action, and fulfilled the intent of funding the research at the outset.

The final step, the translation of the planning process into specific action, requires another set of actors, processes, and agendas. The relocation of a specific facility, development of a program for the elderly, budget reallocation, and so on, will be undertaken in the context of another set of variables.

The collection of data by no means insures a rational planning model in the voluntary sector, but informed planning cannot take place without it. The involvement of a diverse coalition that is versed in the use of data as a planning tool will facilitate broader comprehension and use of the data. The control of information must not only insure effective utilization in the planning system so as to avoid wasting the investment in the study; it must also prevent misuse of the data and the manipulation of data contrary to the Jewish community's "public good."

Widespread participation can prevent such misuse of the data. Shared expertise and sophistication with the data effectively blocks any individual or group from claiming an interpretive hold on the results, and screening or manipulating the data in a way that furthers only their individual or group agenda. Information is a source of power, a good to be collected and traded. An active participatory system of data collection and analysis can prevent an undesirable misuse of the results of the study. Widespread participation produces an important safety check for everyone who should be represented in the study process.

References

Bennis, Warren G. 1966. Changing Organizations: Essays on the Development and Evolution of Human Organization. New York: McGraw-Hill.

Benveniste, Guy. 1972. The Politics of Expertise. Berkeley: The Glendessary Press.

Boguslaw, Robert. 1981. The New Utopians. New York: Irvington Publishers.

Boxerman, William I. 1947. Statistically Speaking. Jacksonville: Jewish Community Council.

Davidoff, Paul. 1965. "Advocacy and Pluralism in Planning." Journal of American Institute of Planners 31: 331-338.

_____ and Thomas A. Reiner. 1962. "A Choice Theory of Planning." Journal of American Institute of Planners 28: 103-115.

Forester, John. 1982. "Planning in the Face of Power." Journal of the American Planning Association 48: 67-80.

_____. 1980. "Critical Theory and Planning Practice." Journal of the American Planning Association 46: 275-286.

Goldstein, Sidney. 1964. The Greater Providence Jewish Community. Providence: General Jewish Community of Providence, Inc.

Gouldner, Alvin. 1968. "The Sociologist As Partisan: Sociology and the Welfare State." American Sociologist 3: 103-116.

Merton, Robert K. 1949. "The Role of Applied Social Science in the Information of Policy: A Research Memorandum." Philosophy of Science 16: 3: 161-181.

Tobin, Gary A. 1982. A Demographic and Attitudinal Study of the Jewish Community of St. Louis. St. Louis: Jewish Federation of St. Louis.

_____ and Nancy Boguslaw. 1983. "Developing a Data Utilization System for Jewish Demographic Studies." Journal of Jewish Communal Service 60: 104-111.

3
Interpreting and Communicating the Results of Jewish Population Studies

Peter B. Friedman

This paper discusses several issues involved in the interpretation and communication of Jewish population study results. It starts from the premise that findings may be used in different ways or for different purposes, one of which is to provide information to assist planning and communal decision-making. This use follows the classic model of doing research in order to facilitate decision-making. Data can also be used to justify decisions previously made or to avoid decision-making (Weiss).

However, a study may also be helpful without having a direct impact upon decision-making. It may broadly educate consumers. That is, it may correct false impressions or provide a different conceptual framework or context for decision-making. For example, a study may provide a better general understanding of the relationship of single-parent families to the Jewish community, which may not directly affect policy.

Alternatively, population studies may serve as a basis for community organization. Here the principal objective is to enhance federation's involvement and connection with the larger Jewish community. This involvement derives from wide discussion of the findings, from presentation of the rationale of federation in undertaking a study of the entire community, and from sharing with organizations results that will assist them to plan their programs and encourage them to look beyond their group perspectives.

There is no single or right approach to interpreting or communicating results. Sometimes more than one interpretation may be consistent with the data. Consequently, the interpretation and communication of results provide an opportunity to exercise choice and judgment. Some judgments are technical; others relate to the values of either the sponsors or researchers or the consumers. In addition, interpretations may always be modified by additional analysis or data. There are also many styles of communication which can be used. The choice depends upon the kind of data, their projected use, and the particular audience addressed.

Because of diversities in interpretation and communication, it is appropriate to go beyond the experience of a single case study, such as the Jewish Federation of Metropolitan Chicago's 1981-1982 Population Study with which I have been associated. Hence, the observations below also reflect reports of other Jewish communities that have recently completed population studies, as well as the observations of researchers, especially those (e.g., Patton; Weiss; Rothman) who have focused on the issue of how interpretation and communication affect the ways findings are used in the policy-making process.

PHASES IN A POPULATION STUDY

Interpretation and communication of a study's results must be viewed within the context of judgments and decisions made at earlier phases. The major phases may be outlined simply thus:

1. Planning for a population study (including developing support for a study, defining the study and its objectives, designing methodology, determining who will be responsible for the study, etc.).
2. Conducting a study (technical aspects involving questionnaire design, sampling, pretest, data collection, coding of data).
3. Analyzing population study data (organizing raw data, univariate and multivariate statistical analysis).
4. Interpreting results.
5. Communicating results.
6. Disseminating results to different consumers and audiences.
7. Applying results (whether directly of indirectly, for decision-making, planning, education, or community organization).

Communication involves the style in which the findings or interpretations are conveyed to consumers. In this model it is regarded as separate from dissemination, which refers to the process by which the findings are made available to different audiences beyond the sponsors or key decision-makers.

The expected ultimate use of the population study may well dictate the communication style and how to present findings to consumers of population studies. These consumers include, in addition to staff and lay leadership of federation, laity and professionals from the local federation agencies, the larger Jewish community, and the general community, to whom results are disseminated for public relations purposes.

Because decisions made during the early phases of a population study are crucial, it is essential that federation staff or lay persons be involved in these decisions even if they do not conduct the study. Discussion of this process below is followed by an assessment of the major issues affecting interpretation and communication. These include alternate varieties of interpretation and communication, how to deal with controversial findings, and sources of misinterpretation.

THE IMPACT OF PLANNING AND CONDUCTING A STUDY UPON INTERPRETATION AND COMMUNICATION

Planning for a population study is often bifurcated: planners initially pay much attention to sampling and research design, questionnaire construction and related issues, without thinking through the issues of interpretation and communication. As a result, sponsors of the study may find themselves with technically accurate data which however cannot provide the information required to address factual questions or communal issues; nor will they have the flexibility to communicate the findings in the most appropriate manner.

Another planning consideration is the need to envision not only the short-term, but also the long-term uses of the data. What may be of immediate interest at the time the study is conducted may become less important than another issue, possibly one which had been temporarily dormant. A few examples of concerns regarding sampling, questionnaire

Sampling

Decisions about sampling involve a number of considerations. For purposes of planning and decision-making, Jewish federations generally think in terms of geographic units (e.g., a region, suburb, or neighborhood) or target groups (e.g., elderly, singles, single parents, those in need of a specific service). In studies using geographically based strata for sampling, a major consideration should be the overlap between sampling strata and planning areas. Ideally, samples should be allocated so that smaller areas can be aggregated into larger areas, since this allows greater flexibility. Where there is special interest in a specific area (such as one undergoing population change, or one regarded as politically significant), researchers will need to allocate the sample so as to assure that there are sufficient cases for projections and analysis.

The Chicago study, for example, which used a Random Digit Dialing sampling approach, overallocated calls to the northwest suburbs, a recently developed area with a growing Jewish population, in order to provide sufficient cases in that area. For communities that do not use area-wide approaches to sampling (e.g., lists of organizational members), a preliminary analysis of the distribution of the sample on a geographic basis should be conducted to insure or to ascertain whether the sample will yield sufficient cases to justify planning decisions.

Although most studies analyze and interpret data relative to different target groups (e.g., the elderly), few, if any, actually take that into consideration in developing the sample. The Chicago population study insured the inclusion of a large number of households headed by the elderly and by singles by focusing on areas in which these households were known to be numerous.

Questionnaire Design and Data Definition

Jewish population studies, like general social surveys, are designed to gather vast amounts of basic information. As a result it is impossible to cover all the issues. Furthermore, tradeoffs take place concerning depth of coverage. Will sponsors and decision-makers require broad coverage of issues with little depth, or vice versa?

If specific data are to be collected, it is important how measures are defined. Take, for example, the issue of poverty within the Jewish community, an issue which has become a more salient concern due to the economy and cutbacks in government funding. How should the study define poverty? Should income alone be the criterion? Whose definition of poverty should be used--the government's, United Way's, academicians', someone else's? Due to respondents' reluctance to divulge exact income figures, most recent studies have relied upon categorical information (e.g., between $5,000 and $10,000) rather than asking the respondent to name specific amounts. As a result, researchers must consider the different definitions and categories of poverty they plan to use in constructing the question. These decisions affect the projections regarding the number of economically disadvantaged.

A related issue is that of determining the basic units of analysis and interpretation. The typical unit of sampling is a household. However, information may be collected about (a) the household as a whole; (b) every individual living in the household; or (c) subgroups within the household (e.g., the respondent only and/or spouse, all adults 18 and over, children under 18, or adults over 65). The decision about which information to collect will have a direct bearing on interpretation.

These examples clearly show that considerable attention must be paid to the issue of analysis/interpretation during the planning and early phases of the study. Sharing these issues at the outset with the lay and professional leadership will avoid the problems that might arise if they first confront these issues as a fait accompli.

VARIETIES OF INTERPRETATION

Analysis and interpretation are two separate but related phases of a population study. Analysis deals with the organization of data and application of statistical formulae and tests, while interpretation involves judgments made about the meaning of the data and its implications for communal policy.

There are at least six styles or forms of interpretation:

1. Highlighting descriptive facts ("fully 30 percent" as opposed to "only 30 percent").
2. Comparing differences or examining relationships among variables ("there is a higher level of synagogue affiliation among those who identify as Orthodox than among Reform Jews").
3. Noting patterns including interrelated trends ("a variety of forces are impinging upon the family: lower birth rate, intermarriage, geographic mobility, etc.").
4. Predicting ("the population size will be relatively stable during the next decade").
5. Providing explanations ("the decline in the Jewish population was caused by decline in birth rate and out-migration of Jewish elderly").
6. Suggesting communal policy implications of the findings, whether general or specific ("given the growth in the number of elderly, there is a need for consideration of more services to the elderly"; "we should provide at least 200 more slots for day care").

One of the major issues in interpretation is the role of the consumers, lay and professional, in interpreting the data. Patton suggests that in order to avoid having consumers reject the findings of the study, they should be involved in working toward those findings; that is, they should be given the data and allowed to struggle with them toward an interpretation. While this may not be feasible, a comparable result may be achieved via a knowledgeable federation staff which engages in open discussion with consumers regarding the basis for a particular interpretation and which is willing to explore others.

Analysis, as opposed to interpretation, requires little intimate knowledge of a community. Anybody with sufficient technical and theoretical skills can analyze data. The validity and credibility of an interpretation, however are greatly enhanced by an understanding of the Jewish community in general and of the local federation and communal organizations in particular.

ALTERNATIVES FOR COMMUNICATING AND DISSEMINATING RESULTS

The communication of study findings is as important as their interpretation. It must be decided (a) what to present, (b) to whom it should be presented among potential consumers, ranging from federation decision-makers, to the larger Jewish community, to the general public, and (c) how to present it. Most population studies and analyses are communicated by a written report. The report, however, is only one means of communication. Audiovisual and oral presentations, workshops, executive summaries, press releases, federation publications, informal reports to budgeting and other federation committees, are all different ways to communicate findings to different audiences. In Chicago, we released preliminary information to federation leadership via a special audiovisual presentation accompanied by a set of tables and graphs that summarized major findings. Subsequent to this presentation, others were made to various federation committees and fund-raising groups for purposes of education and planning. In addition, special presentations were made to agency boards and staff.

While a written report is only one form of communication, it is desirable for these reasons: it is a concrete product of the study, it makes information readily accessible, and it is compact and easily transmitted. There are many styles of reports, ranging from comprehensive overviews of a study to those which are devoted to a particular topic. For example, the 1970-1971 National Jewish Population Study was released primarily through a series of topical reports (such as aging, demographic trends, and Jewish identity). The model for most community population studies has been the comprehensive report. The main advantage of a comprehensive report is that it provides an overview of the results in one place. The combination of a comprehensive report and topical reports is desirable, as this helps maintain interest in the study results and findings.

Comprehensive reports vary in their style and content. Some are over 200 pages long, others shorter; some include recommendations, others do not. Communication style is important, for while good style may not guarantee readership and use, poorly conceived reports and presentations do have a negative impact. In studies of research utilization the issues raised regarding reports and presentations include use of language (particularly, is it free of jargon so the reports can be understood?); their length; their attractiveness (in terms of graphs and illustrations); and their avoidance of "sophisticated statistics which may impede, rather than aid . . . comprehension of research" (Weiss, p. 52).

The Chicago Jewish Population Study, in its preliminary presentation, utilized readily understandable graphs and illustrations (see Figure 3.1 for examples). Most consumers, including professionals, have neither a sophisticated understanding nor an appreciation of quantitative material. By using relatively simple charts, information can be communicated easily. As others have noted, any presentation of data that involves data reduction (as do our charts) runs the risk of oversimplification. However, an accompanying interpretation, going beyond the material contained in the charts, may be used to explore complex factors.

METROPOLITAN CHICAGO JEWISH POPULATION 1981

CITY AND SUBURBS 1951-1981

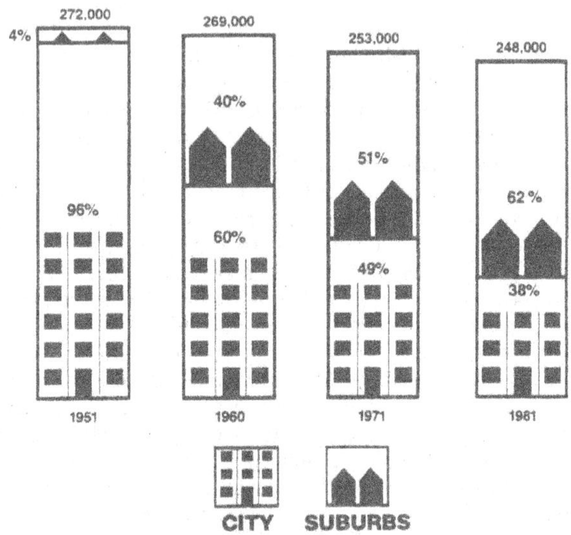

MOBILITY PATTERNS—1971-1981

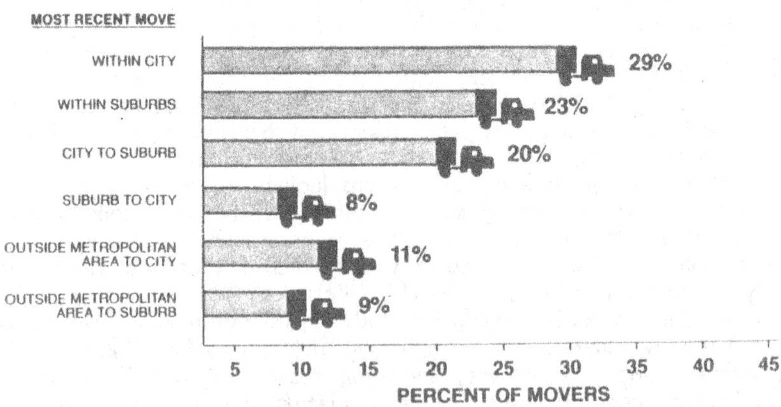

SOURCE: Metropolitan Chicago Population Study 1981-1982, Preliminary Tables, Jewish Federation of Metropolitan Chicago, November, 1982.

In determining what information should be conveyed and how, it is important to distinguish between lay and professional consumers. Professionals in Jewish communal life have a greater in-depth knowledge than lay volunteers simply because of their involvement in the day-to-day activities of agencies, services, or programs. However, in terms of technical skills and understanding of the research methodology and quantitative material, there appears to be little difference between professionals and laity. Data reduction and simplification are necessary for both groups (except for the rare cases of professional researchers who work at agencies or lay persons with a research background).

An even more significant distinction among consumers entails their areas of substantive concern. Both lay leaders and professionals from community centers, family service agencies, and Jewish educational institutions were mainly interested in the results that applied to their own organizations. Thus, the same information could be viewed differently by groups with different perspectives. For example, the family agency would view household comparisons in terms of potential service need and the community center might be concerned with potential for membership and programs.

CONTROVERSIAL FINDINGS

One problem characteristic of communicating research findings is that the findings are often familiar. Thus, the researchers are forced to defend the need for a study to confirm the obvious. However, since data on local Jewish populations are rare (some communities have never systematically studied the Jewish population; others have not studied the population for more than a decade), even findings confirming the familiar are of interest.

Some results, however, may be considered controversial either because they appear to have negative implications for the community, or because they present information that contradicts commonly accepted assumptions.

However, there are ways to present controversial findings which have a potentially major impact upon the Jewish community so that they may be used for planning purposes. One approach is merely to report the findings without interpretation, policy implications, or predictions. This has been done in several studies regarding intermarriage and population change. Another approach is to view the findings within the context of other findings, rather than singling them out for emphasis. For example, one might report intermarriage data while noting other elements of Jewish identification which show vitality, so that a negative finding is counterbalanced by positive ones. Still another approach is to present the findings, but qualify them as contingent upon further analysis or research as the case may be. Finally, results may be presented and viewed as a challenge for policymakers to address. This is certainly the case, for example, with Jewish poverty in Chicago. The findings of the Jewish population study regarding the concerns of the economically disadvantaged and vulnerable were presented within a study, "The Planning Project on Services to Economically Disadvantaged," which included recommendations for a wide range of services and programs.

Findings, however controversial, must be discussed with the leadership so that there is agreement on how to treat them. Then even controversial findings may be presented without fear of damaging the study's credibility.

MISINTERPRETATION

Both sponsors and consumers can misinterpret the findings, and if they do, they usually do so unintentionally. Examples of misinterpretation include:

Misinterpretation from faulty data. This occurs when there are deficiencies in the quality of data collection or when a response bias (e.g., high refusal rate among elderly) leads to a distribution that does not correctly reflect the population distribution. Sometimes biases are known and can be corrected. For example, in Chicago we conducted a followup study of a sample of eligible respondents (i.e., those identified as Jews) who refused to participate in the study. The followup questionnaire was limited to a few questions about the household. It revealed that the elderly were overrepresented among refusals, almost twice the proportion as among completed interviews. The results enabled us to modify the age distribution data.

Overexpansion of inferences about the implications. The large investment often required for a population study and the expectations of its utility foster a tendency to draw inferences far beyond what the data legitimately permit. Inflated statements should be avoided, not simply by limiting oneself to descriptive comments, but by carefully qualifying the kinds of inferences made, recognizing that they may provide a basis for policy-making.

Inadequate analysis or premature communication of findings. Yet another source of misinterpretation occurs where there is a rush to make data available. Sufficient analysis is needed to reveal inconsistencies or to lead to a revised interpretation, especially after the introduction of other variables. Interpretations are always subject to revision based on additional data or reanalysis. Given the pressure to make policy-relevant research available as soon as possible, there will always be a dilemma between communicating findings shortly after the study is completed and holding back to insure that there has been sufficient analysis to assure the quality of the results.

Misinterpretation due to selective interpretation. All interpreters bring their values and particular perspectives to bear on the data they receive. Therefore there is room for distortion in their interpretation--either through inadvertent selectivity, or through their deliberate disregard of findings that clash with their own values or needs.

Over-precise application of findings. Nearly all population studies are based upon probability samples of households within the Jewish community. All samples, because they do not deal with entire populations, are subject to sampling error. We determined that our household estimate of 107,700 households had a sampling error of 5.5 percent with a 95 percent confidence level. That is, if we choose a sample in the same manner, 95 out of 100 times we would be within 5.5 percent of the true figure. Consequently, the actual number of households may be between 101,712 and 113,688 (107,700 ± 5.5 %). Because of our concern about over-precise interpretations we rounded our Chicago Jewish population projection to 248,000. In instances where population projections were made for subgroups (e.g., age groups) we rounded to the nearest thousand or hundred in order to avoid the impression that the sample can give more exact information than it does. The problem of over-precision also arises when making inferences from a small number of cases. The Boston Jewish community study, in attempting to mitigate the problem, noted in each table that data based on fewer than fifty cases should be viewed with caution (Fowler). Finally, misinterpretation occurs when small differences in percentages are regarded as substantively important, when in fact they are not.

CONCLUSION

This paper has emphasized how essential interpretation and communication are to a population study. They should be considered at early stages of the study, since overall judgments and decisions made will affect the options for interpreting and communicating the results. We also have suggested that the manner in which one communicates the findings is sometimes as important as the findings themselves: not only will the style have a bearing upon how the findings or data are used, but it will also help to reduce possible misinterpretation or misuse.

References

Cook, Thomas D., J. Levinson-Rose, and W. Pollard. 1980. "The Misutilization of Evaluation Research: Some Pitfalls of Definition." Knowledge, Creation, Diffusion Utilization (June): 477-498.

Fowler, Floyd J., Jr. 1977. 1975 Community Survey: A Study of the Jewish Population of Greater Boston. Boston: Combined Jewish Philanthropies of Greater Boston.

Kalton, Graham. 1983. Compensating for Missing Data. Ann Arbor: Institute for Social Research, University of Michigan.

Pettigrew, Thomas F. and Donald P. Warwick. 1983. "Toward Ethical Guidelines for Policy Research." A Hastings Center Report, A Special Supplement.

Patton, Michael Quinn. 1978. Utilization Focused Evaluation. Beverly Hills, Calif.: Sage Publications.

Rothman, Jack. 1980. Using Research in Organizations: A Guide to Successful Application. Beverly Hills, Calif.: Sage Publications.

Weiss, Carol H. 1978. "Improving the Linkage Between Social Research and Policy." In Knowledge and Policy: The Uncertain Connection. Study Project on Social Research and Development, Vol. 5. Washington, D.C.: National Academy of Science.

4
Planning Policy and Research: The Perspective of a Federation Executive

Jacob B. Ukeles

The basic case material for the following analysis of the interface between planning, policy development, and research is the 1981 Greater New York Jewish Population Study, carried out under the direction of Professors Paul Ritterband and Steven M. Cohen of the City University of New York. The discussion is in two parts: (1) the politics of Jewish population data and (2) the use of the Jewish Population Study in planning and research.

THE POLITICS OF JEWISH POPULATION DATA

The decision to undertake New York's first Jewish population study in decades was a courageous political decision. First, it was difficult to get the resources. In effect, $150,000 of scarce communal funds had to be diverted from the basic services which most people expected such funds to support. Thus, while there was a wide recognition that the federation needed better data to plan effectively, the setting aside of so large a sum was an agonizing process. Second, but not nearly as important, it was difficult to reach agreement on the questionnaire, sampling design, and overall structure of the survey. Third, there was in the air a fear of data--what some have called the "I would rather not know" syndrome. This attitude has pervaded the Jewish communal response, for example, to the United States census, characterized by unwillingness to surface the religious question lest it show that the Jewish community was substantially smaller than we had believed. An last, there were those who were antianalytic, preferring to rely on intuition and subjective judgment; some felt that the data could not show anything substantially new--"either I know it already, or it is probably wrong." Federation's lay and professional leadership needed to push hard to secure the funding and the necessary agreements to implement this major effort.

Once the field work was completed (in the summer of 1981), the political issue shifted to one of whether to accept the data when they arrived. Although the study seemed like a large expenditure, it involved a relatively low-cost, innovative method of collecting information on an extremely large community. This meant that there was some probability that the data would not be usable. Thus, the first "political" task was to validate the data. The key question as we framed it was "did we want to put Federation behind these numbers?" It was important to recognize that there was a world of difference between a set of numbers put out by social scientists and a set of numbers that would have the imprimatur of Federation. A Federation judgment about how many Jews of what type lived where could have an impact on policy and ultimately on dollar allocations.

We developed a series of independent cross-checks of the results of the survey, comparing each independent estimate of population to survey results. The estimate of Russian immigrants, Jewish day school enrollment, and the percentage of the population estimated to be Jewish as determined in a number of newspaper surveys, all provided a basis for validating the data. Thus we were able to satisfy ourselves--independently of the study directors--that the numbers look reasonable.

We resolved, in advance of the actual completion of the study, that if our independent efforts to validate the data showed that the numbers were not reliable we would not release or use the study. Once we validated the data, there was no question of not releasing the information, but there did remain a substantial question as to how the information should be released. An effective, major public story would maximize the credibility of the study and would promote its use. In deciding on a release strategy, we had to be sensitive to the political impact of the data. In other words, we were aware that if the study showed that the Jewish community was substantially smaller than it was believed to be in the political arena, the publication of the number itself could do damage to the community.

It became obvious fairly quickly that the results for the city--over one million Jews remaining in New York City--would make for a better story than emphasizing the 1.7 million we found in the metropolitan area. The first number was more than most knowledgeable people expected, the second was less.

We did not have accurate trends because there was no baseline in which we were confident, yet it was widely believed that the trends were down. Available studies from the 1950s and early 1960s indicated that there were substantially more Jews in the city, and probably more Jews in the total metropolitan area, than we found in 1981. A headline indicating that the Jewish population was down would not only reinforce the hand of the anti-analysts (those who thought the study should not be done or released in the first place), but could also damage the community politically. Thus, our press strategy and press conference were built around commitment to the city and the New York City story.

In the course of preparing for the press conference, some argued that we should hold back until we had the whole story, that is to say, not only the total number of Jews by county, city, and metropolitan area, but also some of the interesting information about their socioeconomic characteristics and religious behavior. The consensus was that it was more important to develop the initial story than it was to be able to answer detailed questions. The press conference was held and the key headline in The New York Times was "1.1 Million Jews Residing in City, A Survey Shows" (5/5/82).

A serious political problem was that of disappointed localities. By looking at the preliminary numbers, it was obvious that leadership in the Bronx and Long Island, particularly Nassau County, would be very unhappy with the results. Actually, we seriously underestimated the anger in Nassau and the sense there of a political price paid. Conventional wisdom had it that there were over 600,000 Jews in Long Island; our own numbers showed approximately 420,000. There was bad press on Long Island, but the Bronx was relatively quiet. Queens, which showed a higher population than expected, was overjoyed. Overall there was a sense that the New York metropolitan area continued to have a strong Jewish community.

It is important to stress that from a planning point of view the county totals are almost useless. Even in the context of the Long Island controversy, Federation officials repeatedly stressed that whether Long Island had 400,000 Jews or 600,000 Jews would have no material impact on Federation's allocations to Long Island because we shared with local leadership their perception that Federation allocations to Long Island need to "catch up" with needs. On the other hand, the detailed data relating to age, socio-economic characteristics, family status, and affiliation, were viewed as an enormous tool for forward planning for Federation, and it is to the use of the data that I would like to turn.

THE USES OF POPULATION DATA

In thinking about the Jewish Population Study in New York we identified four potential audiences: (1) the academic community (it was understood that the study directors would develop materials on their own for this community); (2) the Jewish community at large; (3) interested professionals and volunteers in Jewish communal work in general and federation agencies in particular; and (4) social planners.

For the Jewish community at large we envisioned a series of subject reports summarizing the basic data. For Jewish communal leaders we envisioned and actually constructed an inquiry response system with an analyst housed at Federation, using a terminal to respond to specific inquiries. With regard to central social policy analysts, we envisioned an approach which would position Jewish population data at the heart of an analytic process. It is this fourth use of the data that I would like to discuss.

For the purposes of this paper, social policy analysis is defined as the presentation of options for lay decision-makers, together with the pros and cons of each option. The process uses explicit criteria, projects the probable consequences of alternatives, and makes explicit value judgments about various outcomes. The approach is issue-oriented and data-intensive. Social policy analysis is viewed as the heart of what a federation headquarters does.

Social policy research, for the purposes of this paper, is defined as the collection, interpretation, and presentation of policy-relevant information. It is the fact component of the fact/value process of social policy analysis described above

The heart of social policy research in a human service environment is information about people in the system. Nothing is more crucial to our efforts than information about population.

Social policy research aims to illuminate difficult policy choices and enrich decision-making. Effective social policy research relies on explicit hypotheses, that is, important policy questions or issues requiring illumination. In the best of all possible worlds, policy hypotheses would have been designed before a questionnaire was designed or tested. This is a widely overlooked step in social policy research in general. Where hypotheses are developed they tend not to be policy-oriented.

In the New York Jewish Population Study, the second best of all possible worlds was obtained--that is, researchers who were sensitive to, and interested in, the application of the data to policy and to seeing the data used.

The development of policy hypotheses is crucial; and not having such hypotheses may result in inappropriate research questions or ill-designed data tabulation strategies. To illustrate:

1. Assume a policy interest in encouraging Jewish practice is part of an identity-building strategy.
2. Assume that a search for relatively easy, pleasant areas of Jewish practice as expressions of Jewish identity put Chanukah and Purim high on the list.
3. Hypothesis: Purim observance is less widespread than Chanukah observance.
4. Hypothesis: One good use of communal resources would be to encourage further observance of Purim.

From the point of view of the sociology of ritual observance, one would not necessarily ask questions about Purim; from the point of view of the policy issue defined above, such data could be important. In the New York study, Purim observance was not one of the questions asked.

New York Federation is assessing the camping needs of children, observing that many relatively low-income children did not seem to be taking advantage of Federation's camping services. Substantial numbers of low-income children are in the right-wing Orthodox community; camps for this group need to be segregated by sex. Federation has two such camps for boys and one for girls. Is another camp for girls needed? Data on sex of children could be important in helping to resolve this issue. To economize, our survey did not ask the sex of children. In the absence of a policy issue relating to camping services such a judgment makes perfectly good sense; in the presence of such an issue, on the other hand, it makes less sense.

Even in the absence of explicit policy hypotheses formulated in advance of the study, the actual results are enormously significant in relation to a wide variety of policy questions ranging from relatively small-scale and immediate issues to long-range and complex problems of resource allocation, priority-setting, and comprehensive strategy.

One of the current issues in New York relates to whether Federation should develop a Jewish marriage referral service (a modernized version of the old-time shadchan or marriage broker). Our hypothesis was that singles were spread all over the metropolitan area. An analysis of the distribution of the number and types of singles by age, previous marital history, and location suggested a great concentration of young Jewish singles in Manhattan, with a complex distribution of other types of singles (widowed, divorced, and older never-marrieds). The classification of singles, using the study, gives one the basis for creating a sample frame for actually convening a set of singles into a panel to discuss in detail their specific needs and concerns as a key component for testing the relevance and usefulness of the marriage referral concept.

Identifying and assessing needs is critical to program design and evaluation. For example, one of the crucial questions in New York is the adequacy of the number of nursing home beds for the Jewish elderly. The issue of the adequacy of the number of beds relates to the need for such service as a function of age and frailty. One can use nationally developed experience with regard to the probability of the need for full-time nursing homes in different age groups to derive an estimate of the needed number of Jewish nursing home beds, which one can compare to the actual number of beds available. Without such basic population data by age, within the elderly community (65-70, 70-75, etc.), this analysis is not feasible.

One of the important policy questions that we need to pursue at a broader level is the distribution of resources by population type and area. Thus, in the future we envision computing dollar expenditure per capita by population type and neighborhood. It is inappropriate to infer that per capita allocations should be equal in all settings; rather the expectation is that the differences between the levels of allocation should parallel explicit policies. For example, it would be hard to justify higher per capita allocations for social services to wealthier neighborhoods as compared to poorer ones. Another broad issue relates to our neighborhood preservation program. We are looking at a series of investments in fifteen target neighborhoods. One of the oft-repeated questions raised by prospective donors is "What is the probability of success?" or alternatively, "What is the risk?". The population study gives us the possibility of constructing a risk index by relating levels of satisfaction and the percentage planning to move in different neighborhoods.

Several other examples of the use of these data are important. In our planning for community centers we have established 50,000 to 100,000 Jewish population as a required base for a full-service center, with 100,000 being more appropriate in high density neighborhoods and 50,000 in low density neighborhoods. The population study gives us the basis for projecting the needed number and potential locations of centers. In our very definition of Jewish neighborhoods, which relates not only to our neighborhood preservation program but also to planning for future services, the population per square mile and the total Jewish population provide an absolutely essential cornerstone to the whole effort to define Jewish communal interests in a neighborhood. This in turn is our criterion for defining a Jewish neighborhood.

The study of population, while the core of social policy research, is not enough. For example, we also need information on service use. Thus, we know very little about which families use camping services and under what conditions. Similarly, we know nothing about the use of Federation or other Jewish camps. Neither do we know anything about satisfaction with existing services or future needs for them. Even so, population analysis is an enormously important beginning to systematic planning for Jewish communal services.

In order to maximize the use of such data, a whole series of other problems has to be overcome. Professional staffs in Jewish communal organizations are not necessarily trained in the use of large-scale data systems, and the lack of sophistication needs to be overcome. Most importantly, we need to inculcate a mindset that says that before collecting a single number we must have some sense of what we will do with it when it arrives; a mindset that says, "Don't ask a question unless you have some idea as to how you will use the answer."

In the final analysis, value judgments are intrinsic to social planning in any system. Recognizing the interaction between facts and values means that we give primacy to policy questions in framing the agenda for Jewish research. Thus, the crucial starting point for Jewish research in the coming decade should not be What is the nature of the Jewish community? but rather, What are the possible options for strengthening the Jewish community? and What information do we need to collect and process in order to sharpen our ability to select and implement the best policy options?

5
Using Jewish Population Study Data for Decision Making: Theoretical Considerations and Practical Experience

Steven Huberman

The year 1923 is a landmark in Jewish organizational research. In that year, the Cleveland Jewish Federation undertook one of the most comprehensive population studies ever conducted. Although done sixty years ago, it can serve as a model for Jewish population studies today.

The goals of the Cleveland survey were twofold: to identify the unmet needs of Cleveland Jewry and to propose solutions. Using the database provided by the survey, the Federation went beyond fiscal functions to social welfare. For example, the survey documented that there were 12,000 children of school age, many of whom were not receiving a Jewish education. In response, the community established a Bureau of Jewish Education to promote student recruitment and improve the quality of schools. The survey found that the "Orthodox" community was growing in power and self-consciousness. The Federation responded by closing its institutions on Shabbat and holidays, making the facilities kosher, and developing an extensive Jewish social and recreational program. In short, the study charted the directions of the Federation for the next twenty years (Gartner).

In this paper, we will explore those factors which promote effective research utilization. We will examine the usefulness and limits of population studies as well as the research requirements of Jewish planning bodies. Finally, we will present case material from one federation (Los Angeles) which has had a comprehensive action research program. Before turning to these issues, it is important to understand the organizational climate of Jewish population research.

SOURCES OF TENSION AND MISUNDERSTANDING

Jewish organizational research differs from much academic research in that it is almost always conducted in an action setting. Fund-raising, budgeting, planning, and service delivery are taking place at the same time as the research. As a result, lay and professional decision-makers often see research as an appendage to these primary responsibilities, or at best as a second level priority.

When an "outside" researcher is hired by a Jewish communal organization, a number of factors may generate and exacerbate tension between the researcher and the staff or lay leaders. These factors include ambiguous role definition, organizational insecurity, and differing expectations.

Ambiguous Role Definition

Research frequently requires that organizational personnel accept new responsibilities. They may be asked to assist in survey design, data collection, analysis, and interpretation, and in general to collaborate in new tasks. These role definitions may not be clear or the division of responsibility may be vague. Organizational staff and researchers may also have conflicting frames of reference. Practitioners are concerned with delivering services. They may perceive research as a diversion or even a threat, and the money, time, and Jewish executive energy invested as of dubious utility. In fact, the study may directly threaten some administrators' jobs because it might uncover gaps and deficiencies in Jewish communal programming. One Jewish community recently undertook a major organizational study which demonstrated that the agency studied was not serving its clients effectively. The study resulted in the dismissal of the agency executive, which later made other agency executives in the community reluctant to encourage further research.

Organizational Insecurity

In a Jewish organization that is undergoing some internal dissension, researchers may be seen as "hatchet men"--agents hired to "do in" a particular group. Fairly typical research practices--protecting the confidentiality of the data and not sharing findings prematurely--may produce suspicion. The troubled nature of some Jewish organizations may make life difficult for the researcher. The effectiveness of the outside researcher may be influenced by such circumstances as how he or she is supervised, the openness of communication within the agency, or things as mundane as bookkeeping arrangements.

One technique for alleviating tension between agency and researchers is to foster the participation of administrators in the research. If they are involved in the planning process, they can gain a proprietary feeling toward the study and a greater commitment to using it. Administrators need to have a better understanding of what the research is suppose to produce. In turn, they can contribute ideas to the project, especially regarding agency norms and realities. In one instance, a Jewish community recently concluded a study which led to significant changes in its management structure. A key to its success was having the researcher share her thoughts on the study design and findings with agency staff on a regular basis. Staff may be regularly asked to comment on the research methodology and accuracy of the collected data.

A clear authority structure can reduce the possibility of friction. An informal contract needs to be negotiated at the beginning of the project so that administrators and researchers recognize the scope and limits of their roles. Everyone should know who is responsible to whom. Disruptions can be minimized with such initial role definitions. Researchers and agency staff can be made to feel that they are a "team." Researchers who provide useful feedback information can get the support of their practitioner colleagues.

Differing Expectations

In addition to the possibilities of administrative tension, conflict may arise from differing expectations held by the researcher and the practitioner. Although the Jewish community has sometimes supported "pure" research, organizations have generally given priority to "applied" studies--research designed to upgrade staff and agency performance. Lay and professional leaders need practical information to enhance Jewish decision-making. The litmus test for successful Jewish organizational research is that it be used.

However, conventional demographic studies can help answer only some policy-oriented questions. Some leaders and staff misunderstand what can be answered by a particular piece of research. It is therefore helpful, if not imperative, to define for organizational clients the strengths and weaknesses of a population study. They must understand from the outset that the population study cannot answer all of the questions on each organization's agenda.

USING POPULATION RESEARCH: SOME ILLUSTRATIONS

Some federations do know how to use population research, as the following illustrations confirm.

1. Finding: One federation discovered that during a ten-year period there was a marked decline in the number of persons under age 10 and over 40, while there was a significant increase in the number of Jews aged 20-30.

   Action: The federation developed a Young Professionals Program, and the Jewish Community Centers started a Young Adult Center in an area of new Jewish concentration.
2. Finding: The same population study indicated marked population relocation. The areas of growth were in new suburban locations. The magnitude of the population relocation far exceeded the projections of federation planners.

   Action: The community designed plans for new multipurpose facilities, and federation agencies opened offices in the new residential districts.
3. Finding: Few Jewish teenagers were enrolled in post-Bar/Bat Mitzvah Jewish schooling. Fewer than half of all Jewish children were being exposed to Jewish education.

   Action: The community developed a program of Jewish studies for high school youth, and the Bureau of Jewish Education conducted a pupil recruitment drive.
4. Finding: A study showed that the image of the Jewish federation was ambiguous. Among all groups there was enormous misinformation about the organization, especially its allocations system.

   Action: The Communications Department formulated a series of media productions to dispel myths about the federation.

These are "success stories" of population research use. However, for a federation or agency to have an effective planning capability, it needs to do more than demographic research in its classical definition. Communities that use research extensively have gone beyond demography to needs assessment.

COMBINING DEMOGRAPHIC AND NEEDS ASSESSMENT RESEARCH

The Los Angeles Jewish Federation has had a comprehensive research program for approximately twenty years and offers a fruitful case study in research sponsorship. The Los Angeles research program has several components--demography, needs assessment, and service utilization profiles. In addition, it has just developed a large-scale system for evaluating agencies and for setting allocations priorities, with population and needs assessment data constituting the key inputs for the Federation's allocations system.

Needs assessment may be defined as a methodology that identifies and analyzes individual, group, and community deficiencies. Human service requirements of geographic areas and target groups are measured in terms of relative importance and intensity. Today Jewish communal funds, staff, and programs cannot realistically accommodate all Jewish human service needs. Hard choices must be made among programs of seemingly equal importance and worth. Many federations are now moving to develop community priorities and to reconsider the level of funding for their programs.

The Los Angeles needs assessment approach supplemented and filled the gaps in its demographic survey. Researchers interviewed "key informants," persons who represented diverse segments of the community and who were knowledgeable about human service or Jewish communal problems (e.g., Jewish organizational professionals, lay leaders, rabbis, Jewish educators, and academics). Many of these key informants were current or potential consumers of Jewish agency services. Since Los Angeles is a vast territory with different geographic population structures, the study was done in each of the five Federation regions.[1]

Key informants in the Los Angeles survey were interviewed regarding approximately fifty problems. They were asked whether each problem existed in their region; the seriousness of the problems; the specific communities most affected; and whether the problems were getting worse. In addition to problem identification, they were asked to select the most serious problems, to justify their selection, and to analyze the adequacy of services addressing these problems.[2]

There are four key elements to how the Los Angeles Federation displays its population and attitudinal data derived from the population study and the survey of key informants for the use of decision-makers:

1. A demographic analysis of each of the Federation regions, and of trends that act across regional boundaries.
2. A regional needs breakdown--a delineation of the most pressing human service problems confronting each region and the population groups most in need of help.
3. The connections between particular demographic trends and the most serious problems affecting Jews in each region.
4. Planning implications from the needs assessment and population study data.

In combining population and needs assessment data, the Los Angeles Federation report took into account several considerations:

1. Data were compiled and displayed in a way that encouraged readers to make their inferences and draw their own conclusions. The summary suggested alternative ways of viewing the accumulated

data for planning purposes and cautioned against generalizing beyond the data.

2. Data on population and on needs were presented wherever possible for each region as well as for the total Los Angeles area, so that regional differences could be taken into account in policy formation.
3. Since the report was intended to be useful for policy-making, the population statistics in the first part were selected and framed so that they had a direct bearing on the needs and problems discussed in the second part.
4. Because of space limitations, the report provided an overview of major needs and problems instead of detailed analyses of only a few selected ones. Separate reports on specific problems or population groups were issued.[3]

For details of how such a study report is drawn up, see the Appendix at the end of this article.

APPLYING RESEARCH TO A FEDERATION ALLOCATION STRUCTURE

What is the secret to managing a successful business? Why do some corporations do extraordinarily well, while others wallow in mediocrity? A recent study of management techniques revealed some straightforward answers (Peters and Waterman). America's best-run companies encourage experimentation and innovation. They are also data-intensive. Research and development are core activities.

The lay leadership of the Los Angeles Federation consists primarily of successful business people. They have recognized that they need to apply the same standards to running a Jewish organizations that they use in running their own businesses. They are committed to experimentation and research. This business orientation is reflected in the creation of the <u>Federation Community Priorities System</u> (CPS).

The Community Priorities System, modeled after similar undertakings in the business world, integrates data on population characteristics and service needs into the Federation allocations structure. Specifically, CPS has six functions:

1. To develop an approach for establishing community priorities and to define the roles of different stakeholder groups in the priorities-setting process.
2. To develop the process for applying collected demographic and needs assessment data and any program-ranking criteria identified to the priorities-setting process.
3. To develop a program and service classification system for Federaation departments and agencies.
4. To develop a format for presenting background information about each high-priority program.
5. To design a plan for applying the priorities to the Federation allocations process.
6. To develop and present the final community priorities report, which includes the list of priorities as determined by the

priority-setting procedure, a methodological statement, and supporting population and needs data.

A grant of $46,000 was awarded in 1982 to the Federation's Planning and Budgeting Department to develop these six elements. The importance of establishing this long-range priorities system was documented by the community's population study. That study showed that (1) the community had grown in size to 500,000, but that household size was shrinking; (2) comparatively, the single and elderly proportions were increasing; (3) Jews were dispersing over tremendous geographic areas; and (4) Jewish identification was eroding. These documented changes encouraged the Federation to reexamine how best to serve the community with the limited resources at its disposal. The CPS process became particularly urgent since the Federation - United Jewish Appeal campaign was not even keeping pace with inflation in Los Angeles.

The initiative for CPS did not come from Jewish agency professionals; it came from lay leaders, many of whom work for top high technology, consumer goods, industrial, and service corporations. These leaders were looking for guidelines for disbursing allocable funds within the Jewish community, and wanted to identify the most pressing Jewish communal needs and problems so as to have a more rational basis upon which to make allocations decisions.

One central element in the priority-setting process has been stakeholder participation. The Community Priorities Committee, a newly established and prestigious Federation committee, consists of lay and professional representatives from key central Federation committees and from each Federation region, along with agency presidents, agency executive directors, and academicians, especially social scientists. They review the Federation research program and help develop the priorities system, seeking extensive lay and agency input. This partnership among various groups has produced a committment to use research data throughout Federation and its network of agencies.

This experience suggests that a Jewish organization looking to generate and use research data should establish a broad-based research committee. Its membership needs to be highly diverse, comprising both practitioners and potential users of Jewish-sponsored research. The group should continue to function after the completion of the specific research project. Finally, the committee needs to supervise the dissemination of the research information and be sure that the data are used.

SUMMARY

This paper has examined the organizational climate of Jewish-sponsored research, arguing that the climate is politically turbulent and action-oriented. Friction between researchers and practitioners may be caused by ambiguous role definition and organizational insecurity. The tension around research implementation can be ameliorated by the participation of administrators in the study design. A clear and unambiguous contract between outside researchers and agency administrators can help set forth mutually understood expectations and responsibilities. A sharing and open relationship between researcher and practitioner can further this sense of collegiality.

We also considered differing expectations about research utility. Practitioners want readily understandable, nontechnical, usable information. They want data which can be quickly translated into social policies and programs.

Last, we cited the Los Angeles Federation as a case study. The Los Angeles Federation has gone beyond demography into a variety of other research methodologies, particularly needs assessment, agency evaluation, and allocations priority-setting.

The Jewish community has no choice but to sponsor policy-oriented research. Ongoing and innovative programs need to be based on a factual foundation. Population research can provide that necessary foundation.

Appendix: Sample Organization and Table of Contents for a Report Combining Population and Needs Assessment Data

Executive Summary. Concise account of the major findings of the study.

1. Introduction

Descriptions of the purpose of the report, the major data sources, and the report's organizations. Discussion of possible uses for various audiences. Insert of a map of the greater Los Angeles area, designating the regions.

Part I. The Jewish Population of Greater Los Angeles and the Regions

Brief introduction to the sections that follow.

2. Demographic Characteristics

Percentage distributions of Jewish inhabitants of greater Los Angeles and each region, including age, sex, birthplace, education, occupation, income, marital status, composition of household, and geographical mobility.

3. Jewish Characteristics

Percentage distributions for the following characteristics, for inhabitants of greater Los Angeles and each region: religious identity; religion of parents, spouse, and children, including education of children in Jewish schools or programs; synagogue affiliations of household; degree to which residence is in a Jewish neighborhood; including attitudes toward living in a Jewish neighborhood; extent of contact with Jewish friends and close relatives; subscriptions to Jewish newspapers or magazines; affiliation with Jewish clubs and organizations; and contributions to Jewish charities or other Jewish causes.

4. Summary

Brief summary of the major findings reported in the preceding two sections, especially with regard to regional differences. Discussion of implications linking this part of the report with the next.

Appendix (continued)

Part II. Problems, Needs, and Services Currently Provided

Brief introduction to the sections that follow.

5. Jewish Social Problems and Needs

Percentage distributions of key informant opinion on twenty-two selected social problems that potentially affect Jews in greater Los Angeles, but which are not restricted to Jewish communities. Judgments reported regionally for all of the following aspects: existence of the problems and, for those judged the most serious, the extent of their seriousness, recent improvements or declines, and the adequacy of Jewish and non-Jewish agency programs addressing them.

6. Jewish Communal Problems and Needs

Percentage distributions of key informant opinion on twenty-five selected Jewish communal problems that are specific to Jewish communities. Judgments reported regionally for all of the following aspects: existence of the problems and, for those judged the most serious, the extent of their seriousness, recent improvements or declines, the Jewish population groups most affected, and the adequacy of Jewish agency programs in addressing the problems.

7. Social and Communal Problems Joined

Percentage distributions and rankings based on key informant opinion of the seriousness of the nearly fifty problems discussed in the preceding two sections and of the population groups considered to have the greatest need for additional resources. Judgments reported regionally, and primary attention given to the problems judged by expert opinion to be the most serious. Summary of suggestions and recommendations on how to deal more effectively with the most serious problems.

8. Summary and Conclusion

Brief review of the major findings in the preceding three sections. Discussion of implications for Community Priorities System and action planning.

Appendix A. The Population Survey

Description of technical aspects. Inclusion of tables too detailed to fit into the main text, or tables on peripheral topics. Inclusion of original questionnaire.

Appendix B. The Needs Survey

Description of technical aspects. Inclusion of tables too detailed to fit into the main text, or tables on peripheral topics. Inclusion of original questionnaire. [4]

Notes

1. A full treatment of the Los Angeles needs assessment model is contained in Andron.
2. Step-by-step directions for conducting a needs survey are analyzed in Neuber.
3. UCLA professors Adrianne Bank and Robert Wenkert collaborated on developing the "Sample Organization and Table of Contents for a Report Combining Population and Needs Assessment Data."
4. The Los Angeles population survey was designed and directed by Bruce A. Phillips. The needs survey was developed and implemented by Steven Huberman and Saul Andron.

References

Andron, Saul. 1982. "Going Beyond Demography: Generating a Base for Federation Priority Setting and Decision-Making." Paper presented at the CJF Social Planners Institute.

Gartner, Lloyd. 1978. History of the Jews of Cleveland. New York: Jewish Theological Seminary.

Neuber, Keith. 1980. Needs Assessment: A Model for Community Planning. Beverly Hills, Calif.: Sage Publications.

Peters, Thomas J. and Robert H. Waterman, Jr. 1982. In Search of Excellence: Lessons from America's Best-Run Companies. New York: Harper and Row.

6
Federation and Population Studies

Lester I. Levin

Federations generally engage in research studies in order to answer immediate questions of concern to the Jewish community. Examples include where to locate a new Jewish community center; whether there is a need to expand the home for the aged; and what are the current service gaps. This type of research is narrow in scope and related to program and service issues. It contrasts with studies of broader subjects such as Jewish identity, intermarriage, and family breakdown. This is not to suggest that federations are not interested in or do not utilize academic research. Increasingly, we are seeing federations serving as stimulators, cosponsors, and consumers of traditional "basic" research.

By themselves, population and demographic studies do not answer complex community planning and budgeting questions, but properly used, they can be most helpful in the federation process of problem-solving and decision-making. Federation community planning requires and uses a variety of data including service statistics, reports from service providers and key informants, as well as national data collected and disseminated by the Council of Jewish Federations (CJF) and other national agencies. In many instances this readily available information is quite adequate for community planning purposes. Most federations operate in small and intermediate communities, with Jewish populations under 30,000. The federation system (federation and agencies) and the sense of "community" in Jewish communal life provide easy access to highly reliable impressionistic and hard data.

Since 1970, the number of federations engaging in a formal, ongoing planning process has increased from ten to sixty-five, and currently there are approximately 100 professional staff people nationwide with primary responsibilities for planning. Recently, smaller federations have shown an interest in developing an effective planning capacity, and CJF has published a special manual to assist them.

The scope of federation planning is also changing. Initially, federation planning was primarily related to service planning and used to determine the gaps between service needs and available services within the federation system. Today, federation planning is also concerned with priority-setting; effectiveness of service (outcomes); and coordination. In addition, federation planning often encompasses the entire Jewish community beyond the agency service network.

To a large degree, we can attribute the growing interest in population and demographic studies to the changes in federation planning described above.

THE FEDERATION EXPERIENCE WITH POPULATION STUDIES, 1947-1978

During the years 1947 through 1978 over fifty federations conducted population studies (see Appendix). In addition, the Council of Jewish Federations conducted the National Jewish Population Study, which was completed in 1971.

Alvin Chenkin of the CJF staff has analyzed these studies with respect to their objectives, the use made of the findings, and their value to the community. His work dealt with the integration of the study findings into the community planning process rather than evaluating technically the study process itself. There is much to learn from his analysis. Some examples follow.

Objectives

In undertaking population studies, federations may have either a single limited objective or broad goals:

1. Specific or limited goals:

   Decide where best to locate a Jewish community center. Determine whether the community needs a home for the aged. Provide support data to develop community priorities.

2. Broad or diffuse goals:

   Develop demographic data for community planning. Develop demographic data to assist Jewish service agencies in program development. Measure population growth or decline to reevaluate community priorities.

For many communities the National Jewish Population Study provides useful and adequate demographic information for community planning. Exceptions, however, are those communities which have been significantly affected by population loss or gain and shifts of population within the community. The Sunbelt communities and major Jewish population centers are the most common examples of these types of communities where local population studies may be needed to provide supplemental data essential to effective federation fund-raising, planning, and budgeting.

Many local population studies confirm national trends which were identified in the National Jewish Population Study (NJPS), such as the increasing proportion of aging and the shift in occupation patterns from entrepreneur and managers to professional categories. These trends had obvious planning significance to which many communities responded--for example, by expansion of services for the elderly.

Why Studies "Fail"

Problems encountered in past population studies, which led to complaints and "failures," resulted from one or more of the following:

1. Inadequate consideration of the pros and cons of a study. Often, the decision to do a study was made without a feasibility or exploratory consultation, as provided by the Council of Jewish Federations. This consultation considers the kinds of information desired, information available from existing sources, alternative methods of getting additional information, the nature of the decisions and their dollar expenditures for which the study findings would be used, and other relevant factors to help the community determine the advisability of a population study.

2. Failure to use and exploit existing local and national data. Good use of such data may make a study superfluous, or reduce the scope of a study to specific target areas.

3. Study done outside of a planning process. Federations which do not have an ongoing planning structure and process often have difficulty in implementing the study. Although the study may have some immediate application, it is usually not "mined" and is often forgotten after a year or two.

4. Little or no community involvement in preparatory steps before study. This usually results in the completed study being treated as an outsider's report. The lack of credibility weakens the value of the study and makes it difficult to implement. It is particularly important for the lay committee to be involved in the preparatory stage of the study, working very closely with the consultant. It is at this stage that the purpose is clarified and then translated into technical form (questionnaire, sample, interview methods). In many communities, the study findings will be used by Jewish communal agencies, synagogues, and organizations, as well as the federation. Their input during the preparation period is important and should give the study greater credibility and usefulness. Particular attention should be given to what information is needed and what use will be made of the information.

5. Confusion or lack of clarity about the purpose of the study. As discussed earlier, population studies can be used for a variety of purposes: to ascertain the size of the community, its demographic characteristics, and its mobility patterns; to explore attitudes about communal issues; and to delineate service needs. To accomplish any or a combination of these requires careful design planning, which cannot be done if the purposes are not specified in advance.

6. Unrealistic expectations. Some federations expect the study to provide solutions to one or more community problems, as if the study were a panacea. They are not prepared to analyze the findings and utilize them in a dynamic planning process.

7. Lack of understanding of types of studies and their uses, values, and limitations. Planning departments conduct a variety of studies, including studies of general needs; target populations (elderly, singles, working woman); consumer attitudes; and user

(client) satisfaction. As discussed above, a population study may be broad in scope or limited to a few areas. It is important that the study fit the use intended, and that it be seen as only one of the tools of the planning process.

8. Overload of information. Some past studies provided more than the community wanted or was ready to deal with. A specific study would have been more useful than a broad population study.

Confusion About Population Studies

Based on our numerous recent contacts with federations, it is obvious that there is a great deal of confusion about what a population study is, when and how to use it, and what its limitations are:

1. Population counts. Sometimes a federation wants a population study as a means of determining how many Jews live in the community. They are uncomfortable with their present estimates and want more exact figures. Often, they assume or expect that a formal study will be 98 to 100 percent accurate. Related to the desire for increased accuracy is the assumption that there are significant numbers of Jews unknown to the Jewish community ("non-list Jews") and "if we only knew them, we could solicit them; they would affiliate and become active." It is important for communities to understand that Jewish population counts are educated guesses at best, and that identification of new prospects is but a first step in involvement. We must be careful not to use population studies to raise expectations unrealistically.

2. New information. Communities expect to learn something new from a population study and not just to confirm their impressions. They also want to feel that the new information is worth the cost of securing it. Planners and consultants bear a major responsibility in fulfilling these expectations or advising the community of limitations. Consideration should be given to alternate means of collecting data, full use of existing local data, comparable data from other communities, and the potential impact of the new information.

3. The "kitchen sink" study ("We want to know more"). Early conversations with federations wanting to have population studies done often begin with "We want to know more about our community." When we ask, "More about what?" the answer is likely to be "Everything." This answer is probably our first clue that the federation is not ready for a population study. Unless we go beyond this level of generality, we will produce an "all but the kitchen sink" study, which is doomed from the outset.

4. Putting the cart before the horse. Some federations have initiated population studies before developing a planning process. Often, they expected the population study to be a panacea and, not surprisingly, were disappointed with the results. As implied

earlier, the most effective population studies emanated from planning concerns and were implemented by the planning process. Some population studies have elicited information which the community had no intention of using. When this happens, the entire process is endangered, community dollars may be wasted, and federation credibility can be impaired. Thoughtful planning and preparation can prevent this. Particular attention needs to be given to what information is required and how it will be applied.

USING THE NATIONAL JEWISH POPULATION STUDY TO DEVELOP A COMMUNITY PROFILE

Based on these examples and numerous consultations, it is obvious that the National Jewish Population Study and recent community and national studies have not been used to their full extent. Before embarking on a population study, a community should review existing information to determine its relevance and adequacy. As an example, the NJPS developed the distribution of the Jewish community by major age groups, as shown in Table 6.1.

TABLE 6.1
Percent Distribution of Individuals by Major Age Groups

		Estimates	
Age	1971 %	1981 %	1991 %
0-4	5.73	7.24	6.67
5-14	17.01	11.50	15.17
15-29	24.03	25.72	17.77
30-64	42.08	41.84	46.22
65 +	11.50	13.70	15.17

This national profile predicts a steady increase in the number of individuals 65 and over and a decrease in ages 5 to 14 (from the 1971 base). The trend information for 1981 which has been substantially confirmed by numerous national and local studies, provides signals to individual federations and agencies in planning for the elderly and school age populations in their communities. Numerous communities have used this trend information effectively in developing increased services for the elderly and in preventing the overexpansion of programs and facilities for the school age population.

Using the NJPS distribution profile, a federation can develop a working population profile of its own community, which has numerous uses in planning. Table 6.2 shows the theoretical age distributions in a Jewish community with a population of 10,000.

TABLE 6.2
Population Profile for Typical Jewish Community of 10,000 Individuals

Age	1971	1981	1991
0-4	570	720	660
5-14	1,700	1,150	1,410
15-29	2,400	2,570	1,780
30-64	4,200	4,180	4,620
65 +	1,150	1,370	1,500

By converting the percent distributions to the number of individuals in various age categories, smaller communities can more easily determine how well the profile fits and/or how comfortable they are using the profile for planning purposes. When discrepancies are obvious or easily identified from available records (membership lists, service statistics, agency experience, etc.), adjustments can be made. The smaller the community, the more likely that these adjustments can be made satisfactorily without a formal population study, from available data and key informants. In a community of 10,000, estimates within 3 to 5 percent accuracy will change the total results by 300 to 500 individuals. When these numbers are distributed into their respective age categories, however, they become less significant.

The numerical profile makes it easier for a community to identify the target populations it wishes to consider more closely. Assume a community wants to explore the needs of the elderly. Table 6.3 shows the figures for the elderly as a proportion of the total population.

TABLE 6.3
Jewish Elderly: Percentage of Total Jewish Population

	1981	1991	Change
NJPS estimated %	13.7 %	15.0 %	+1.3 %
Number individuals in community of 10,000	1,370	1,500	+130

The projected increase of 1.3 percentage points from 1981 to 1991 in a community of 10,000 would result in an additional 130 elderly individuals (a 10 percent increase in the elderly population), which is not an overwhelming figure when considered in terms of service planning and development. At most, it would usually indicate a possible increase of six more individuals requiring skilled nursing care, and approximately twenty more individuals needing community-supported housing.

Though the projected percentage increase in the elderly from 1981 to 1991 might not have significant impact, the suggested figures of 1,370 and 1,500 individuals 65 and over provide the community with a basis for collecting and analyzing available data on the elderly such as:

1. How many individuals 65 and over can be identified from current lists (federation, agencies, synagogues, membership organizations, etc.)?
2. How many elderly are participating in current programs and services?
3. How many are on waiting lists?

The 1971 NJPS developed special information reports on six areas relevant to community planning, in addition to demography and national and regional population counts. These reports dealt with intermarriage, mobility, Jewish identity, Jewish education, and Jewish communal services. A number of federations have used this information to assess their present services, identify service gaps, expand or develop new services, and determine priorities. Their use of NJPS information has prevented unnecessary and costly studies, and demonstrated the usefulness of NJPS, particularly as benchmark data.

OTHER SOURCES AND TECHNIQUES

Some of the information federations want for planning purposes may be extracted from local non-Jewish sources, such as the U.S. Census, the United Way, the local Chamber of Commerce, colleges and universities, utility companies, and market research. These services are collecting information continuously, and federations may be able to utilize their studies. There is a need to accumulate more experience in using these resources, from which guidelines can be developed for local communities.

Throughout the year, federations sponsor major community events (annual meetings, Super Sundays, telethons) which might be used to conduct limited surveys, using the exit interview technique. In addition to collecting data, federations need to develop better methods of disseminating information, so that it is readily accessible to more communities.

Federation planners and social scientists need to work together to develop a common language and definition of the components of the study and planning process. They need to have a common understanding which can be transmitted to the laity. Some of the areas of confusion in which CJF is currently providing consultation and which may be appropriate for joint exploration are in defining and describing such key concepts as planning, population study, needs assessment, and indicators.

As planning by federations continues to expand, the need for current and reliable information will increase. Population studies can provide much of this information, if they are properly designed. There is hope that the current cooperative efforts of planners, demographers, and researchers will lead to more integration of planning and population studies within the Jewish community.

Appendix

Communities which conducted population studies through 1978, and the year in which conducted, are shown below. These studies vary greatly in terms of scope, methodology, type of direction, and budget. The differences are the result, in part, of varying community goals, and in part the changes in approach over the time period covered (1947 to 1978).

Akron	1974	Milwaukee	1964
Allentown	1976	Minneapolis	1972
Atlanta	1947	New Orleans	1953, 1958, 1973
Atlantic City	1975		
Baltimore	1968	Norfolk	1974
Boston	1965, 1975	Oakland	1970
Camden	1965	Omaha	1976
Canton	1955	Passaic	1949
Chicago	1970*	Paterson	1964
Cincinnati	1970*	Pittsburgh	1963, 1976
Cleveland	1970*	Portland, Ore.	1971, 1977
Columbus, Oh.	1969	Providence	1964
Dallas	1974	Rochester	1961
Erie	1977	St. Petersburg ca.	1972
Flint	1967	Salt Lake City	1976
Hamilton, Ont.	1978	San Diego	1975
Hollywood, Fla.	1971	San Francisco	1959
Houston	1956, 1976	Seattle	1978
Indianapolis	1948	Shreveport	1970
Jacksonville	1947	Springfield, Mass.	1968
Jersey City	1978	Tampa	1958
Kansas City	1976	Trenton	1949, 1961, 1976
Long Beach	1962		
Los Angeles	1948, 1953, 1959	Vineland	1977
		Washington, D.C.	1956
Lynn, Mass.	1956	Waterbury	1970
Metro. New Jersey	1948	Wilmington	1962
Miami	1970*	Worcester	1957

*"Add-on" study utilizing interviews from the National Jewish Population Study and from a supplementary sample.

PART TWO

Issues in Data Collection and Analysis

The six articles in this section focus on select topics in data collection. Not only are they highly relevant to the concerns of the researcher, but planners could also benefit considerably by learning some of the more technical problems that confront the analyst.

The first paper provides an overview of sampling strategies. Its author Bruce A. Phillips has conducted more American Jewish community studies in recent years than anyone else. His paper compares the sampling techniques, population estimates, and weighting schemes for nine recently conducted studies. He concludes that local conditions--size of community, budget, accuracy of lists, and other factors--preclude the establishment of any firm and fast rules for ideal sampling strategies. Instead, techniques need to be sensitively adapted and applied for each study.

The article by Paul Ritterband and Steven M. Cohen provides a detailed examination of the sampling design and population estimation techniques employed in the largest local Jewish population study to date. The Greater New York Jewish Population Study exemplifies many of the problems encountered in other studies, if perhaps on a grander and more complex scale.

Bruce A. Phillips and Eve Weinberg recount their experiences in actually conducting the interviewing in several Jewish community studies. Their distillation of their experiences will provide useful lessons for even the most seasoned survey researchers.

Calvin Goldscheider has recently completed a monograph analyzing population trends among Boston Jews in which he imaginatively compares the community's Jews and non-Jews using the same study (the 1975 Boston Jewish Community Study). Goldscheider makes a compelling case for collecting data on a community's non-Jews concomitantly with the random sample survey of the local Jewish population. He argues that without such data one cannot determine whether Jewish population trends, relationships, and processes are distinctively "Jewish," or whether they are more a reflection of parallel phenomena among socially and demographically comparable non-Jewish groups.

Ira Rosenwaike has been successfully analyzing death records to obtain information on elderly population size, geographic distribution, patterns of illness, and related matters. In "Using Death Records for Estimating the Jewish Elderly Population in Local Areas," Rosenwaike presents an extremely low-cost and reasonably accurate technique for obtaining considerable information about a locale's aged Jews without going through the major expense and effort of a full-blown population study.

Last, Bruce A. Phillips presents several methods of updating Jewish community studies. "A Note on Updating and Followup Studies," while not dismissing the need for periodic complete Jewish population studies (as Boston and other communities have wisely decided to do every ten years), suggests some low-cost approaches to gathering useful interim information between major studies.

7
Sampling Strategies in Jewish Community Studies

Bruce A. Phillips

Detailed information about the sample designs of Jewish community surveys has been circulated largely by word of mouth or through unpublished statements produced by the sponsoring federation. As a result, Jewish communal researchers (especially those new to the field) have not had the experiences of other researchers readily available to them. Neither have the methodological advances made in the field of Jewish communal research been available to sociologists with similar methodological concerns in other areas of inquiry. The techniques employed by the major Jewish community studies conducted in the 1980s are described and compared in this paper so as to make them accessible to both groups of researchers.

Eight of the nine studies described here (Los Angeles, Chicago, St. Louis, Denver, Phoenix, Milwaukee, Cleveland, and Las Vegas) were conducted in the 1980s, and taken together they represent a new generation of Jewish communal research. (I leave description of the tenth study--New York--to a separate paper in this volume, written by the researchers.) The ninth study, Boston, was originally conducted in 1965 and later replicated in 1975. In many ways this study pioneered new directions, which became models for the other studies discussed. All ten studies represent a new generation of Jewish communal research characterized by methodological innovation and a commitment to including the broadest possible cross-section of the Jewish community. In addition to documenting the current state of the art of Jewish community survey technique, this paper also discusses the rationale for the choice of methodology and the tradeoffs that must be made when developing such a survey.

Sampling is the most problematic area of Jewish communal research. The researcher must choose between a true probability sample in which every Jewish household in the community has a known probability of selection, and some kind of list sample where only Jewish households on some kind of list are sampled. In a pure probability sample, randomly selected households are screened to locate Jewish households. This procedure is called "sampling to locate rare populations" and has been used to locate other rare populations such as unemployed black males (Sudman).

There are two basic kinds of list samples: lists made up from membership rosters and lists of "Distinctive Jewish Names" (DJNs) compiled from telephone directories, motor vehicle registrations, and other sources directly accessible by computer technology. The list sample is less expensive than the screening sample, but has the disadvantage of excluding those Jewish households who for some reason do not appear on the list.

Each of the studies discussed approached the sampling problem differently, but they can be grouped into three generic kinds of sample designs: pure screening samples (Los Angeles, Chicago, Milwaukee, Phoenix, and Denver), modified screening samples (Boston and Cleveland), and nonscreening samples (St. Louis and Las Vegas).

SCREENING SAMPLES

Screening samples are economically feasible only when conducted by telephone, and only recently have adequate methodologies and procedures for telephone surveys become available. During the early 1970s the rising cost of conducting surveys and the increasing reluctance of potential respondents to open their doors to strangers combined to bring about an interest in telephone surveys. A technique called Random Digit Dialing (RDD) was developed to overcome the potential bias introduced by sampling only from telephone directories. An RDD sample combines the three digit telephone prefixes in the community with four other digits generated at random by computer. The resulting sample of seven-digit phone numbers includes both listed and unlisted telephones, as well as commercial, residential, and nonworking numbers.

Two sets of decisions have to be made in an RDD screening sample: what geographic areas of the community to include and how to allocate the sample among the prefixes. The division of the community into specific geographic areas or strata is typically made on the basis of the distribution of the Jewish population in the community. Geographic conventions already widely accepted by the general community are also taken into consideration. The boundaries thus combine definitions based on Jewish population concentrations with geographic boundaries that are meaningful in the larger community. These geographic divisions must then be translated into their corresponding telephone prefixes. This is not necessarily a straightforward procedure since the telephone companies do not usually allocate exchanges according to recognizable geographic boundaries. Incorporated municipalities within metropolitan areas often have unique prefixes, but some prior research on the geographical distribution of prefixes is usually required within the city limits of that metropolitan area in order to properly include urban neighborhoods within the stratification scheme.

Chicago

The Chicago sample used nine strata, based in part on the "community areas" designated by the University of Chicago. The community areas were grouped into Jewish planning areas according to planning needs and the distribution of the Jewish population. Strata containing communities of particular planning interest were oversampled (i.e., the proportion of interviews conducted in those strata was higher than the share of Chicago Jewish households found in them). Other strata in which Jews make up only a small percentage of the population were undersampled in order to reduce the cost of locating Jewish households. Data about the distribution of Chicago Jewry were available from the National Jewish Population Study (conducted in 1970) which included a special sample for Chicago and from update studies conducted during the intervening years.

The sample was divided into ten replicates or equal-sized groups of randomly generated numbers. Each replicate included all the prefixes used in the study and thus constituted an independent random sample on its own. This made it possible to end the study after any given replicate was exhausted. After reviewing the first three completed replicates the sample was modified by eliminating prefixes that did not fall into one of the geographic strata, eliminating two strata of very low Jewish density where screening costs were considered excessive, and adding further replicates to six strata where it was evident that the original ten replicates would not produce the required number of completed interviews.

Los Angeles

The geographical strata in Los Angeles were determined by a Federation decision to decentralize by creating five regions which would participate directly in planning and allocation decisions. The geography and topography of Los Angeles are the major factors used to define the Federation regions. In Chicago, areas of low Jewish density were undersampled to conserve funds. By contrast, in Los Angeles, the same sorts of areas were oversampled because they required their own separate samples for regionalized planning. Half the budget and a quarter of the 825 completed interviews were allocated to these two low Jewish density areas which together constitute only 14 percent of the Jewish population. This decision had some fortunate scientific fallout, as it turned out that one of these regions had an overrepresentation of both intermarrieds and single-parent families. At the same time, the opportunity to learn more about subareas of the heavily populated San Fernando Valley region was lost, since that sample could not be made large enough for adequate geographic and subsamples.

The sample was further stratified according to the distribution of residential numbers by prefix within each regional stratum (based on the model described by Waksberg). The sample size for each individual prefix was determined using a three-stage process. First, the aggregate Jewish density for each region was computed from prior estimates of Jewish population made using a DJN technique. Next, the total number of residential households needed per region was computed by dividing the desired number of interviews for the region by its Jewish density (i.e., Jewish households as a proportion of all residential households). In the southern region, for example, a 3 percent Jewish density overall meant that 3,333 residential telephone numbers were needed to locate the required 100 Jewish interviews. In the third step, the total sample size was computed by taking into account the volume of nonresidential numbers that could be expected to appear in the sample. Seymour Sudman suggests that a simple random sample of randomly generated telephone numbers is only 20 percent residential, but a sample stratified by prefix proportional to the distribution of residential telephone numbers is closer to 50 percent residential. In the southern region, this meant that 6,666 telephone numbers were needed to produce 3,333 residences.

Information about the distribution of residential numbers (including unlisted numbers) was obtained from the two telephone companies that serve Los Angeles, and each of the five geographical strata was then further stratified by prefixes proportional to the distribution of residential phones. Returning to the southern region example, this means that if 2 percent of all residential numbers in the southern region were located in a given prefix, then 2 percent of the 6,666 numbers needed should be allocated to that prefix.

Thus, the size of the sample that would be needed was predicted ahead of time, rather than monitored as in other RDD studies described. The predictions were accurate in three out of the five regions. The Jewish density of the metropolitan region (which includes the old Jewish neighborhoods) was found to have been overestimated by the DJN technique. As a result, a new sample (or replicate) had to be generated in order to obtain the required number of interviews. In the eastern region the Jewish density had been underestimated, and too many interviews would have been collected had it not been for a coincidental offsetting error introduced by the telephone company data.

Denver

Unlike Chicago and Los Angeles, no previously existing hard data about the geographic distribution of Jews were available in Denver. Without such hard data, the sample could not be stratified by geographic area as it could be in Chicago and Los Angeles. The sample was instead stratified initially only according to the distribution of residential prefixes (as was the case within the Los Angeles regions) and the first phase of the screening was used to gather data on the distribution of Jewish households throughout Denver. About one month into the study and a third of the way through the original sample, the prefixes were grouped by "hit rate" (Jewish households as a percentage of all telephone numbers in the prefix) into four strata. The cost of locating and interviewing a Jewish household in each of the four strata was then computed. The remaining budget was then compared with the remaining number of interviews needed, and it was decided to discontinue interviewing in the fourth stratum where the cost of completing interviews was far more expensive than in the other three.

The fourth stratum of phone prefixes was the geographic area called the Boulder Corridor, an area of rapid growth for Denver overall where Jewish growth was also expected. By coincidence, the seventy interviews conducted in this area turned out to be disproportionate within the sample as a whole, which means that the area was probably oversampled from the perspective of sampling efficiency. Still, when the popular assumption of Jewish growth in the Boulder Corridor is taken into consideration, the expense of demonstrating that Jews were in fact not moving in was at least in part justified, although it is clear in retrospect that the first wave of the sample could have been smaller, as these decisions could have been made on the basis of fewer screening calls.

Planning areas were created after the fieldwork was completed. Both the number of completed interviews per zip code and the local conventions of community identification were taken into consideration in combining zip codes to create planning areas.

Milwaukee

No prior geographical stratification was required for Milwaukee, which is both smaller and more concentrated geographically than the other communities discussed. As with Denver, planning areas were created after data collection was complete. The original proposal called for a random digit sample similar to that used in Chicago. A pilot study (done as a first replicate) showed that the Jewish households were all listed in the directory, making it possible to use a sample of listed residential telephones for the sample frame. Listed numbers were divided into equal replicates in the same way that the random telephone numbers were divided in Chicago. Those prefixes which yielded no Jewish interviews in the early replicates were dropped from the later replicate to reduce study costs.

Phoenix

Information about the distribution of Jews in Phoenix was available from two market studies conducted in Phoenix with a questions on religion, and from a data set that showed the distribution of Distinctive Jewish Names in Phoenix by zip code, originally purchased for fund-raising from a direct-mail database company. The market study data and local convention suggested four planning areas or strata: Central Phoenix, Tri-Cities, Scottsdale-Paradise Valley, and Sun City. The names generated from the direct-mail database indicated a major Jewish concentration in the Glendale-Peoria area, and this was made a fifth stratum. The sample was allocated in proportion to the Jewish population (as based on the market study), with Glendale-Peoria and Sun City being oversampled. The former was oversampled because it was an unexpected population concentration, and the latter because it is primarily a retirement area and thus of special planning interest.

A random digit sample was divided into equal replicates, following the Chicago and Milwaukee models, so that screening would end when the required number of interviews was obtained. It became apparent within a few weeks of screening that the DJN list produced for the Federation by the direct-mail firm had greatly overestimated the Jewish density of Glendale-Peoria. This area was then added to the Phoenix stratum, and its quota of interviews allocated proportionally to the other strata (with the exception of Sun City which was already oversampled).

MODIFIED SCREENING SAMPLES

Two communities chose to reduce the cost of the survey by combining random screening with a list sample. In Boston the list was made up of federation givers and members of organizations and synagogues. In Cleveland both memberships and DJNs were used to compile the list.

Boston

The methodology used in the 1975 Boston study was originally developed for the 1965 study. Morris Axelrod and Floyd Fowler, who conducted the 1965 study (Fowler alone worked on the 1975 study) were the first Jewish researchers to go beyond lists of known Jews, explaining that "every unit in the population being studied must have a known, non-zero, chance of selection" (Axelrod, Fowler, and Gurin, p. 4).

The Jewish population study was a component in a community-wide health survey conducted for the United Way. Standard demographic data were collected for both Jews and non-Jews, with federation items included for Jewish respondents. The interviews were conducted in person as part of an areal sample covering the Boston SMSA.

Cleveland

Random Digit Dialing was employed in the eight "core communities" of Cleveland (Cleveland Heights, Shaker Heights, South Euclid, University Heights, Beachwood, Lyndhurst, Mayfield Heights, and Pepper Pike) where Jewish density is higher. In the noncore areas Jewish organizational lists were combined with Distinctive Jewish Names. The telephone exchanges associated with the eight core communities extended slightly beyond their geographic boundaries, and a "core exchange area" was created by adding to the core community the 4 percent of the households with core exchanges who live outside the core communities. The average Jewish density of the core communities is 31 percent. Adding the very low Jewish density noncore households with core exchanges reduced the overall Jewish density of the core exchange area to 22.5 percent. The core exchange area, with 85 percent of the Jewish population, was undersampled in order to oversample the noncore areas, which contain an estimated 15 percent of the Jewish population. The noncore Jews were found to have a higher proportion of households that had recently moved to Cleveland and a lower proportion of organizational members than the core areas, which suggests that an RDD sample would have turned up an even higher percentage of these two unlisted populations (they were probably included in the sample because they have distinctive Jewish surnames). Nevertheless, the use of multiple lists and cross-checks convinced Federation personnel that the sample was adequately representative, and that the potential refinement of an RDD sample did not warrant its additional cost.

NONSCREENING STUDIES

Two communities chose to use a list methodology exclusively, but for opposite reasons. Las Vegas is a very new Jewish community with a federation organized only a few years prior to the study by its one professional staff member, the executive director. With limited accumulated resources and funds and no previous experience in planning, undertaking even a small demographic study represented a major commitment. St. Louis, by contrast, can trace its Jewish roots well back into the nineteenth century, and the federation had greater professional and financial resources to invest in the study. These resources facilitated not only list sampling, but the conduct of very comprehensive in-person interviews.

Las Vegas

As part of its outreach efforts, the Las Vegas Federation had begun contacting unaffiliated Jewish households by using volunteers to contact all Jewish-sounding names in the Las Vegas directory. Because of the rapid growth of this Sunbelt community, updated new directories with more new Jewish names would appear every few months. The volunteers would call and inquire whether the household would like to receive the Federation's Jewish newspaper. The majority said yes; some indicated that they were Jewish but did not want the paper; and others stated that they were not Jewish. (A number of Mormon households with Jewish-sounding surnames--such as Levine --were contacted in this process.) The first two groups were added to the Federation list to create a DJN sample frame.

In New York, the DJN sample was weighted against the screening sample to eliminate a possible bias introduced by the DJN method (see the next article in this volume). Las Vegas could not afford even a small RDD study, and the Denver study was used instead to approximate a true probability sample of Las Vegas. The Las Vegas sample was reconstructed in Denver by computer. The Denver interviews were constructed by selecting all cases with a listed DJN (all 800 phone numbers were researched in a cross-listed directory) and all federation contributors. A series of tables was run comparing the Las Vegas subsample with the Denver total RDD sample as a whole on key variables such as age, family structure, intermarriage, and length of time in the community. In recreating the Las Vegas sample within the Denver data, the question was posed: How would the Denver study have been different if it had been conducted using the Las Vegas methodology? Weights were then computed for each of the dependent variables to answer the opposite question: How would the Las Vegas sample have looked if it had been conducted using RDD?

The validity of this approach depends on the degree to which Las Vegas resembles Denver, and without an RDD sample in Las Vegas, this is not known. However, the bias introduced by using a weighting scheme developed in Denver is certainly less than the bias introduced by leaving the sample in its pure DJN form.

St. Louis

The St. Louis study was built from organizational lists. Unlike other studies that have used lists, St. Louis sought to maximize coverage by compiling and merging all available lists and adding to them known Jews from other sources. While some smaller organizations did not cooperate, over 150 lists were ultimately merged. These included temples and synagogues, the St. Louis Jewish paper, agencies, organization chapters, boards of directors, elderly persons living in retirement housing, resettled Soviet immigrants, and day school families.

Efforts were also made to include Jewish households not appearing on any of these lists. Old lists going back to 1965 were compiled from synagogues, the Jewish Community Centers Association, and agencies. Records of marriages performed by local rabbis were also collected from the synagogues, along with lists of confirmands and nonmembers who had purchased high holiday tickets. Distinctive Jewish Names from the telephone directory were also included in the frame, along with a "snowball" sample of Jews known to key informants. All the lists were then merged and duplications eliminated. This last step sounds deceptively simple. Variant spellings of names, address changes, and marital dissolutions were but a few of the factors that had to be considered in the process of "merging and purging" the lists.

TRADEOFFS

Each of the surveys utilized a different methodology in response to different needs, budgets, and settings. One goal of the Brandeis University conference in November 1982 was to standardize community studies. However, as we have seen, hopes of progress toward this goal need to be tempered by recognizing differences in size, history, and composition among different Jewish communities. All these factors must be taken into account when constructing a sampling plan.

Nonscreening Samples

Coverage and accuracy are the classical problems associated with list samples. The extent to which certain groups in the population are excluded from the lists detracts from the ability of the sample to accurately represent the population. Lists can get out of date, and certain groups (such as recent movers or single women who have married) are more likely to disappear from lists. The exclusion of Jewish households not on the federation lists was the reason all the communities rejected this traditional model outright.

St. Louis sought to overcome the problem of coverage by expanding the list to cover all organizations, previous members of organizations, and individuals who ordinarily would not appear on federation lists. The St. Louis report on methods acknowledges this problem. Recent movers who are difficult to trace in the directories were less likely to be included in the sample; and, according to the report, Jews who "have never had an affiliation with any Jewish organization, even as children, will be excluded." These were not considered to be major problems for the study, however, because "there is no evidence...that recent migrants as a group have lower affiliation rates than longer-term residents." The unaffiliated households not included are considered "the most marginal people in terms of the study purposes" (Tobin, p. 80). The proportion of recent migrants and unaffiliated in St. Louis, which is an old, stable, midwestern city, is considerably lower than in the rapidly growing Jewish communities of the West.

The process of compiling, comparing, and merging lists was expensive: two years and over $15,000 (not including computer time) were spent in putting together the master sampling list. This cost is probably somewhat less than a comparable RDD sample, but does not take into consideration the cost in federation staff time necessary for contacting and working with the other organizations involved. The St. Louis study, then, accepted the failure to cover some small number of unaffiliated Jews in order to (1) conduct a longer, in-person interview; (2) gather comprehensive data about patterns of organizational cross-membership; and (3) obtain information about the number of previously affiliated households that have left St. Louis.

The Las Vegas sample was the least costly, and probably also the weakest of the studies discussed here. Ideally, the sample would have mixed RDD and DJN sampling within the same community, but costs even for this refinement were prohibitive. The availability of a better sample in a presumably comparable community (Denver) allowed this newly emerging community to begin its planning on the basis of some data. Careful attention was given to explicating the limitations of the sample design.

True Probability Screening by Telephone

The random selection of general households screened by telephone to find Jewish households is the most popular methodology. Chicago, Los Angeles, Denver, and Phoenix used RDD to generate the sample. Milwaukee found it could use directory listings instead of randomly generated numbers. The interest of Jewish researchers in this methodology reflects the increasing interest of survey researchers in general. Recent experiments with RDD have found no bias introduced as a result of the telephone interview. However, the general literature reports some evidence that elderly households are less likely to have telephone service. This issue, especially as it pertains to surveys of Jews, needs to be investigated further.

The major drawback in random screening is its higher cost. Most data collection costs, in fact, are typically expended just on locating the Jewish households to be interviewed. On the other hand, two substantial advantages are purchased by the higher cost of a RDD study. The first is coverage: several subpopulations were included in the Los Angeles, Denver, and Phoenix samples that would have been underrepresented in either an organizational list sample or a DJN sample, such as intermarrieds, recent movers, and young singles. The second is credibility: it is more difficult to take issue with controversial findings when the sample design has taken no short cuts and made no compromises.

Modified Screening

A compromise solution between screening and list sampling may be the direction of the future. The Boston study was the first to attempt this by integrating randomly selected Jewish households with federation lists. The great majority of the interviews were from the list sample, which creates a problem. Even though the randomly selected households were weighted, the relatively small number of interviews conducted at random introduced some additional sampling variation and limited the extent to which detailed analysis of the unaffiliated (appearing only in the random sample) could be performed.

The procedures by which the New York study combined RDD with DJNs are discussed in the next article. The subsequent weighting is cumbersome, because of the number of different weights necessary to take into account regional sampling units, listed versus nonlisted households, and DJN and RDD cases. Another issue here is the uncertain degree to which DJNs differ from RDD samples. The evidence from two studies which made such an investigation is contradictory. An independent DJN sample (N = approximately 1,800) in New York was compared with the main RDD sample (N = approximately 1,800) with only three statistically significant differences: Israelis, recent Russian immigrants, and intermarrieds were underrepresented in the DJN sample (because Jewish women married to non-Jewish men will not have a distinctive Jewish name). In Denver, however, a subsample of DJNs was created by researching all 825 sample phone numbers in a reverse directory (only 6 percent or about forty-eight cases had a listed DJN). This small subsample was then compared with the total RDD sample. A number of statistically significant differences resulted. It is not known to what extent these differences result from different DJN lists used (New York had a larger list), from different methodologies (New York had a large, independent sample of DJNs, while in Denver the DJN sample was small and created post-hoc), or from actual differences in communities. Further and more rigorous experiments in this area are needed. But the modified screening sample (where the telephone prefixes with very few Jews are dropped from the sample) is clearly a promising survey method. It combines the statistical surety of a probability sample with the relative economy of list sample.

WEIGHTING AND JEWISH POPULATION ESTIMATES

A good sample provides an accurate representation of the population at the smallest reasonable cost. Sampling efficiency is the ability to preserve representativeness, controlling sampling variation (a statistical concept) while finding a less expensive way to create the sample. Stratified sampling is the most common procedure for making a sample more efficient. Stratification means that proportionally more households in one group (or stratum) are contacted than in other groups (or strata). When the strata are geographical areas, stratified sampling makes it possible to include numerically smaller communities about which information is needed. Most of the samples discussed here employed either prefix stratification or geographical stratification or both. The following discussion of weighting could have been included with the description of each community's methods, but those descriptions were already fairly complicated; and, as weighting is a more technical issue, it is discussed separately here.

Los Angeles and Denver

The Los Angeles sample was stratified in a two-step process. Five geographical strata (two of which were oversampled) were created in the first step and the prefixes associated with them were identified. Fortunately, the telephone companies and the Federation both divide the county up in the same way; each of the Federation regions corresponds to a separate bank of prefixes and even has its own telephone directory. Next, the sample was distributed according to the distribution of residential prefixes within each region, introducing a second set of prefix strata.

The Denver sample was initially stratified by the distribution of residential prefixes, with one community (Boulder) oversampled. Later in the study, some forty prefixes with low Jewish density were dropped.

Both geographical and prefix biases were introduced. The geographical bias was created by oversampling certain areas (the Southern and Eastern region in Los Angeles, and Boulder in Denver). The prefixes were similarly oversampled since prefixes with more residences had a greater chance of inclusion in the sample. Both biases were corrected simultaneously by adapting a weighting scheme suggested by Joseph Waksberg, one of the original innovators of Random Digit Dialing (1978). Each interview was assigned a weight according to its prefixes, using the following formula:

$$W_i = \frac{K}{(pfx_i)(hh_i)}$$

where:

W_i = the individual prefix weight;

pfx_i = the number of phone numbers generated for that particular prefix;

hh_i = the number of different residential phone numbers in the household;

K = the largest number of phone numbers generated for any given prefix (so that the smallest prefix weight is 1).

Because the range of phone numbers generated for the different prefixes is so great, the weighting scheme causes the computer (using the

WEIGHT command in SPSS) to count over 5,000 cases which can introduce artificially high levels of statistical significance. To avoid this problem all tables originally were run twice: weighted and unweighted. During the analysis of the Denver data a second, simpler solution was introduced: W_i above was divided by a second constant which lowered the count of cases to within about 20 of the actual number.

Chicago

The Chicago study was stratified by stratum and the number of different telephone numbers in the household. After first correcting for the prefix overlap among the strata (procedures not described here), a stratum weight was computed as follows:

$$W_i = \frac{\text{number of Jewish households in stratum.}}{\text{sample size in stratum}}$$

This fraction was in turn corrected for nonresponse by multiplying it by another:

$$\frac{\text{number of Jewish households in stratum}}{\text{number of interviews in stratum}}.$$

Because the replicates for each of the geographical strata in Chicago contained equal sample sizes for each prefix, there was no need to correct for the prefix bias as was the case in both Denver and Los Angeles.

Milwaukee and St. Louis

The Milwaukee sample was not stratified, and thus required no weighting. Similarly, the St. Louis study, because it worked from lists, needed no stratification. Every element in the sample was given an equal probability of selection by removing all duplicate households from the master list.

Las Vegas

The Las Vegas sample was weighted using the Denver data. A Las Vegas subsample was created in the Denver database by collecting all cases which either were federation givers or which were found to have a listed DJN (all 800 phone numbers were checked against a criss-cross directory for this purpose). This subsample was than compared with the Denver sample as a whole on a number of dependent variables to produce a correction weight. The computation of the weight for synagogue membership is demonstrated in Table 7.1.

Using the WEIGHT program in SPSS, the case was weighted according to whether the household was currently a member, previously a member, or never a member. These weights were used whenever synagogue membership was the dependent variable. Weights were constructed in this way for all the dependent variables used in the analysis.

TABLE 7.1
Computation of Weight for Synagogue Membership

Synagogue membership status	A Las Vegas subsample in Denver	B Denver RDD sample	Correction factor [B / A]
Currently a member	65.8 %	39.1 %	.59
Previously a member	11.4	15.6	1.37
Never a member	22.8	45.3	1.99
TOTAL	100.0 %	100.0 %	

Population Estimates from Screening Samples

Estimating the Jewish population of a community is at its best an inexact science, and at its worst pure speculation. The problem with Jewish population estimation methods is that there is rarely an accurate count of Jewish households available against which to test the estimation method. Next to the census, the ideal situation would be a survey conducted in the community including a question on religion. In New York, for example, the researchers could check their estimates against results from pure RDD telephone surveys conducted for local newspapers by major polling organizations. The sample of general households contacted in a screening study to find the Jewish households can also be used in this way. The Los Angeles, Denver, and Phoenix surveys used the large number of screening calls made as an independent survey of the community with one question only: Is the household Jewish? The result is an estimate of Jewish households as a percentage of the larger number of households in the community. This is in turn multiplied by the total number of households in the community to arrive at an estimate of the Jewish households.

Population estimates at lower levels of geographic specification than the community itself create a problem, since they have to be constructed from the Jewish sample itself. Since the number of interviews in any given zip code tends to be small, the statistical basis for making a zip code level estimate is weak. In Los Angeles an independent estimate of the number of Jewish households on a zip code basis was purchased from a statistical database company (created using a computed DJN technique). The estimate of the number of Jewish households in each region from the screening calls was compared with the regional estimates from the database company. It was consistently found that the database company had identified about half the number of Jews in each region. It was then assumed that this fraction was consistent across all zip codes within the region, and the zip code estimates provided by the database company were adjusted accordingly. In Denver and Phoenix the estimate of Jewish households was limited to planning areas by dividing the estimated number of households by the planning area distribution of the sample itself.

SUMMARY AND CONCLUSION

All of the surveys discussed faced the same basic choice: how to balance the statistical confidence of a probability sample against its greater cost. Even when rejecting a true probability sample, each survey director paid careful attention to the potential introduction of sample bias and took great pains to demonstrate that such a possible bias had either been eliminated or controlled.

One of the purposes of the Workshop in Jewish Population Studies at Brandeis University's Center for Modern Jewish Studies was to standardize local Jewish population studies so that they can be compared. However, the variety among the nine studies described here suggests that different situations inevitably call for different solutions to common sampling problems. If we want local Jewish community studies to be more comparable to each other, we must first have a better understanding of the effects of different sampling methodologies. But no single community can be expected to take on the task of funding such rigorous methodological experiments. Some central body such as the Council of Jewish Federations or the Center for Modern Jewish Studies itself might consider such a role as other communities conduct local surveys.

A Jewish community's understanding of itself depends in part on a comparison with other communities. It is important that our comparisons and conclusions not be distorted by methodological differences.

References

Axelrod, Morris, Floyd Fowler, and Arnold Gurin. 1967. A Community Survey for Long-Range Planning. Boston: Combined Jewish Philanthropies of Greater Boston.

Sudman, Seymour. 1976. Applied Sampling. New York: Academic Press.

Tobin, Gary A. 1982. A Demographic and Attitudinal Study of the Jewish Community of St. Louis. St. Louis: Jewish Federation of St. Louis.

Waksberg, Joseph. 1978. "Sampling Methods for Random Digit Dialing." Journal of the American Statistical Association 73 (March): 40-47.

8
Sample Design and Population Estimation: The Experience of the New York Jewish Population Study (1981–1984)

Paul Ritterband and Steven M. Cohen

The Greater New York Jewish Population Study, initiated in 1981, is to the best of our knowledge the largest random sample design population study of a diaspora Jewish locality conducted to date. Commissioned by the New York Federation of Jewish Philanthropies-UJA, the study is based on data collected from 4,505 households in the five boroughs of New York City (the Bronx, Brooklyn, Manhattan, Queens, and Staten Island) and three adjourning suburban counties (Nassau, Suffolk, and Westchester).

This paper reports on the study's sample design, its population estimates, and their corroboration. We report some of our initial plans and thinking as well as what we ultimately did. The design and implementation of the study was a great deal messier than this paper suggests; we repeatedly tinkered with our design as we encountered unanticipated difficulties. This paper reports on our experiences with some of the jagged edges smoothed out for simplicity and brevity.

DRAWING A SAMPLE

In preparation for our sample design, we considered several alternative methods for drawing the sample of New York area Jews. These methods have been used in one form or another in previous studies. In general, the order in which we present them moves from the least expensive and probably least precise to more expensive and accurate methods.

The overall cost-benefit framework entails a number of considerations. On one side of the ledger is the dollar cost in locating an eligible member of the sample. But the simpler (i.e., cheaper) methods for locating eligible respondents also tend to imply larger costs in terms of bias (over- and underrepresenting certain types of respondents) and efficiency (extent of error variance; more efficient estimates are those with smaller error

----

The authors wish to emphasize that the research on which this paper is based was a collective enterprise. We received crucial support from Richard Link, our sampling consultant; Herbert Hyman, our survey design consultant; Sidney Goldstein, our Jewish community survey/demography consultant; Donald Feldstein, our first professional liaison at Federation; and Jacob Ukeles, our current liaison. We owe a debt of gratitude to all of them.

variances, that is, those which command greater confidence in their accuracy).

In sum, the "best" method is the one which is cheap, unbiased, and efficient, or, as an alternative to the latter criterion, one whose biases and efficiency are easily and accurately estimable. As we shall see, there is a a tradeoff between expense and other criteria.

Master Lists of Jewish Households

Many Jewish population studies derive their samples from master lists of Jewish households. Intermediate and small-size communities are able to gather fairly complete lists of Jewish residents by merging lists of donors and members of synagogues, Y's, or other Jewish institutions, and by asking community activists or randomly sampled Jews whether they know of recent migrants to the area. By and large, the larger the city and the larger the Jewish population, the less useful are master lists. In large cities, such lists tend to represent not only relatively small fractions of the Jewish population, but are biased as well in that they overrepresent the types of Jews who affiliate with Jewish communal institutions: married couples with children, the affluent, the residentially stable, and the Jewishly committed.

The New Orleans Jewish Community Study reported a discrepancy of only 1 percent between names which appeared on the master list and those which showed up through probability sampling. However, it is clear that in the New York area, master lists would have given us extremely biased distributions of Jews. Too many Jews would simply not show up on the master list.

Studies of larger Jewish communities such as Los Angeles or Boston employed some combination of master lists and areal sampling. Los Angeles surveyors used random areal sampling for neighborhoods with dense (35 percent or more) Jewish population and samples from the Jewish master lists for Jews living in less densely Jewish areas. Boston used a master list for the bulk of its sampling frame. The remainder were sampled on a random basis. The huge expense of locating Jews via the latter method meant that only a small number of respondents could be sampled in that manner. As a result, the Boston data require weighting the area-sampled Jews by very large weighting factors. This in turn makes the findings and analysis less reliable.

Moreover, the Boston experience points up the problems inherent in use of a master list for a large-sized Jewish community where no more than half the area's Jewish households may find themselves on the list. Listed Boston Jews were markedly different from their nonlist counterparts. The former were considerably older, more affluent, and more frequently involved in Jewish communal activities (Fowler).

In light of these considerations, we do not recommend the use of a master list for large cities.

Distinctive Jewish Names Listed in the Telephone Directory

The DJN procedure entails selecting from published telephone directories people whose name suggests they are probably Jewish. Such a method raises two issues: First, what is the bias entailed in selecting people with common Jewish names? Second, what is the bias entailed in selecting individuals listed in the telephone directory?

Initially, we believed that there was reason to think that Jews with common Jewish names might be different from other Jews for a number of reasons. We thought it likely that Jews without common Jewish names include all the individuals and their descendents who changed their name to avoid overt Jewish identification. Though name-changing for this purpose probably took place most frequently one or two generations (or more) ago, there is nevertheless a correlation between parents' and children's orientations to Jewish life. As a result, we thought we might expect somewhat higher levels of assimilation among Jews without common Jewish names (although it should also be recalled that names that "sound Jewish"--e.g., end in "-berg," "-baum," or "-itz"--are not the most common names held by Jews).

Even if the use of common Jewish names proved workable, we felt that their selection from published telephone directories might be undesirable. Research on the use of telephone directories reports that perhaps 30 percent of large metropolitan household residential telephones are unlisted (Glasser and Metzger, 1972, 1975; Kahn and Groves). These are in large part recent migrants rather than (as might be supposed) deliberate unlistings. More precisely, telephone books, when published, appear seven to eight months out of date, and suffer an attrition rate--in terms of increasing unlistings due to movers--of about 2 percent a month in areas such as New York (Sudman). As a result, depending in part on the currency of a particular directory, the following groups might well be underrepresented in the telephone directory sample: young people, the divorced, and the separated; singles; apartment dwellers; and residents of areas with high turnover (Bruner and Bruner; Glasser and Metzger, 1972, 1975; Fletcher and Thompson). In short, these are the people most likely to move in any period between the collection of information for the telephone directory and its use by survey samplers.

In light of these problems and in light of the initially large budget expectations we rejected the exclusive use of DJN lists in phone books.

Modified Random Digit Dialing

To overcome the difficulties (i.e., the sample biases) associated with using telephone directories, sampling experts have concurred that Random Digit Dialing (RDD) is required to obtain an unbiased sample of telephone subscribers. RDD, in its purest form, works in the following manner: One first obtains a list of working three-digit telephone exchanges from the telephone company. A computer program then generates a list of random numbers, each such number being four digits long. This list of random four-digit numbers is then linked with a random list of the working exchanges producing a list of random telephone numbers.

Interviewers would next call each number on the list to determine whether it is an eligible household. If the household is eligible, the interview proceeds. This procedure is repeated until the requisite number of interviews has been completed (see Klecka and Tuchfarber; Tull and Albaum; Waksberg).

In a Jewish population study, pure RDD would be costly because of the low proportion of eligible telephone numbers, that is, Jewish residential households. A large proportion of numbers fall into other categories:

nonworking numbers; business numbers; and non-Jewish households. The most recent estimates reported that only 38 percent of randomly dialed telephones in large metropolitan areas are household members (Kahn and Groves); of course, an even smaller proportion are Jewish households. Thus, if Jews constituted one-seventh of the metropolitan area population, then we would expect approximately 5 percent (i.e., 0.14 times 0.38) of the completed calls to reach Jewish households, or in other words, it would take twenty completed calls to reach one Jewish household using a pure RDD method. Telephone surveyors report that nonresponding numbers normally require at least three to five call-backs. Thus, taking into account business phones, busy signals, nonworking numbers, and other problems, we estimated that it might take thirty, forty, or more attempts to reach a single Jewish household.

To reduce the expense of pure RDD, we modified the method to reduce the number of calls to noneligible numbers. We wanted to eliminate exchanges in which there was a negligible Jewish residential population. We took our list of Distinctive Jewish Names and noted their distribution among the telephone exchanges in the sampling unit. In all, for each county, we enumerated a total number of DJN entries equal to thirty times the number of exchanges, an arbitrary but reasonable number. Thus if there were 167 exchanges in a county (as in Brooklyn), then we extracted 30 times 167 (= 5,010) entries from the county phone book and examined the distribution of those 5,010 entries among the 167 exchanges.

These names were organized by exchange, and the number of names per exchange was tabulated, with the exchange with the most names listed first, the exchange with the next most second, and so on. We found that the DJNs clustered in exchanges such that 90 percent of the names were located in approximately one quarter of the exchanges. Thus, in our example (Brooklyn) approximately 4,500 of the names fell into about 40 exchanges while the remaining 500 names fell into the other 127 exchanges. Thus, in the 40 exchanges we have an average of around 112 DJNs per exchange, while in the other exchanges we have around 4 DJNs per exchange.

We restricted our telephoning only to those exchanges which had approximately 90 percent of DJNs. This device results in an enrichment of our exchanges of around four to one, since we would expect on the average only 30 names per exchange if there were not clustering. Eliminating the low-yield exchanges gives a potential source of bias, since we have systematically eliminated approximately 10 percent of the potential population from being called. But we believed that in the interest of survey efficiency, the benefits of a four-to-one yield in completed interviews per call more than compensated for this possible source of bias.

The advantage of this adaptation over pure RDD is that one spends much less time dialing ineligible numbers. Thus, in Manhattan one is unlikely to make large numbers of calls to business districts or to areas with low Jewish densities.

At the point of actually collecting data we found that our budget was such that we could not use the modified RDD method for all of our data collection. We used modified RDD along with DJN mail-back and telephone samples. By that time, Harold Himmelfarb of Ohio State and associates had presented their work on the characteristics of DJN and non-DJN Jews. They found that, if anything, non-DJN and DJN Jews from the 1971 National Jewish Population Study had similar scopes on Jewish commitment. As an aside, we too found in subsequent analysis that on practically every critical variable --demographic, socioeconomic status, Jewishness, service usage--the RDD and DJN samples were virtually identical. Where they differed was in their representation of three subsamples: Israelis, recent Russian immigrants, and the intermarried (particularly women). Since the DJN sample under-represented these three groups, we would upweight the groups so as to set the proportions of Israelis, Russian immigrants, and intermarried households in the DJN sample equal to those in the RDD sample. (See Appendices A and B for statistics on calls and dispositions.)

POPULATION ESTIMATES

Our first candidate for a population estimation procedure was a varient of the methods since employed by the Denver, Cleveland, and other Jewish population studies. That is, we initially proposed using our call record sheets as the source of data for population. Briefly, the method calls for taking the number of completed calls to Jewish households as the numerator and the total numbers reached as the denominator. Since each exchange has a theoretical possibility of 10,000 phone numbers, the fraction is multiplied by 10,000. More than one exchange is used; therefore the product of the fraction times 10,000 is multiplied by the number of exchanges. The DJN as sampling frame contained 90 percent of the Jewish households; therefore the estimate is multiplied by 1.1, giving the number of Jewish households in the sample area. This number is then multiplied by the average Jewish household size, giving an estimate of the number of Jews.

While this method is straightforward and reasonable, our statistical consultant (Dr. Richard Link) advised us that it would allow for substantial error variance. Thus, we ultimately opted for a different (though related) procedure.

Table 8.1 presents the detailed data that we used to arrive at estimates of Jewish households and Jewish persons. In the first column we give the name of the sampling unit. The sampling units (whole counties, and oversampled neighborhoods within four of them) are defined by zip code boudaries (see Appendix C). The number of Jewish households was estimated by multiplying four factors:

Column B: <u>Listed DJNs</u>: The number of households listed in the telephone directories whose family names qualify as Distinctive Jewish Names.

Column C: <u>Correction for non-DJNs</u>: This factor takes into account the proportion of Jews who do not have distinctive Jewish names. According to our list, about 31 percent of all Jews bear DJNs.

Column D: <u>Correction for non-Jews with DJNs</u>: Since not all people with Distinctive Jewish Names are themselves Jewish (although they may be descended from Jews), we had to shrink our population estimates accordingly.

Column E: <u>Correction for nonlisting</u>: The proportion of people who do not list their telephone numbers in the directories varies from neighborhood to neighborhood. The correction factor takes this variation into account and expands the estimate in accordance with the number of nonlistings in each sampling unit.

TABLE 8.1
Estimating the Number of Jewish Households

A Sample Unit	B Listed DJNs	C Correction for Jewish non-DJNs (constant B divided by 0.31)	D Correction for non-Jews with DJNs (constant C times 0.92)	E Correction factor for nonlistings
Bronx	13,194	42,561.29	39,156.39	0.1311
Staten Island	2,657	8,570.97	7,885.29	0.2250
Suffolk	9,796	31,600.00	29,072.00	0.1561
Westchester	12,233	39,461.29	36,304.39	0.1842
Upper West Side	10,653	34,364.52	31,615.35	0.1230
Upper East Side	12,966	41,825.81	38,479.74	0.1593
Murray Hill	3,941	12,712.90	11,695.87	0.1605
Lower East Side	5,392	17,393.55	16,022.06	0.1308
Greenwich Village	3,955	12,758.06	11,737.42	0.1129
Other Manhattan	8,695	28,048.39	25,804.52	0.1552
Boro Park	6,705	21,629.03	19,898.71	0.1172
Flatbush	11,313	36,493.55	33,574.06	0.2088
Brighton	5,466	17,632.26	16,221.68	0.1782
Other Brooklyn	21,746	70,148.39	64,536.52	0.2090
Forest Hills-Rego Park	7,044	22,722.58	20,904.77	0.2513
Flushing	7,148	23,058.06	21,213.42	0.1991
Other Queens	21,806	70,341.93	64,714.58	0.1923
North Shore	1,517	4,893.55	4,502.06	0.2279
Other Nassau	28,831	93,003.23	85,562.97	0.1561

$$\text{Number of Jewish Households} = \frac{B \times 0.92}{0.31(1 - E)}$$

Each of the correction factors in Table 8.1 merits separate explanation.

Listed DJNs

The first entries in our calculations for each sampling unit consist of the number of households bearing distinctive Jewish names listed in telephone directories in each sampling unit. The A. B. Data Company of Milwaukee supplied us with these data from their list of DJNs. In all, their list, at that time, consisted of approximately 1,600 names which can be identified as DJNs. (Their files have since grown to incorporate 37,000 names and from 40 to 50 percent of Jewish households.) Using reverse phone books and similar devices they have put on computer tape the names and addresses of all telephone book household entries bearing these names. They then aggregated the names for each zip code giving us the number of DJN households for each zip. For our purposes, we then summed the zip codes for each sampling unit (i.e., neighborhood or county).

Correction for Non-DJNs

After determining the number DJNs for each sampling unit, we then had to calculate the number of Jewish households represented by the DJNs. For example, suppose that rather than using the A. B. Data list we simply counted the residential Cohens for each sampling unit. Suppose further that somehow or other we knew that the name Cohen was borne by one out of a hundred Jews or Jewish households. We would then take the number of Cohen entries for the sampling unit and multiply it by 100 to get the number of listed Jews. We would be using Cohen as an indicator of all Jews. In practice we had a list of approximately 1,600 names. We now had to determine what proportion of all Jews bear those names. In other words, what is the distribution of DJNs in a population of Jews?

To make this determination we examined the distribution of our DJNs in the population of Federation-UJA contributors. That list consists of 179,085 entries. The Federation-UJA computer center made a count for us of each of the names found on their list. We determined that our 3,315 DJNs constituted 31 percent of the total entries on the federation-UJA givers list. To get a first approximation of the number of listed Jewish households we divided the telephone count (column B) by 0.31.

Correction for Non-Jews with DJNs

For a variety of reasons--intermarriage, conversion, historical accident--not all people bearing Jewish names are in fact Jewish. The A. B. Data list was checked in the Boston area where Combined Jewish Philanthropies telephone solicitors found that 8 percent of people bearing Jewish names were not Jewish. To correct for non-Jews with DJNs, we multiplied by the proportion of persons bearing distinctive Jewish names who are Jewish (= 0.92).

TABLE 8.2
a. Estimates of Population of Jewish Households and Jewish Persons for New York Area Counties

A Sample unit	B Number of Jewish households	C Mean Jewish household size	D Number of Jewish persons in households	E Total Number of Jewish persons	F Jewish households as percentage of all households	G Jewish persons as percentage of all persons
8-county total	699,800	2.34	1,642,300	1,670,700	18	16
New York City	513,900	2.16	1,114,600	1,113,100	18	16
3 suburban counties	185,900	2.84	527,700	537,600	17	15
Bronx	45,100	2.08	93,700	95,800	11	8
Brooklyn	166,200	2.46	409,100	412,900	20	19
Manhattan	157,900	1.70	267,800	276,300	19	19
Queens	134,500	2.33	313,700	317,100	19	17
Staten Island	10,200	2.97	30,300	31,000	9	9
Nassau	107,000	2.84	304,300	308,300	25	23
Suffolk	34,400	3.01	103,700	106,200	9	8
Westchester	44,500	2.69	119,700	123,100	14	14

TABLE 8.2 (continued)
b. Estimates of Population of Jewish Households and Jewish Persons for Selected Neighborhoods Within the Counties

Upper West Side	36,000	1.78	64,200	not available
Upper East Side	45,800	1.74	79,800	
Murray Hill	13,900	1.48	20,500	
Lower East Side	18,400	1.69	31,100	
Greenwich Village	13,200	1.48	19,500	
Boro Park	22,500	2.79	62,900	
Flatbush	42,400	2.38	101,000	
Brighton	19,700	2.33	46,000	
Forest Hills-Rego Park	27,900	2.01	56,000	
Flushing	26,500	2.21	58,800	
North Shore	5,800	2.87	16,800	

B. Number of Jewish households obtained by multiplying (a) Distinctive Jewish Name count supplied by A.B. Data) by (b) correction factor for DJNs (= 1/0.31 = 3.2258), by (c) correction factor for non-Jews with DJNs (1.00 - 0.08 = 0.92), by (d) correction factor for nonlistings (obtained from surveys) for each county or neighborhood.

C. Jewish household size = number of Jewish persons living in Jewish households (obtained in the sample survey).

D. Jewish persons in households = Jewish households times Jewish household size.

E. Total Jewish persons = Jewish persons in households plus correction for institutionalized population estimated by projections from U.S. Census, county by county.

F. Percentage of total population = Jewish population (individuals or households) divided by total countywide U.S. Census estimates (individuals or households).

Correction for Nonlisting

Some households do not list their phones. In our Random Digit Dialing survey we determined the proportion of our respondent households in each sampling unit which were not listed. The nonlisted proportion for each sampling unit is given in column E. We divided our estimates by the proportion listed (listed = 1.00 minus unlisted). For example, if 12 percent of the sample reported unlisted phones, we divided by 0.88 (1.00 minus 0.12 = 0.88).

From Households to Persons in Households

Now that we have the number of Jewish households, Table 8.2 shows how we calculated the number of Jewish persons in households and *in toto*. For the purposes of our analysis, and for our screening during the interviewing process, a Jewish household is one in which one or more persons in the household is Jewish. We entered in column C the average number of Jewish persons in the households in each of our sampling units, a number somewhat smaller than the average total number of persons in the households. We then multiplied this entry by that in column B to arrive at our estimate of the total number of Jewish persons residing in households in each of our sampling units (column D).

The Institutionalized Population

The numbers which we have been working with in Table 8.2, columns B, C, and D are based upon Jewish households and Jewish persons in Jewish households. In addition to those residing in households, the census also calculates those residing in "group quarters," i.e., institutionalized persons. We have followed census definitions and procedures in making our calculations and estimates. In Table 8.2 we incorporate general U.S. Census statistics so that we take into account both household and group quarters populations.

In Table 8.2, column D we have the total number of Jewish persons in households, and in column E the number of Jewish persons in households and group quarters. The census is not able to tell us the composition of the group quarters population; we do not know how many are in hospitals, old age homes, prisons, or military bases. Thus we cannot differentially weight to take into account the probable Jewish fraction of that population. To compensate for our not having taken into account the Jewish institutionalized population, we have computed a multiplier of household population (column D) to arrive at total Jewish population. We then entered the number of Jewish persons in households (column E) and multiplied it by the correction factor for the group quarters population.

CHECKING THE METHODS

Our estimates of Jewish population were checked against several external and internal sources.

Comparisons of the Total Results with External Surveys

Both The New York Times and The New York Daily News conducted RDD surveys during 1981. They have made their results available to us. The Daily News surveys were conducted monthly; they interviewed respondents in the five boroughs plus Nassau, Suffolk, Westchester, and Rockland counties. The New York Times survey was conducted during the week of December 7-14, 1981, and was restricted to the five boroughs alone. To increase sample size and thus decrease sampling error we combined the Daily News and New York Times samples for the city. Doing that we found that 18.8 percent of the households were estimated to be Jewish (based upon a combined sample of 2,712 cases), as compared with our estimate of 18.3 percent Jewish households in the city (see Table 8.2, column F). The 0.5 percent discrepancy is well within the allowable error.

For the suburbs our problem was somewhat more difficult. First, Rockland County is included in the Daily News surveys, and we could not separate out the Rockland contingent from the data for the other three suburban counties. We believe that Rockland has a somewhat smaller proportion of Jews, and we know that the total Rockland population (approximately one-quarter million people total) is significantly smaller than that of the other counties. In addition, we should note that the Daily News survey's sample base for the suburban counties is much smaller (N = 834) than that for the five boroughs, making for a larger sampling error. We estimated that Jewish households constituted 16.8 percent of all households in these counties, while the Daily News survey estimated 14.7 percent in the four suburban counties. Though the discrepancy is greater than that which we found for the city, we are satisfied that it is well within the expected error range.

After we completed our checks with the New York City newspaper polls, the data were checked against internal data held by Federation. These data were not made available to us prior to the checks so there was no way in which we might have "cooked" the data. The two internal checks were Russian Jews and Jewish school enrollments.

Russian Jews. NYANA/Federation estimates that there are between 40,000 and 50,000 new Jewish immigrants. The study--based upon the very small percentage of Russian families in the sample--projects an estimate of about 47,000 Jewish persons in Soviet Jewish recent immigrant (post-1968) households.

Jewish school enrollments. The Bureau of Jewish Education (BJE) makes an annual survey of Jewish school enrollments and we developed our own estimates from the sample survey. The BJE reported a Jewish day school enrollment of 56,671 pupils while we estimated a day school enrollment of 66,000 pupils. We were disturbed by the discrepancy and attempted to find its source. We asked the BJE statistical/census person if their figures included the enrollments in what we termed ultra-Orthodox yeshivot. The answer was no. The Satmar Hasidim do not report their enrollment figures to the BJE. However, Satmar did report their numbers to the State of New York (through the BJE) so as to receive school lunch subsidies. In all Satmar reported 7,000 pupils. When added to the BJE numbers we have an "external" estimate of close to 64,000 pupils, as compared with our 66,000 estimate.

Our supplementary school enrollment estimate (i.e., Talmud Torah/Hebrew school and Sunday school) was 81,000 while the BJE estimate was 55,000. That is a large discrepancy and we have been trying to find the source.

Protest and Correction

Academic sociologists routinely expect peer review. We welcomed Federation's checks on our numbers, for neither we nor the Federation wanted to go public with shaky numbers. What we were not really fully prepared for was the reaction of some of the Jewish communal leadership in Nassau and Suffolk counties. Our Nassau-Suffolk combined estimate was 426,000 Jews while the local Jewish communal leadership estimate was "at least 650,000."

"Misplacing" 225,000 Jews is no trivial matter. The Nassau-Suffolk people were fighting mad. One of the leaders was quoted in The New York Times (July 13, 1982) as saying:

> It was a crude mythology [sic; presumably a misprint for methodology] looking for names that end in itz and such.... Scientifically, I can't comment, but personally I don't buy it.
>
> We're out here; we're aware of shifts and changes in population that the Federation could not possibly have addressed.... Do they know Dix Hills? Do they know the large Jewish population there?

Long Island's Newsday, a large daily paper, reported that the Nassau-Suffolk people had decided to conduct a survey of their own. What distressed the Nassau-Suffolk people was not simply our allegedly misplacing up to a quarter of a million Jews; they expressed the fear that Federation would decrease funding for Long Island's Jewish communal agencies.

Newsday (July 13, 1982) then commented as follows:

> Although the Federation's figures are lower than the estimate of the United Y's, they do approximately agree with the data of the Newsday polls. The Newsday total estimate of Jews in the two counties [is] about 445,000. In its numerous polls on other subjects, Newsday routinely asks the religious affiliation of persons who are selected at random.

A subsequent recheck of our population estimates demonstrated that, in fact, there was some legitimacy to the complaints of the Long Island communal leaders. Due to a misclassification of several zip codes on the Nassau-Suffolk border, we had overestimated the Suffolk population and underestimated the Nassau population. As a result, we issued new estimates, correcting the misclassified zip codes. While the total Nassau-Suffolk population estimates remained essentially unchanged, we in effect shifted about 60,000 Jews from Suffolk to Nassau, where they belonged.

The experience demonstrated two important lessons. First, population estimates are indeed politically and emotionally charged. As a result they will come under greater scrutiny than other results emerging from the study. Second, the objections of communal leaders to certain findings should be taken seriously. While their alternative explanations or interpretations may not always be accurate, their repeated and strenuous objections should be cause for rechecking one's work.

Appendix A: Disposition of RDD Calls

	Number	Percent
Residential, no Jews	13,349	46.0
Business	2,764	9.5
Number changed	1,855	6.4
Not in service	3,325	11.5
Refuses to say if Jewish	1,258	4.3
Jewish but refuses interview	712	2.5
No answers (call-backs)	2,907	10.0
Broken surveys	89	0.3
Other (pay phone, claimed duplicate)	90	0.3
Completed (Jewish interview)	2,661	9.2
	29,010	100.0

Residential completed calls

	Number	Percent
No Jews	13,349	74.2
Refuses to say	1,258	7.0
Jewish but refuses	712	4.0
Completed (Jewish interview)	2,661	14.8
	17,980	100.0

	Number	Percent
No Jews	13,349	79.8
Jewish but refuses	712	4.3
Completed (Jewish interview)	2,661	15.9
	16,722	100.0

Appendix B: Distribution of Cases by Sample Method, Means of Contact, and Telephone Status

Weighted		Unweighted
	RDD	
33	listed mail	21
3,139	listed phone	2,214
1,158	unlisted phone	426
4,330	total	2,661
	DJN	
1,441	mail	1,068
1,180	phone	758
2,621	total	1,826
	unaccounted for	
25		18
6,975	grand total	4,505

Appendix C: Sampling Districts and Zip Codes

Sampling Districts	Zip Codes
Westchester	105xx, except 10509, 10512, 10516, 10524, 10537, 10541; 106xx; 107xx; 108xx
Bronx	104xx
Upper West Side	10023, 10024, 10025
Upper East Side	10021, 10022, 10028
Murray Hill	10010, 10016
Lower East Side	10002, 10003, 10009
Greenwich Village	10011, 10014
Other Manhattan	All other 100xx
Staten Island	103xx
Boro Park	11204, 11218, 11219
Flatbush	11223, 11229, 11230
Brighton	11235
Other Brooklyn	All other 112xx
Forest Hills-Rego Park	11374, 11375
Flushing	11354, 11355, 11365, 11366, 11367
Other Queens	11004, 11005; 111xx; 113xx; 114xx; 116xx, except 11696
North Shore	11030, 11040, 11050
Other Nassau	All other 110xx; 115xx; 11696; 11709, 11710, 11714, 11732, 11735, 11753, 11756, 11758, 11762, 11765, 11771, 11783, 11791, 11793, 11797, 118xx
Suffolk	All other 117xx; 119xx

References

Bruner, James A. and G. Allen Bruner. 1971. "Are Voluntarily Unlisted Telephone Subscribers Really Different?" Journal of Marketing Research 8: 121-124.

Fletcher, James E. and Harry B. Thompson. 1974. "Telephone Directory Samples and Random Telephone Number Generation." Journal of Broadcasting 18:2: 187-191.

Fowler, Floyd J. 1977. 1975 Community Survey: A Study of the Jewish Population of Greater Boston. Combined Jewish Philanthropies of Greater Boston.

Glasser, Gerald J. and Gale D. Metzger. 1972. "Random Digit Dialing as a Method of Telephone Sampling." Journal of Marketing Research 9: 59-64.

______. 1975. "National Estimates of Non-listed Telephone Households and Their Characteristics." Journal of Marketing Research 12: 359-361.

Kahn, Robert L. and Robert M. Groves. 1977. Comparing Telephone and Personal Interview Surveys. Ann Arbor: Survey Research Center, Mimeo.

Klecka, William R. and Alfred J. Tuchfarber. 1978. "Random Digit Dialing: A Comparison to Personal Surveys." Public Opinion Quarterly 42: 105-114.

Reissman, Leonard. 1958. Profile of a Community. Jewish Federation of New Orleans.

Rogers, Theresa F. 1976. "Interviews by Telephone and in Person: Quality of Responses and Field Performance." Public Opinion Quarterly 40: 51-65.

Sudman, Seymour. 1973. "The Uses of Telehone Directories for Survey Sampling." Journal of Marketing Research 10: 204-207.

Tull, Donald S. and Gerald S. Albaum. 1977. "Bias in Random Digit Dialed Surveys." Public Opinion Quarterly 41: 389-395.

Waksberg, Joseph. 1978. "Sampling Methods for Random Digit Dialing." Journal of the American Statistical Association 73: 40-47.

9
Data Collection Procedures in Random Digit Dialing Screening Studies: Interviewers and Respondents

Bruce A. Phillips and Eve Weinberg

The paucity of models has been one of the primary obstacles to researchers interested in using Random Digit Dialing (RDD) to locate and interview Jewish households. Researchers who have conducted RDD Jewish population studies have done so almost completely independently of each other. While is methodologically reassuring for these researchers to discover that they have developed similar solutions to common problems, it would have been better not to have reinvented the same wheel. In this paper the study directors of the Los Angeles, Denver, Phoenix, Chicago, and Milwaukee Jewish community surveys have collaborated in describing some of the strategies and conventions they have found useful.

The rationale for the expense incurred with an RDD or other screening survey is that it most accurately represents the variety of the Jewish community, since every Jewish household has an equal chance of selection. Not every Jewish household, however, is equally disposed to participate in the survey, and thus the success of the research very much depends on the rapport the interviewer is able to establish with the respondent. This paper discusses four sets of decisions that have to be made regarding data collection: selecting interviewers, presenting the study to the respondent, answering the respondent's questions, and selecting the eligible respondent in the household.

THE CHOICE OF INTERVIEWERS

There are three kinds of interviewers available for Jewish community surveys: volunteers; paid but largely inexperienced interviewers recruited from the community; and staff members of professional survey organizations.

Given the voluntary nature of federations, volunteers could, in theory, constitute the interviewing staff. As supporters of the federation, they are conscious of the importance of reducing costs, and could be expected to welcome the task. Further, their identification with the work of the federation itself should make them convincing interviewers. There are two problems, however, with using volunteers. The first is the stability of the interviewing staff. Interviewing is not typical of the kind of involvement that most volunteers are used to. While they might be attracted to the idea of talking to respondents, the paperwork and frustrations that are a major part of survey interviewing often prove burdensome. In a Random Digit Dialing or other screening sample, the amount of work entailed in locating the Jewish respondents is pure drudgery for volunteers who are accustomed to finding meaning and fulfillment in their volunteer activities. The Los Angeles and Las Vegas studies attempted to reduce study costs by using volunteer interviewers, but they had to abandon these plans when it became apparent that the interviewing would never be completed.

Using volunteer interviewers can present serious problems even in studies that require no screening. Previous experience in studies outside the Jewish community have found that volunteer interviewers work effectively only in studies where the interview is short (no longer than ten minutes), where all respondents are asked the same questions (no branching questions based on answers to prior questions), and where the survey period is short (no longer than four weeks).

The second major problem with using volunteer interviewers entails interview quality. The use of volunteer interviewers limits the scope of the questions because they are more likely to know or be known by the respondent, precisely because of their activity in the community. Sensitive questions, about personal history and income, for example, thus must be excluded from the survey in order to maintain confidentiality.

The Los Angeles and Denver studies used paid interviewers recruited from the community (as noted above, an earlier effort to use volunteers in Los Angeles had failed). The model for recruiting and training community-based interviewers comes from community health surveys conducted in poverty areas using local interviewers from the same communities.[1] Although the original purpose of this model was to provide employment and job training to the poor, its adaptation in Denver and Los Angeles helped to hold down study costs since inexperienced interviewers are paid less than professional interviewers, and there was no overhead to pay as in the case of a survey organization. Using community-based interviewers proved to be workable and economical, but this model was not without problems. Inexperienced interviewers need much more training and require closer supervision than do experienced interviewers. Community-based interviewers are also more likely to interview ineligible respondents (e.g., non-household heads), take down incomplete verbatim responses, and make errors in record keeping and paperwork.

Whatever the interviewing model used, it is advisable to assign interviewing tasks according to skill when conducting a screening study. In Phoenix and Milwaukee the best interviewers were assigned only to the actual interview, so as not to waste their talents and enthusiasm on screening. In Milwaukee a local interviewing firm was employed to conduct the screening and to do interviews when an available Jewish respondent was found. Those Jewish interviews requiring call-backs were conducted using interviewers who had demonstrated their skill working on the Chicago study. These more experienced interviewers were also able to elicit successful interviews from a large number of "not availables" and refusals encountered by the Milwaukee-based screening staff.

PRESENTING THE STUDY TO RESPONDENTS

The presentation of the study to potential respondents is the most sensitive aspect of data collection. Jewishly marginal respondents might feel threatened by the Jewish sponsorship of the study, while those concerned with anti-Semitism will want to be assured of its legitimate Jewish sponsorship. Still others might choose to express their antipathies toward the federation through noncooperation with the study. The presentation of the study to the potential respondent must navigate through all these shoals.

The first choice to be made in presenting the study to respondents is whether to declare outright that it is a Jewish study; the second is whether to specify sponsorship by the local federation. The Boston and Phoenix studies did not initially specify that the study was intended to locate Jewish households, but used a "blind screen" instead. Since the Boston study was conducted as a community health study by the Survey Research Center of the University of Massachusetts (Boston Campus) in coordination with the local United Way, the study was presented to potential respondents in exactly those terms. Those respondents who turned out to be Jewish answered additional Jewish-related questions (household and demographic data had already been collected for all respondents). The Phoenix study was conducted by the Behavior Research Center, a well-known polling and market research firm in the Southwest. The screening was conducted as a market segmentation study so that BRC and the federation shared the cost of locating Jewish households in Phoenix; this was the only way that the Phoenix Federation could afford an RDD study. The segmentation study included a question about religion ("How many of the persons in your household consider themselves to be Protestant, Catholic, Latter Day Saints, Jewish...?"). Those households with one or more Jews were then called back two to three weeks later with an introduction that specified both Jewish content and federation sponsorship.

In Los Angeles, Denver, and Las Vegas there was concern that federation visibility could hurt participation in the study since respondents familiar with the federation might suspect that they were being asked for money. In all three studies the federation sponsorship was minimized by using the name for the study itself:

> Hello, I'm [FULL NAME OF INTERVIEWER], from the Denver Jewish Population Study. In this study we're calling a scientific sample of all possible phone numbers in the greater Denver area.

The interviewer then verified the phone number, established that a residence had been reached, and continued to explain:

> We are interested in interviewing households with one or more Jewish persons. The interview is completely anonymous, and the information will be used by the Denver Jewish community to identify social service needs and plan better services. Are there any Jewish persons living in this household?

Should the interviewee want to know more about the study (see the next section), federation sponsorship was acknowledged.

The recontact of screening-identified Jewish households in Phoenix and the initial contact of all households in Chicago specified both the research organization and the federation. Both introductions are reproduced here.

<u>CHICAGO:</u>

Hello. Is this [NUMBER DIALED]?

> This is [NAME OF INTERVIEWER] from Policy Research Corporation in Chicago. We are conducting a household study. Have I reached a business or a residence telephone? We are calling a scientific sample of phone numbers in the Chicago metropolitan area.
>
> Policy Research Corporation is a survey research firm conducting a study sponsored by the Jewish Federation of Metropolitan Chicago. We are interviewing in households with one or more Jewish persons. The purpose of the study is to help the Federation learn about the needs in the Jewish community and to help the Federation plan better services. Are there any persons living in your household who are Jewish?

PHOENIX:

The Phoenix introduction included two questions which were intended to establish the legitimacy of the study:

> Hello, I'm ________ calling from the Behavior Research Center of Arizona. We have been hired by the Jewish Federation of Phoenix to conduct a community needs study. The purpose of this study is to help the Federation plan to provide better services for the Phoenix Jewish community. There are no right or wrong answers, and all of your answers will be held in confidence.
>
> A. Did you receive a flyer in the mail from the Federation about the study? [A flyer had been sent to all Federation contributors informing them about the study and asking their cooperation should they appear in the sample.]
>
> B. Do you recall seeing anything in any paper about this study? [Articles about the study had appeared in both the Jewish and general press.]
>
> To make sure I am speaking with a qualified household, are there any adults in your household who consider themselves Jewish?

The Milwaukee study (also conducted by Policy Research Corporation of Chicago) began by using an introduction identical to that used in Chicago. Later on, some experiments with wording were carried out and the conclusion reached that most respondents really did not care about federation sponsorship while some were confused with sorting out the difference between the survey organization and the federation. Accordingly, that part of the introduction which presented the credentials for Policy Research Corporation was dropped.

RESPONDENT QUESTIONS

Explaining the study to potential respondents in an RDD screening study is the most sensitive aspect of data collection. The respondent cannot see the interviewer, and the interviewer cannot present credentials to the respondent. The very nature of the phone call is itself unusual: a stranger who is looking for Jews. Finally, the potential respondent may have strong negative feelings about the sponsoring organization or even about being Jewish. These are conditions that are less likely to obtain in general social surveys.

The kinds of questions that respondents ask and the objections they most often raise can be grouped into two categories: general questions or objections about being in a survey, and specifically Jewish questions and objections. The replies interviewers were provided with are presented below.

General Questions and Objections

Respondents in an RDD study (particularly those with unlisted phone numbers) wish to know how they were located. The fact that federations normally contact Jews in order to raise money adds another complication. Interviewers in Chicago and Milwaukee were provided with the following replies:

> We had the computer select numbers at random in a scientific manner. In fact, some of the numbers are not even working telephone numbers. When we dial the number we have no idea whose number it is. When someone answers, we ask if anyone in the household is Jewish, and if there is, we do an interview in that household.
>
> We promise you that the information and opinions you give will be kept strictly confidential.
>
> No one interviewed will be identified by name or phone number, and the interview will be seen only by members of the research team.
>
> Your answers will be combined with those of others to establish the statistical results.
>
> The report of the study will be in statistical form, such as X percent of the people over 65 told us such and so; or Y percent of young adults said so and so.

In Denver interviewers explained that "We have a random sample of phone numbers which were generated by computer. Many of the numbers turn out to be businesses, and many are non-Jewish residences. A few numbers turn out to be Jewish households, such as yourself." If the respondent was still skeptical, the interviewer would often simply read directly from the call sheet the disposition of the numbers called immediately before the respondent. Respondents worried about being asked for funds were reassured as follows: "Your name was not taken from any list; in fact, we don't even know your name. The questionnaire is entirely anonymous and confidential."

Potential respondents in a Jewish survey have many of the same reservations about being interviewed as they would in a general survey. The Milwaukee interviewers used the following replies for "put-offs":

> <u>"I don't have the time"</u>
> We don't need to conduct the study all at once. We could do some now and some later at a time convenient to you. Two shorter ten minute talks might be better for you. Would that help?

"Mail it to me"
That would be great, but unfortunately this survey is set up for telephone interviewing. It's got a lot of instructions and skip patterns that the interviewers are trained on for an entire day. Stuff like, if you're 70 years old we skip the section on the nursery school-aged kids, or if you're married, we don't ask the section on blind dates and singles bars, that type of thing. It really is faster this way, and I'll go just as quickly as I can. (We can stop anytime and pick up later, but the computer can't use a partly done survey.)

"Too old to do you any good"
This study isn't just for the young people. Older people are just as much a part of the Jewish community as the younger ones are, and your situation and opinions are very important to planning services in different parts of the city (or decreasing services in areas that don't need as much service).

"Can't you call somebody else?"
These phone numbers we have are just randomly generated by a computer so it's very important that when we do reach a household with one or more Jewish people living there we do get your unique opinions. You see, you represent more than just your own household, because the phone numbers that get called in the sample represent other Jewish households that don't get included in our random sample. (And yours just came up randomly on the computer.)

Jewish Objections

Some respondents are reluctant to be identified in a survey conducted by the Jewish community. Surprisingly, the potential respondents who are affiliated are no more likely to participate in the survey than those who are not affiliated. In Denver, Phoenix, and Los Angeles (where affiliation is lower than in Chicago and Milwaukee) there were unaffiliated respondents who found the survey to be a novel, and welcome, contact with the Jewish community, and affiliated respondents who felt they already had done enough for the Jewish community.

In Milwaukee the following explanations were used to persuade a reluctant respondent who stated either that he or she was not active in the Jewish faith or not interested in Federation:

Let me tell you a little bit more about the study. It's like something that the Census Bureau might do, but since the government can't ask religion, Jewish communities have to do their own type of census.

The Federation is the sponsor, but the data gathered will be made available in statistical form to all Jewish organizations in the Milwaukee area, not just the Federation. They're only overseeing the project.

If you're not involved in some kinds of activities, then that information alone will help the Jewish community plan where they can

> possibly cut some programs and services and save some money. A study like this hasn't been done for about 20 years in the Milwaukee area, so it's important to find out the general area of active Jewish people and less active Jews for community planning purposes.

In Denver, where almost a third of the Jewish households have lived in the community for five years or less, special attention was given to explaining what the Federation is and how it wanted to use the information:

> "Who is sponsoring the study?"
> The study is sponsored by the Endowment Fund of the Allied Jewish Federation of Denver. The Allied provides social, cultural, and recreational services for the Jewish community of Denver, such as Jewish Family and Children's Service, and the Jewish Community Center.
>
> "How will the information be used?"
> First of all, the information will be used to put together a profile of the Denver Jewish community, kind of like a census. This will tell us how the Jewish community in Denver is changing. The findings from the study will also be used to plan social, cultural, and recreational services for the Denver Jewish community.

In Denver, as in Milwaukee, it was anticipated that some respondents would use lack of interest in the services provided as a reason to refuse. The following reply was provided to interviewers:

> "But I don't want any services from the Denver Jewish community"
> Even if you do not use the services provided by the Allied Jewish Federation, it is still important that you participate in the study. Because you were selected as part of a random sample, your attitudes, opinions, and experiences will be used to represent hundreds of other Denver Jewish households.

Far more common than the respondent who did not want any federation services was the respondent who wanted to verify the sponsorship of the study. In Denver, Phoenix, and Los Angeles the switchboard was alerted to route all calls of inquiry to the planning department. The Denver reply, below, makes reference to the extensive publicity the study had been given in the community:

> "How do I know this is for real?"
> Perhaps you may have seen or heard one of the television or radio programs about the study. There have also been some newspaper articles (Denver Post, Rocky Mountain News) as well as public service announcements. If you haven't seen any of our publicity, you might wish to call the Allied Jewish Federation of Denver to verify the study. My name is _________, and the number of the Allied is 321-3399. I'd be happy to call you back in a few days after you've verified the study.

In Chicago and Milwaukee reluctant respondents were given the name and phone number of the federation planning director. Interviewers tried to set a specific time for a recontact after the respondent had verified the survey.

RESPONDENT SELECTION AND ELIGIBILITY

Last, we wish to address the criteria for selecting Jewish respondents in an RDD screening study. Although the problem is complex and sensitive, we believe the solutions are fairly straightforward.

Defining a Jewish Household

The rationale for an RDD screening study is to give every Jewish household the same probability of inclusion. Since the procedure for locating a Jewish household requires the interviewer to ask if there are any Jewish persons in the household, we have decided (Los Angeles, 1979; Chicago, 1981; Denver, 1981) initially to accept the respondent's self-definition. In other words, if the respondent thinks that he or she is Jewish, then the interview is conducted. The Jewish status of the household can be verified as part of the editing process. Both authors accept as Jewish anyone who has a Jewish parent or grandparent and considers himself or herself to be Jewish.

Although the marginal cases included in this way turn out to be few in number, they are interesting and serve to illustrate the variety of households that appear in an RDD screening study. In Los Angeles, for example, a non-Jewish woman was included who was divorced from a Jewish man. She had custody of his child by his first marriage, and was raising the child as a Jew. This was counted as a Jewish household. In both Denver and Phoenix there were several instances of Jewish individuals with non-Jewish parents who had been raised either as "nothing" or as non-Jews, but chose to identify as Jews through a strong sense of personal connection to a Jewish grandparent (or in one case, a Jewish stepfather). Although Phillips did not choose to include in his studies Jews for Jesus (about 1 percent of all the self-defined Jewish households contacted in Denver and Los Angeles), he did include Jewish Buddhists. This rationale was based on an observation by Marshall Sklare that Buddhism was never perceived as a religious identity competitive with Judaism.

Obviously included as Jews by these criteria are persons who have no halakhic Jewish status (almost 10 percent of all Jewish family members in Denver and Phoenix are not halakhic Jews). Since the Federation uses self-definition rather than halakhic status as the basis for service delivery, this procedure is not only legitimate but appropriate. Given the furor over Jewish status in Israel, it is interesting that the Orthodox leadership in Denver, Chicago, and Los Angeles have not raised this as an issue.[2]

Selecting the Eligible Respondent

In general social surveys, respondent selection is generally done at random from among all adults in the household. In the National Jewish Population Study, all information was collected about every Jewish household member. In the studies described here, limited demographic information (e.g., age, sex, marital status, relationship to respondent, and whether

Jewish) was collected about all household members, but detailed demographic data and socioeconomic variables such as occupation and education were collected only for respondent and spouse. The rationale was to allocate more time (and therefore questions) to other areas of the study. Lost, however, is occupational and educational information about grownup children living with their parents, elderly parents living with their children, and Jewish roommates of single Jewish respondents. Peter Friedman of the Chicago Federation has observed in retrospect that this would have been valuable information to have, since it would provide more complete information about the individuals (as opposed to households) in the Jewish community.

In Milwaukee, Chicago, and Phoenix, the choice of respondent alternated between males and females and was limited to Jews. In Los Angeles and Denver, whoever answered the phone was interviewed in an effort to reduce refusals. The decision to have roughly equal numbers of male and female respondents was made with consideration to attitude questions, as was the decision not to interview non-Jewish spouses.

The inclusion of non-Jews as respondents in Denver and Los Angeles created problems for some of the attitude questions (e.g., attitudes toward Jewish giving, planned fertility, and Jewish identity), but it also illustrated the value of talking to non-Jewish spouses.[3] The attitudes of the non-Jewish spouses were, in many cases, very different from those of the Jewish respondents.

It is clear that intermarriage is an established fact of Jewish life. To better understand the dynamics and implications of this phenomenon, Jewish social researchers should probably think in terms of talking to more rather than fewer non-Jews, particularly about issues such as childbearing (intermarrieds in Denver were found to have fewer children than in-marrieds) and childraising (intermarrieds often say that they raise their children as Jews, but do not give them a formal Jewish education).

SUMMARY

In this paper we have shared some of our experiences as well as some of the techniques we have developed in Los Angeles, Denver, Chicago, Milwaukee, and Phoenix Jewish population studies. We noted the pitfalls of using volunteer interviewers. We gave detailed suggestions as to how to open the interview so as to overcome some of the most typical inhibitions to participating in the survey on the part of potential respondents. And we discussed criteria for eligibility and selection of respondents. No doubt there is more to learn in each of these areas, but we hope we have provided a useful starting point.

Notes

1. See Eve Weinberg, Community Surveys with Local Talent: A Handbook, Chicago: National Opinion Research Center, 1971.
2. Sergio DellaPergola of Hebrew University and other researchers have recommended using the broadest definition of Jewish identity possible in order to ascertain accurately processes of assimilation and intermarriage. Thus, interviewers should ask if anyone in the

household ever was Jewish or had parents who were ever Jewish. However, researchers who want to go beyond merely ascertaining whether such dropout Jews exist must address two issues: (1) Interviews conducted with the children of intermarrieds who no longer consider themselves Jewish cannot be used for planning. The supporting federation is thus paying for interviews it cannot use. If there is an institution that wishes to look into the progeny of intermarriages, then the issue of cost sharing must be addressed; and (2) We would construct a set of screening questions to identify the assimilated children of intermarriages, but what would we ask them further? The usual questionnaire employed in community studies would not be usable in these cases. The demographic questions would pertain, but they would not provide very interesting information. In order for such a study to make sense, there would have to be an additional investment in a second questionnaire.

3. See, in this regard, Calvin Goldscheider's article in this volume on the merits of simultaneous surveys of non-Jews.

10
Including Non-Jews in Jewish Community Samples: Substantive and Methodological Issues

Calvin Goldscheider

SAMPLING ISSUES IN JEWISH COMMUNITY STUDIES

The availability and quality of data on American Jews and their communities have been continuing problems for social scientists, planners, and policy-makers. There are few general data sources, such as censuses or vital statistics, where Jews can be identified; no comprehensive lists of Jewish households exist as a basis for sampling; and there are no agreed-upon techniques for obtaining a representative and continuous picture of American Jewry. Creative strategies have been used in some areas to supplement membership listings of Jewish organizations with "marginal," nonaffiliated Jews, and develop alternative designs (e.g., Random Digit Dialing) where no lists are useful. In general, all sampling strategies have limitations and biases, particularly for small populations with specific social, economic, and demographic characteristics.

Samples of the Jewish community could be obtained as part of larger surveys of the total population. However, since Jews are not randomly distributed geographically or socially and their proportion of the total population is small, the largest general samples contain too few Jews for detailed analysis. Moreover, large government-sponsored national surveys, such as the National Family Growth Surveys and the National Longitudinal Study have specialized samples--young couples or high school graduates--which while valuable lack either a community focus or a sufficient number of cases for analysis in depth.

We therefore have to rely on local Jewish community studies for our analysis of changes and variations among Jews and particularly for policy and planning. At the community level, questions of how to obtain a representative sample of Jews, what information to include in the survey, and how the data should be analyzed have been critical. Issues of sample design per se have rarely been discussed at the local level and the central considerations have revolved around cost and efficiency. Scientific, academic, and analytic concerns have rarely been in the forefront of survey sampl issues in Jewish community studies.

The research project reanalyzing data from the Boston Jewish Community Studies of 1965 and 1975 was made possible by the generous support of the Center for Modern Jewish Studies, Brandeis University. The encouragement of Steven M. Cohen in the preparation of this paper is gratefully acknowledged.

SUBSTANTIVE REASONS FOR INCLUDING NON-JEWS IN JEWISH COMMUNITY STUDIES

The argument for obtaining a sample of the Jewish community as part of a survey of the total community, Jewish and non-Jewish, has almost always been made on the basis of procedural considerations. Since it is difficult to obtain a representative sample for most American Jewish communities based on organizational lists or using other methodologies, it is desirable to draw a large sample of the general population and screen for Jewish households. Even where organizational lists are available and form the basis for a core sample, it is desirable to obtain a supplementary sample based on a general survey to pick up more (or the most) unaffiliated, marginal Jews.

This paper addresses the question of including non-Jews in Jewish community surveys from another angle. We argue not on sampling grounds but on substantive considerations. We pose the issue in reverse: There is a need to include non-Jewish populations as part of Jewish community surveys, de-emphasizing the treatment of Jews as part of total population surveys. Whatever sampling strategies are developed, they need to be justified on their own merits and require evaluation in terms of coverage, representativeness, and quality. We take the position that all sampling strategies should be designed to insure the collection and analysis of comparable data for Jews and non-Jews, using similar questionnaires, administered in similar contexts, at the same time, within the same communities. Given a focus on obtaining data which will be used to understand the Jewish community, our question becomes: Why is the cost of including non-Jews in samples of the Jewish community worthwhile? We shall demonstrate that studies solely focused on Jews without direct comparisons with non-Jews result in a limited understanding of the Jews and their communities. Not including non-Jews in surveys of the Jewish community implies one of two possibilities: (1) that those obtaining information about Jews to analyze Jewish communities or plan Jewish communal activities and services have no interest in placing the understanding of Jews within the context of reliable and systematic social scientific evidence; or (2) that there is no appreciation of why the costs of including non-Jews in Jewish community surveys are justified. Our premise is that Jewish community surveys are in large part undertaken to understand Jewish communities and Jewish populations, and to build from social scientific evidence various policies, plans, and activities which meet the needs of the community. We argue that the costs of including non-Jews in Jewish community surveys are warranted and that in fact there is no substitute for systematic empirical comparisons between Jewish and non-Jewish populations.

This paper illustrates two facets of the issues involved: (1) how the inclusion of data on non-Jews facilitates an in-depth analysis of key issues in American Jewish life, and (2) how the absence of comparable data on non-Jews may distort our understanding and interpretation of Jewish behavioral patterns. The examples used are drawn exclusively from a larger research project, focusing on the 1975 Boston surveys which included Jews and non-Jews.[1] The issues that were examined included family patterns, population processes, and social stratification. In this study, the advantages of the detailed data collected were presented and systematic comparisons with non-Jews were made. There is no need to repeat these specifics here. The focus in this paper is on using the results of the Boston study to highlight the critical analytic value of Jewish/non-Jewish comparisons for understanding the Jewish community. I shall go further and argue that without including non-Jews in Jewish community samples, we are limited in our analysis of Jewish life in America and in the development of policy guidelines for Jewish institutions.

The illustrations will be taken from several substantive themes: (1) marriage patterns, particularly issues associated with the timing of family formation; (2) kinship structure as reflected in household composition; (3) reproduction and contraceptive usage; (4) migration; and (5) social stratification.

The most conspicuous analytic issue requiring comparative data on non-Jews is the extent of Jewish exceptionalism. Two interrelated questions are involved: In what way are Jews different from non-Jews? and What factors account for the uniqueness of Jews? In particular, do differences between Jews and non-Jews reflect socioeconomic and demographic characteristics of the groups, the ethnic bonds and networks linking members of a community to each other, or cultural values and norms which differentiate among groups?

Marriage Patterns

We start with an example from family formation differences between Jews and non-Jews. In general, surveys of Jewish communities have shown that Jews marry relatively late; the more educated marry later than the less educated; and some delayed marriage seems to characterize younger compared to older cohorts of Jews. With refinements and extensions, these findings indicate what may be learned from comparisons among Jews. Comparisons between Jews and non-Jews allow for an examination of whether Jews have a distinctive marriage pattern, whether differences between Jewish and non-Jewish marriage patterns solely reflect the particular social, economic, and demographic characteristics of these groups, and whether differences between Jews and non-Jews extend to the level, timing, and pattern of family formation.

A preliminary glance at Jewish/non-Jewish differences in the timing of family formation shows that Jewish women marry at slightly older ages than non-Jewish women. However, crude comparisons between total Jews and total non-Jews do not take into account the internal heterogeneity of both groups. While Jewish women marry later than the average for all non-Jewish women, their age at marriage is identical to that of Protestants, and earlier than those of Irish Catholics and blacks. Similarly, a comparison of Jewish and non-Jewish males over age 40 would have confirmed the later age at which Jews first marry. A detailed and careful examination shows that such a conclusion would have been unwarranted, since there are no differences between Jews and Italian and Irish Catholics.

Systematic and detailed comparisons of Jewish and non-Jewish marriage patterns leads to a major conclusion for understanding recent changes in American Jewish life: Most Jewish women are neither delaying marriage beyond childbearing nor are they particularly marrying at later ages compared to women of other ethnic and religious groups. The later ages at marriage of Jewish women have little direct relationship to issues of Jewish continuity; nor is the timing of marriage for Jewish men problematic.

The heterogeneity among Jews and among non-Jews extends beyond ethnic-religious differences. Residential, socioeconomic status, and other social, economic, and demographic differences characterize Jews and non-Jews. In the Boston study, we control automatically for region and metropolitan area. In turn, we also can presume similar labor markets, opportunity structures, access to educational institutions, and residential areas. However, we need to control for socioeconomic differences between Jews and non-Jews for two reasons. First, we want to isolate the specific factors that account for differences between groups. For example, those with higher educational levels, in general, marry later. Jews have higher educational levels than non-Jews. Controlling for educational levels will show whether age at marriage differences between Jews and non-Jews reflect the different educational levels of the two groups or whether differences remain within educational levels. A second reason to examine the socioeconomic variation within groups is to identify whether the relationship between particular variables is similar for both groups. For example, we can ask: Does the relationship between educational attainment and delayed marriage among non-Jews apply to Jews as well? If our empirical answer is affirmative, then one factor associated with later age at marriage among Jews is educational attainment.

Here again findings from the Boston study reveal some surprises when comparisons between Jews and non-Jews are made. For example, controlling for educational levels, Jewish women do not marry at later ages than non-Jewish women. Higher educational attainment results in delayed marriage for all women--Jews and non-Jews alike. In contrast, Jewish men of all educational levels marry later, so that higher levels of education have little effect on their marriage timing. But educational attainment does affect the timing of marriage among non-Jewish men. This implies that educational attainment has different meanings for the marriage patterns of non-Jewish and Jewish men.

Jewish/non-Jewish comparisons also help resolve measurement problems. For example, the income measure collected in the Boston data referred to family income. Both nonresponse and questions about accuracy of reporting raised the reliability issue. Hence, when no relationship between income and age at marriage was found among Jewish women, the finding could be dismissed as a measurement problem. When a positive relationship between income and age at marriage among Jewish men was found, the conclusion might have been that the income measure was a poor indicator of socioeconomic status or resources among women. Without comparisons to non-Jews, however, the possibility could not be ruled out that what was found was not a measurement problem for women but a gender specific relationship. Comparing the patterns for non-Jews revealed a clear positive relationship between income and age at marriage among non-Jewish women and men. Hence, the issue was neither a simple measurement problem nor gender specific. It was, indeed, a pattern which characterized Jewish women specifically. In short, the meaning of income was different for Jewish women than for Jewish men and for non-Jewish women. In this case, Jewish exceptionalism was gender specific, extending to both the pattern and the relationship between the particular characteristic (income) and age at marriage.

This analysis was not only an academic exercise to show the value of comparisons. More importantly, comparisons between Jews and non-Jews controlling for socioeconomic status led to the conclusion that the potential conflict between marriage, education, and childbearing was resolved in very different ways among racial, religious, and white ethnic groups. For Jewish women, the resolution was to marry relatively early for their class-education group and delay childbearing within marriage. There are important implications of that family formation pattern for a wide variety of institutions and activities within the Jewish community. That Jewish women resolved this potential conflict differently from others is of paramount significance in understanding life cycle patterns and for relating community institutional planning to these patterns.

Kinship Ties and Household Composition

It is widely accepted that Jews place a high value on family life. In part, the argument has been made that an emphasis on family or kinship ties among Jews is the result of years of group persecution as a minority group, values which emerge from particular features of Jewish culture and religion, and generations of living in small, closely knit communities. Certainly, these explanations could be qualified or challenged with a number of counterarguments. However, a clearer challenge rests with the evidence showing that we often attempt to account for a Jewish pattern which either does not exist or is not particularly Jewish. What if comparisons between Jews and non-Jews reveal that Jewish and non-Jewish groups have similar kinship-family patterns? What if these non-Jewish groups do not share Jewish cultural values, the history of Jewish minority status, or persecution and segregation?

The Boston data allow us to examine selected aspects of kinship ties among Jews and non-Jews. In the process of systematic comparisons, the data reveal a much more complex pattern which is both gender- and age-related and which sharpens our perspective on where Jewish exceptionalism is most conspicious. We start with young Jewish males who are more likely to move away from their family and less likely than non-Jews to start their own nuclear households. Early nest leaving coupled with later family formation is a feature more of Jewish than non-Jewish males. This finding is significant in two contexts: First, it suggests that family-kinship ties are not particularly characteristic of young Jewish males, at least in terms of continued residence in the household of orientation or in terms of leaving home to establish a new family. Moreover, the longer period of time between leaving home and starting a family, and an even longer period of time before having children, has major implications for understanding the Jewishness of American Jews. Since Jewishness and family formation are intertwined in complex ways, changes in family formation have major implications for the expression of Jewishness. The time gap has increased among recent cohorts and, therefore, the "Jewishness" crisis is more keenly felt. There is no evidence that these patterns are permanent over the life course. Hence, there is a strong basis for expecting an upturn in Jewish expression and activities as marriage and family formation occur.

At the other end of the life cycle, older Jewish men who are not part of a nuclear household (e.g., who are not married, living with spouse) tend to live alone compared to a significantly larger proportion of non-Jews who live with their relatives. Clearly the values of extended Jewish families do not apply to Jewish males at least in terms of residential patterns. It seems that values associated with independence and autonomy are more powerful than those of family and kin.

These patterns do not characterize Jewish women. Again, comparisons between Jewish and non-Jewish women help clarify the issues. Young Jewish women are more likely to be in nuclear households than non-Jews but are less likely to have children (i.e., they are in husband-wife, not husband-wife-children households). Jewish women not in nuclear households leave home in higher proportion than non-Jewish women. Indeed, young non-Jewish women who are not forming new households are more than three times as likely to live with relatives as are Jewish women.

Moreover, there are life cycle differences between Jewish and non-Jewish women. Among older women, a higher proportion of Jewish women who are not in a nuclear household live with relatives compared to non-Jewish women. While it is clear that most Jewish women not in nuclear households live alone (fully 73 percent), it is not at all clear whether that is a high or low level. Indeed, it is a low figure relative to non-Jewish women. Fully four times as many Jewish as non-Jewish women live with relatives. The higher proportion of kinship of residence patterns among older Jewish women does not characterize younger Jewish women, Jewish males, or nonJewish men or women. Hence, the issue of greater family-kinship patterns and inferences about the Jewish value on family living arrangements are particular to older Jewish women. While older Jewish women have patterns closer to older Italian than to Irish women, this form of family extension is particularly characteristic of Jewish women compared to all other racial, religious, and white ethnic groups included in the Boston study.

In general, the nest-leaving pattern of younger Jewish women is associated with education. For the most part only less educated young Jewish women live with their family; the college educated who are not married live alone or with nonrelatives. The residential choice among less educated young Jewish women appears to be to form new households by marrying or to remain at home living with parents. For the more educated, the choice is to marry or move out away from the family. Hence, the less educated move out to marry; the more educated move out to live independently. Nevertheless, compared to non-Jews, Jewish women of all educational levels are more likely to move away from their parents' home and live alone. Non-Jewish women with a high school education who are not or have not been married are more likely to live with their family. At the upper educational levels, differences between Jewish and non-Jewish women revolve around issues of the timing of childbearing, not household composition, living arrangements, or marriage.

Very sharp contrasts characterize the household patterns of Jewish and non-Jewish males. Less than 10 percent of the Jewish males with some college education who are not in their own nuclear household live with relatives, compared to four times that level among comparably educated non-Jewish males. The greater independence of Jewish than non-Jewish males from families of orientation characterizes all educational levels.

Again, the biases of the income measure becomes less problematic when Jewish/non-Jewish comparisons are made. These data show, for example, that the greater concentration of older Jewish women in extended households is not simply a function of lower income. Older Jewish women (unlike their non-Jewish counterparts) live with their relatives not because they cannot afford to live alone but for other reasons.

Reproductive Patterns and Contraceptive Usage

Comparing the reproductive patterns of Jewish and non-Jewish women further illustrates the need to include non-Jews in samples of the Jewish community. Overall, Jews have smaller families than non-Jews and most studies show that these differences are not solely accounted for by the differential socioeconomic characteristics of the groups. The Boston data allow us to go beyond these findings. Two important relationships emerge from detailed comparisons between Jewish and non-Jewish women. First, among non-Jews (Protestants as well as Catholics), there is a clear inverse relationship between educational attainment and family size expectations. In contrast, the most educated Jewish women have the largest family size goals. Hence, at higher educational levels, family size expectations of Jews and non-Jews converge. Clearly a prediction of the Jewish pattern from the non-Jewish pattern would be incorrect. More important, the concern regarding overall low Jewish fertility and the inferred lower levels of fertility among the more educated needs to be reexamined. Jewish exceptionalism relates to overall levels of fertility and to different relationships to educational attainment.

A second pattern relates to labor force participation of women and fertility. Generally, there is a negative relationship--women who work have fewer children. In part, this relates to the incompatibility of work and family roles, and choices between careers and childbearing and child-rearing activities. This general finding has been applied by inference to Jews and suggestions have been made about the even lower fertility expected of Jewish women as more enter into the labor force. There is but a short leap from that inference to population projections predicting the demise of American Jewry sometime in the next century.

Careful comparisons between labor force participation and the fertility of Jewish and non-Jewish women point to opposite conclusions. There is no general relationship between work activities of Jewish women and their fertility. The effects of working are largely on the timing of childbearing, not eventual family size. Protestant and Catholic women who work have smaller family size expectations than those who do not. Given the serious methodological complexities in measuring labor force participation of women, such systematic comparisons need to be made within one data set, obtained for the same labor market, and using the same analytic techniques.

Beyond the methodological value and analytic necessities, comparisons between Jews and non-Jews are critical for our understanding of the patterns of Jewish continuity. The conclusion we reach is that the Boston data provide no support for the argument that the work patterns of young, educated, career-oriented Jewish women pose a demographic threat to Jewish continuity. (Indeed, other data show that the work patterns of Jewish women--unlike those of non-Jewish women--reinforce ethnic contacts and have become one basis of Jewish continuity.) As with the relationship between education and fertility, inferences from the literature on the relationship between work and fertility would have been an incorrect characterization for Jews.

In a similar way, comparisons of the contraceptive usage patterns of Jews and non-Jews show the higher levels of sterilization (for contraceptive purposes) among Jews. This finding emerges from direct comparisons between Jews and non-Jews in the Boston study. It is the reverse of what would have been concluded on the basis of a comparison of Jews in Boston with national data on Protestants and Catholics. In general, comparisons of disparate data sets are most problematic; there are differences in the wording of questions (in this case usual rather than current use), the sub-population sampled (currently versus continuously married and with different age-duration specifications), the context of the questionnaire (a single question on contraceptive usage in the context of religion and health compared to a battery of questions in the context of reproductive and contraceptive histories). The lesson to be learned is not necessarily that the Boston population (Jewish and non-Jewish) is unique but that comparisons need to be made within one study. Comparisons between one data set and another will often be less than definitive, since we do not know whether differences which emerge are due to the peculiarities of the data set or are real patterns. Hence, it is often not clear whether there is a need to explain differences that are found or whether the findings can be dismissed on methodological grounds.

Migration

Migration is another important substantive area where comparisons between Jews and non-Jews yield important insights about Jews. The redistribution of the American Jewish population and its continuing concentration are central features of Jewish life in the United States. Yet, the consequences of the migration patterns which result in population redistribution have rarely been appreciated or studied systematically. Attempts, for example, to compare the National Jewish Population Survey data on migration with U.S. Census Bureau materials were frustrated by definitional differences and migration duration variations. No details therefore are known nationally about the determinants and consequences of internal migration patterns among Jews. No one community study, even when comparisons between Jews and non-Jews are made, can characterize the migration patterns in all communities: many Jewish communities have lost populations just as many have gained; cities, neighborhoods, and regions have been transformed over the last several decades. Clearly, the migration patterns of Boston Jewry do not characterize declining centers of Jewish population, communities smaller or larger, or those with different economic opportunity structures, or newly formed communities in other geographic regions. Nevertheless, the inclusion of non-Jews within the Boston sample allowed for the clarification of how different the migration patterns of Jews were, how selective inmigrants were, and what patterns of residential concentration characterized Jews in the mid-1970s. Given the importance of migration for the changing demographic and socioeconomic composition of Jewish communities, it is vital that comparisons with non-Jews be included to understand the patterns. Again, planning for the Jewish community is dependent on knowledge about the sources of continuity and a conception of needs. Without systematic comparisons between Jews and non-Jews neither our analysis nor our planning can be complete.

Socioeconomic Status and Social Class

The final substantive area that illustrates the value of Jewish/non-Jewish comparisons is socioeconomic status and social class patterns. The concentration of Jews in particular jobs, higher income categories, and higher educational levels has been well documented, as has their upward social mobility. These patterns can be observed even with general comparisons between data sets. In-depth comparisons between Jews and non-Jews require, however, the inclusion of non-Jews in the samples of Jewish communities.

The concentration of Jews in professional and managerial positions does not fully capture the much greater concentration of Jews in specific occupations within these broad job categories. Shared statuses and occupational networks support and reinforce community institutions and ties, family and neighborhood bonds, social class and political interests. Of no less importance is the increasing concentration of Jews over time in a more limited number of occupations. The growing occupational homogeneity and concentration among Jews contrast sharply with the occupational divergences among Protestants and Catholics. In our context, this finding could not have been documented convincingly if we were comparing Jews in Boston to census data for the United States or other national surveys.

The importance of this growing concentration should not be underestimated. The transformation of American Jewry resulting in occupational commonalities at high socioeconomic levels has become a major basis for group cohesion. That these patterns are different among Jews and non-Jews becomes critical in the evaluation of Jewish continuity.

A similar conclusion emerges when we go beyond issues of upward mobility to examine the mechanisms of generational socioeconomic transfers. Comparing intergenerational, occupational, and educational linkages between fathers and their children among Jews and non-Jews allows us to pinpoint where occupational transfers differ. Generational outflows in occupational and educational patterns are significantly different among Jews and among Catholics and Protestants.

The data comparing Jews and non-Jews reveal another overall pattern important in evaluating Jewish continuity. Over time, there has been much less occupational assimilation of Jews within the broader occupational structure than is often portrayed. Indeed, comparisons show patterns of crystallization of social class differences between Jews and non-Jews. There is no empirical support for the argument that occupational differences between Jews and non-Jews are converging. The class-ethnic overlap distinguishing Jews from Catholics and Protestants implies the development of social bonds, economic networks, and common lifestyles within each group. These patterns are powerful sources of communal continuity.

In interesting ways, these patterns of overall difference between Jews and non-Jews do not apply to women. For example, the rates of labor force participation of Jewish women are very similar to those of non-Jewish women, when life cycle and educational factors are taken into account. The key differences are in the high concentration of Jewish women in the professional category and in specific jobs within that category. These jobs tend to be dominated by Jewish women; hence, working outside the home brings Jews in greater, not lesser, contact with other Jews.

DIFFERENCES AMONG JEWISH COMMUNITIES

We know that Jewish communities vary: Boston is not New York, and neither is it Los Angeles, Miami, or Chicago. Two types of explanations account for differences among Jewish community patterns: factors associated with distinctive Jewish demographic, social, economic, and institutional structures, and factors associated with the broader context of the community of which the Jews are a part. In the first category, items range from the idiosyncratic (time of immigrant arrival in the local community, communal leadership, local institutional strength) to the size, age-generational composition of Jewish communities, economic structure, and migration patterns.

How can we analyze whether differences are solely or mainly the result of local Jewish differences? Often we have no choice but to remain vague; most often we focus on only one community and make no comparisons. When comparisons across communities are made, we tend to concentrate mainly on the Jewish component.

An example of the value of comparing non-Jews and Jews when examining more than one Jewish community emerges clearly with an illustration from the Boston survey. An examination of the self-employment of Boston Jews shows the very high levels relative to some overall national figure. In turn, largely because data were available in identical form around the same date, the Boston data were systematically compared to data from the Jewish community in Rhode Island. The evidence showed that levels of self-employment were lower among the Jews of Boston than among the Jews in Rhode Island. In part, these differences reflect the age-generational, demographic, and economic differences between the two Jewish communities, their sizes and institutional structures. However, in order to go beyond this very general level and clarify whether the differences were mainly a result of Jewish or general factors, comparisons with non-Jews were essential. Indeed, Protestants and Catholics in Rhode Island had higher self-employment levels than Protestants and Catholics in Boston. Although Jews had higher levels of self-employment than non-Jews in both areas, the differences were proportionally the same, despite different levels between areas. The inclusion of non-Jews in both Boston and Rhode Island sharpened the search for an explanation beyond the specific features of Jewish communities to more general factors associated with occupational markets and economies of the two areas, opportunity structures, the level of in-and out-migration, and the socioeconomic selectivity of those moving out and moving in. These factors together, not specific features of the Jewish community, account for the higher level of Jewish self-employment, and the higher level of self-employment among Jews and non-Jews in Rhode Island compared to Boston. Neither universal Jewish values on occupational independence nor uniform patterns across communities characterize American Jews. To the extent that self-employment patterns are related to ethnic networks and intergenerational continuity, these exceptional Jewish patterns (at different levels for different communities) are of particular importance for Jewish continuity.

THE HIGH COST OF OMITTING NON-JEWS FROM JEWISH COMMUNITY STUDIES

These substantive and analytic illustrations lead to the overall conclusion that the omission of systematic subgroup comparisons of non-Jews with Jews limits our understanding of the Jewish community. The costs of such omissions are too high to justify the exclusive focus on Jews. Indeed, to understand the Jewish community is to be able to plan and serve its needs. All planning and policies have implicit frameworks and conceptions about the nature of the community and its population and how best to relate effectively to them.

The systematic collection and analysis of data on the Jewish community and on Jews are necessary conditions for planning and policy. The absence of comparable data on non-Jews has led in the past to limited analysis and understanding of the Jews in America. The exceptional value of including non-Jews in Jewish community samples is to allow for comparisons with identical data sets addressed to populations in the same community, at the same time, with identical questions, and similar processing procedures. In that way, whatever biases exist characterize all groups equally.

As communities plan new studies and restudies for the 1980s, we need to take another look at the sampling considerations which have guided us in the past, and we need to consider the value of including comparable non-Jewish populations in our surveys of the Jewish community.

Note

1. The project is set forth in detail in a monograph entitled Social Change and Jewish Continuity, to be published under the auspices of the Center for Modern Jewish Studies, Brandeis University.

11
Using Death Records for Estimating the Jewish Elderly Population in Local Areas

Ira Rosenwaike

Those interested simply in a crude estimate of the size, geographic distribution, and a few other characteristics of the Jewish elderly in their area need not turn to the high-cost random sample survey. Instead they may derive elderly population estimates from local death records. Research in Jewish mortality has been relatively neglected (Goldscheider). Before presenting the technique, it seems appropriate to review the use of the death record in a general context as well as in its specific application to Jewish populations.

JEWISH MORTALITY STATISTICS

Death registration in the United States is a function of the individual states and certain other registration areas. A high level of uniformity in record content obtains throughout the nation. In virtually all areas, death certificates include the decedent's sex, age, marital status, place of residence, state or country of birth, usual occupation, and cause of death, as well as the names of the funeral home and of the cemetery or crematory.

Mortality statistics of Jewish populations provide information valuable for many purposes: numerators for the calculation of age-specific death rates, source data for preparation of life tables (providing measures of longevity), data useful for epidemiologic studies examining differences between Jews and non-Jews that might give clues to the etiology of particular diseases; and public health studies examining the health of "high risk groups" or evaluating specific programs (Peritz and Tamir). In addition, many studies have utilized mortality statistics to construct estimates of the Jewish population in American cities.

A major use of Jewish mortality statistics in recent decades has been in epidemiologic studies, particularly those relating to cancer. Cancer mortality among Jews in the United States has been reported by Newill, Seidman (1970, 1971), Haenszel, and Greenwald. Leukemia is among the specific types of cancer which have been studied in Jewish populations (MacMahon and Koller; Feldman et al.). The pattern of lung cancer among Jews has also received close attention (Seidman, 1966; Wynder and Mantel; Herman and Enterline).

The relative importance of various causes of death among Jews in New York City was examined in the 1930s by Bolduan and Weiner and in the 1950s by Liberson. Differences in mortality among Jewish residents by socioeconomic class, also in New York, were examined by Seidman et al. The attraction of New York City for researchers is twofold. First, the city contains by far the largest number of Jews in the United States. Second, New York City is the only registration area in the nation in which the health department classified all deaths by religious affiliation of cemetery of burial--thereby providing unique data for the study of Jewish mortality.

A few studies have produced age-specific death rates and life tables for American Jews. As is well known, no official censuses provide separate counts of Jews, nor is religion ever included on death records anywhere in the United States. In a few instances, however, in conjunction with sample surveys or local community consenses that ascertained the detailed age and sex distribution of the Jewish population in particular cities, investigators derived detailed statistics of Jewish deaths from the records of funeral directors. The principal studies of this type are those of deaths collected by Goldstein (1966) in Providence, Rhode Island, from mid-1962 to mid-1964, and by Fauman and Mayer (1969) in Milwaukee and Detroit during the five-year period 1961-1965. The latter asserted that the combined life table they produced on the basis of the Providence data "can be considered to be the most reliable estimate of mortality rates in the Jewish population in the United States." The mortality pattern observed was similar to that reported in two earlier studies of North American Jewish populations, those by Spiegelman and by the New York Bureau of Jewish Social Research: lower death rates among Jews than among the non-Jewish population at young ages, higher death rates among Jews than non-Jews at older ages. Specifically, Jewish males and females in all three cities--Detroit, Milwaukee, and Providence--had lower life expectancy at age 65 than comparable United States whites. Similarly, Canadian Jews at age 65 had approximately the same average life expectancy as Jewish males and females in the United States and markedly lower life expectancy than Canadian males and females generally (Fauman and Mayer, 1969). Data for New York City provide further corroboration of this mortality pattern: age-specific death rates (standardized for socioeconomic class) indicated that non-Jewish females at ages 65-74 years and 75 years and over had death rates 7 percent and 18 percent lower, respectively, than Jewish females; among males, non-Jews had 4 percent lower mortality at ages 75 and over, but 8 percent higher mortality at ages 65-74 (Seidman et al.).

In the first half of this century statistics of Jewish deaths were frequently collected in American cities for the purpose of computing estimates of the total Jewish population. As early as 1902 Barnett developed a method which he applied to Baltimore; variations on the theme often appeared, particularly in New York City (Chalmers; New York Bureau of Jewish Social Research). The full flowering of the method, however, seems to have occurred in the Midwest where attempts at population construction from death statistics were made by social scientists utilizing data for Chicago in 1930 and for Detroit in 1939-1941 (Jaffe; Fauman and Mayer, 1955). After the 1930s the death record technique was seldom used, replaced by newer techniques of population estimation and, in those communities where financial resources permitted it, by the preferable approaches of actual canvasses of the total population or sample surveys. A recent commentator on current techniques of population estimation fails to mention the death rate method (Phillips).

The problems associated with the death rate method were well explicated in the 1930s and 1940s by Lurie and Robison. Lurie commented on an application of the method in Baltimore where Jewish deaths were tabulated by age groups and an estimate made for the population in each age group using the age-specific death rates obtained for Jews in New York City. He found

> considerable probability of error in each of the age group computations; for example the death rate for females, age ten to fourteen is placed at one per 1,000. There were four deaths in that age and sex group in Baltimore in 1925 and, therefore, it is estimated that there were 4,000 Jewish females in that age group. A difference of a single death in this group would change the estimates by 1,000 persons. A variation of a single death in each one of the eleven age groups for each sex would have affected the estimate by 10.6 percent.... There would be a larger probability of error in cities with a smaller Jewish population [than Baltimore] if this method were to be used.

Improvements in mortality rates during the twentieth century were concentrated at the young ages; accordingly, the continued use of the death statistics approach for estimating population would have meant smaller and smaller numbers of deaths to represent Jewish populations in the young and middle ages. Data for New York City illustrate this dramatic shift. In 1931 only 32 percent of Jewish decedents were aged 65 years or over; by 1953 the proportion had reached 60 percent (Liberson). Statistics for 1979-1981 indicate more than 84 percent of those decedents who were New York City residents and were buried in Jewish cemeteries were age 65 years or over (New York City Department of Health). But since the 1979-1981 figure refers only to city residents, and suburban areas tend to have somewhat younger populations than cities, this figure may overstate the share of Jewish decedents above 65 years of age. Nevertheless, the proportion must be in the vicinity of three out of four deaths.

POPULATION ESTIMATION

In recent years special attention has been focused on the elderly, in large part because the relatively rapid growth of this population has been accompanied by mounting health care and social needs. Goldstein (1981) has pointed out that whereas the United States as a whole faces serious problems due to an aging population, the problems may be still more serious within the Jewish community where a rise in the percentage of persons 65 and over from 11 percent in 1971 to over 15 percent by the early 1990s is anticipated.

The heavy concentration of deaths among persons 65 and above provides the logical foundation for the method described here. Deaths occur with high frequency only among persons of advanced age and it is only for estimating the number of such persons that the number of deaths represents a sensitive indicator.

This paper outlines a method for estimating the age and sex composition of the subgroup 65 years and over in the Jewish community. It presents a comparatively simple and inexpensive technique for preparing estimates not only of the elderly in the total Jewish community but also in major geographic divisions. These estimates will be sufficiently reliable for most planning uses. The procedure is not original but represents a new variation of the older procedure discussed above that was in use for many decades.

Estimates of the population aged 65 years and over are derived by reversing the procedure of computing death rates: given the number of deaths occurring in a population in a given time period and the death rate in that population, its size can be determined by dividing the number of deaths by the death rate. To produce this estimate a researcher needs two sets of data. The first is a reliable count of deaths of Jewish residents 65 years and over by age and sex for the years around the date for which estimates are to be prepared. The second is a schedule of age-sex specific death rates for the Jewish population during the same time period. This, of course, is not available, but proxy figures may be used. The sources of these two sets of data will now be discussed.

There is general agreement that the great majority of deaths of Jews can be identified through two items of information on the death certificates: the name of the cemetary of burial and the name of the funeral director (Fauman and Mayer, 1969). Liberson concluded that "close to 95 percent of all Jewish [decedents]" in New York City were buried in Jewish cemeteries. As noted earlier, the New York City Department of Health is the only such office in the nation in which the place of burial reported on the death certificate is coded (as Catholic, Protestant, Jewish, crematory, etc.). Manual review of the death records in other cities has produced higher estimated levels of completeness: in a study in the St. Louis area the researcher concluded that "three funeral directors handle, as far as could be determined, pratically all Jewish burials. They are also usually in charge of the limited number of Jewish cremations" (Gorwitz). A mortality study in Rhode Island concluded that "reliance upon the records of the Jewish funeral director provides almost 100 percent coverage for all Jewish deaths occurring in Greater Providence or among Providence Jews who die elsewhere and are buried in Providence" (Goldstein, 1966).

Because a small number of funeral homes fill out the death certificates of Jewish decedents in all but the very largest Jewish communities, the most feasible strategy for the demographer usually will be direct contact with the directors of those homes to review the death records and devise needed counts by age and sex. This was the approach taken in mortality studies in Detroit, Milwaukee, Providence, and St. Louis, where three, two, one, and three funeral directors, respectively, accounted among them for almost all Jewish interments (Fauman and Mayer, 1969). To supplement this approach, or to substitute for it in situations where an alternative is desirable, death records for metropolitan areas, counties, or cities can be reviewed at the vital records offices of state, county, or municipal health departments (see U.S. Department of Health, Education and Welfare). In many instances, due to political fragmentation of a geographic area, review of the records in the state health department office, which maintains central files of deaths throughout the state, is recommended. For example, this might be the preferred method for a study of deaths in greater Boston since the metropolitan area is composed of dozens of cities and towns. On the other hand, when the boundaries of a Jewish community approximate those of a county (as for example, in San Diego), review of records in a county health department is recommended.

It is important to emphasize that in many states death certificates are regarded as confidential records and their availability to the public is restricted. However, the documents are available for review by qualified researchers if it can be demonstrated they will be utilized in studies of scientific merit. As a rule, before permission is obtained for examination of the files, researchers must indicate that the end product of their review will be statistical data only and that no names of individuals will be copied. In this connection it is important to note also that some knowledge of epidemiology is an invaluable prerequisite for the analysis of mortality, particularly by cause of death. Most such studies cited here, for example, were conducted by physicians or epidemiologists.

During manual review of the death records, certificates of male and female decedents 65 years of age and over determined to be Jewish should be grouped by ten-year age intervals: 65-74 years, 75-84 years, 85 years and over. At the same time appropriate subgroups representing the major geographic subdivisions of the metropolitan area can be identified. Deaths over a three-year period are preferred to numbers for a single year, since in most communities the numbers of deaths in age-sex groups in a single year are small (especially so for geographic subdivisions); furthermore the general level of mortality can fluctuate from year to year due to "flu" epidemics. The use of three-year averages thus produces more stable rates. In smaller Jewish communities, say those with fewer than 10,000 or 12,000 individuals, the use of five-year averages is recommended.

ESTIMATES OF AGE-SEX SPECIFIC DEATH RATES FOR THE STUDY YEARS

It goes without saying that we do not know the age-specific death rate for population being studied. To compute age-specific death rates reliable population figures are needed--precisely what we are trying to estimate here. A national study might produce such rates--in fact, this was one of the stated goals of the National Jewish Population Survey (Goldstein, 1973)--but such rates have not appeared to date. In order to approximate the rates, we assume that the male and female death rates for the white population 65 years of age and older of the nation as a whole during the study period are roughly equivalent to the death rates among Jews in comparable age groups. National data are published annually by the U.S. National Center for Health Statistics.

One question appropriate at this point is, "Why not equate local Jewish death rates with the rates of the city or metropolitan area being studied?"

There is comparatively little variation in death rates of whites aged 65 years and over among metropolitan areas. More pertinent, however, age-sex-race specific death rates for local areas are seldom available, except for census years. When they are available for other dates, they are usually not as reliable as death rates for the total United States because the population figures used in the denominator are estimates which may sometimes be quite off the mark due to migration.

No valid answer can be given to the question "Is it justified to assume age-sex specific death rates for American Jews are approximately

TABLE 11.1
Illustration of population Estimate by Death-Rate Technique for Jewish Population Aged 65 Years and Over: New York City

Sex and age	Jewish deaths, New York City		Average death rates, 1979-1981 per 1,000 U.S. white population	Estimated Jewish population, 1980 (2) ÷ (3)
	Total, 1979-1981 (1)	Average annual, 1979-1981 (2)	(3)	(4)
Males:				
65-74 years	5,298	1,766	39.5	44,700
75-84 years	6,953	2,318	85.9	27,000
85 years and over	4,170	1,390	185.2	7,500
Total	...	...	...	79,200
Females:				
65-74 years	4,497	1,499	20.5	73,100
75-84 years	8,631	2,877	51.7	55,600
85 years and over	6,755	2,252	142.7	15,800
Total	...	...	...	144,500
Grand total, 65 and over	...	...	...	223,700

Source: Derived from data in New York City Department of Health (1982) and U.S. National Center for Health Statistics (1982).

the same as those of United States whites aged 65 years and over?" Indeed, an answer to this question certainly represents one of the major research needs today. However, if we look at the most recent trustworthy statistics, admittedly dating back to the early 1960s and before, we find that Jewish death rates in all age-sex groups 65 years and older in the combined Detroit-Milwaukee-Providence study were somewhat above those in comparable white populations (Fauman and Mayer, 1969). In the very extensive New York City study (in which population figures were estimated) Jewish females had higher death rates than other whites in the age groups 65 and above, whereas Jewish males aged 65-74 years had lower death rates and Jewish males 75 and over had higher death rates than other New York whites (Seidman et al., 1962).

We must assume then, at least until more current information becomes available, that the death rates for United States whites 65 years and over are minimum estimates of Jewish death rates at comparable ages and that in all likelihood the Jewish death rates are somewhat higher. Accordingly, when the counts of Jewish deaths in local areas are divided by the current age-sex specific death rates for United States whites the resulting estimates of the elderly Jewish population must be considered as maximum estimates.

Using the methods described above, an example of an estimate of the Jewish population aged 65 years and over for New York City is shown in Table 11.1. The figures of Jewish deaths come from the cemetery of burial item traditionally coded by the New York City Department of Health. The numbers are therefore undoubtedly slightly smaller than those that might have resulted through consideration of the additional information provided by the funeral director item on the death certificate. However, compensating errors (undercount of the number of Jewish deaths and understatement of the Jewish death rate by utilizing the national levels) may partially offset one another. The procedures described yield an estimate for the total New York City Jewish population age 65 years and over in 1980 of about 223,700. Estimates for this total should be relatively more accurate than estimates for subgroups of the population. The average error in the total population should be within a few percentage points of the true figure.

Since a sample survey of the Jewish population residing in households in metropolitan New York was conducted in 1981, it is of interest to compare the results of the technique outlined here with the estimates from the survey. A total of 198,500 persons aged 65 years and over were reported in a tabulation of the population of New York City by age (Ritterband and Cohen). Not all of the population was placed in an age group, however. Whereas 92.37 percent of the city's estimated Jewish population of 1,119,000 was classified by age, the ages of 7.63 percent were unknown. Assuming that the proportion not classified by age was the same for those 65 and over as for the total population, the adjusted number of elderly residents of New York in 1981 becomes 214,900. The latter figure is only 3.9 percent less than the death-rate technique estimate. Considering the one-year difference in time (the death-rate technique centers on 1980), the fact that persons living in institutions were excluded from the New York survey, the sampling variation associated with the survey, and the range of error associated with the various assumptions that are part of the death-rate technique, the close correspondence of the two independent estimates appears to justify the use of the death-rate estimate for estimating the elderly population. Application of this technique in other metropolitan areas will undoubtedly lead to further knowledge about its accuracy and limitations.

GENERAL COMMENTS

Two further comments on the usefulness of the calculated estimate of the population 65 and over in comparison with other data sources are necessary. First, we have stated that, size of the community permitting, deaths over any three-year period are acceptable for averaging. However, certain three-year periods are preferred to others. A three-year period around a census year, say 1979-1981, permits the construction of estimates of the Jewish population 65 and over for a time period (1980) which can readily be compared with the total population 65 and over in the same geographic area. The percent elderly Jews constitute of the total elderly population in a densely Jewish neighborhood, for example, can be calculated. A second favorable three-year period in which to apply the procedure is the period around the year in which a local community survey is conducted. For example, if a survey is taken in 1983, deaths in the three-year period 1982-1984 can be ascertained. The resulting estimate of the aged population can be useful in evaluating the survey findings.

A minor disadvantage of the mortality technique is the time lapse involved. Typically it takes some time for death records to be processed and filed at the health department, so that records for a particular year are not available for research use for at least several months after the close of the year. For example, an estimate of the Jewish population 65 and over in 1983 might not emerge until the latter part of 1985. But it is unlikely that agencies requiring such estimates would find the delay to be a problem. There seems little doubt that a method of population estimation that can provide results quickly and inexpensively in comparison with existing alternatives can be of service to many.

References

Barnett, George E. 1902-1903. "The Jewish Population of Maryland." American Jewish Year Book, pp. 46-62.

Bolduan, C. and L. Weiner. 1933. "Causes of Death among Jews in New York City." New England Journal of Medicine. 208: 407-416.

Chalmers, Henry. 1916. "The Number of Jews in New York City." Publications of the American Statistical Association 14: 68-75

Fauman, S. Joseph and A. J. Mayer. 1955. "Estimation of Jewish Population by the Death Rate Method." Jewish Social Studies 17 (October): 315-322.

_____. 1969. "Jewish Mortality in the United States," Human Biology (September) pp. 416-426.

Feldman, Joseph G., Stanley L. Lee, and Barbara Seligman. 1976. "Occurrence of Acute Leukemia in Females in a Genetically Isolated Population." Cancer 38: 2548-2550.

Goldscheider, Calvin. 1982. "Demography of Jewish Americans: Research Findings, Issues, and Challenges." In M. Sklare (ed.), Understanding American Jewry. New Brunswick: Transaction Books, pp. 1-55.

Goldstein, Sidney. 1966. "Jewish Mortality and Survival Patterns: Providence, Rhode Island, 1962-1964." Eugenics Quarterly 13: 48-61.

_____. 1973. "Sources of Statistics on Jewish Vital Events and Migration in the United States." In Papers in Jewish Demography, 1970. Jerusalem: Institute of Contemporary Jewry, The Hebrew University.

_____. 1981. "Jews in the United States: Perspective from Demography." In J. B. Gittler (ed.), Jewish Life in the United States: Perspectives from the Social Sciences. New York: New York University Press, pp. 31-102.

Gorwitz, K. 1962. "Jewish Mortality in St. Louis and St. Louis County, 1955-1957." Jewish Social Studies 24 (October): 248-254.

Greenwald, Peter. 1975. "Cancer in United States Jews." Cancer Research 35: 3507-3512.

Haenszel, W. 1971. "Cancer Mortality among U.S. Jews." Israel Journal of Medical Science 7: 1437-1450.

Herman, Bertram and Philip E. Enterline. 1970. "Lung Cancer among the Jews and Non-Jews of Pittsburgh, Pennsylvania, 1953-1967: Mortality Rates and Cigarette Smoking Behavior." American Journal of Epidemiology 4: 355-367.

Jaffe, A. J. 1943. "A Study of Chicago Jewry (1930) Based on Death Certificates." In S. M. Robison (ed.), Jewish Population Studies. New York: Conference on Jewish Relations, pp. 131-151.

Liberson, David. 1956. "Causes of Death among Jews in New York City in 1953." Jewish Social Studies 18 (April): 83-117.

Lurie, H. L. 1934. "Some Problems in the Collection and Interpretation of Jewish Population Data." Jewish Social Service Quarterly 10 (June): 263-268.

MacMahon, B. and E. K. Koller. 1957. "Ethnic Differences in the Incidence of Leukemia." Blood 12: 1-10.

Newill, V. A. 1961. "Distribution of Cancer Mortality among Ethnic Subgroups of the White Population of New York City, 1953-1958." Journal of the National Cancer Institute 26: 405-417.

New York Bureau of Jewish Social Research. 1928. Jewish Communal Survey of Greater New York.

New York City Department of Health. 1982. Unpublished tabulations of deaths, 1979-1981.

Peritz, Eric and Ada Tamir. 1979. "Remarks on the Mortality of Ashkenazim, with Data on European-Born Jews in Israel." In R. M. Goodman and A. G. Motulsky (eds.), Genetic Diseases Among Ashkenazi Jews. New York: Raven Press, pp. 415-424.

Phillips, Bruce A. 1982. "Research Needs of Local Jewish Communities: Current Trends and New Directions." In M. Sklare (ed.), Understanding America Jewry. New Brunswick: Transaction Books, pp. 245-260.

Ritterband, Paul and Steven M. Cohen. 1982. "The Social Characteristics of the New York Area Jewish Community." Typescript.

Robison, Sophia M. 1943. "How Many Jews in America?" Commentary 8 (August): 185-192.

Seidman, H. 1966. "Lung Cancer among Jewish, Catholic and Protestant Males in New York City." Cancer 19: 185-190.

_____. 1970. "Cancer Death Rates by Site and Sex for Religious and Socioeconomic Groups in New York City." Environmental Research 3: 234-250.

_____. 1971. "Cancer Mortality in New York City for Country-of-Birth, Religious and Socioeconomic Groups." Environmental Research 4: 390-429.

_____, L. Garfinkel, and L. Craig. 1962. "Death Rates in New York City by Socio-Economic Class and Religious Group and by Country of Birth, 1949-1951." Jewish Journal of Sociology 4 (December): 254-272.

Spiegelman, Mortimer. 1948. "The Longevity of the Jews in Canada 1940-42." Population Studies 2: 292-304.

U.S. Department of Health, Education and Welfare. 1979. "Where to Write for Birth and Death Records: United States and Outlying Areas." Washington, D.C.: U.S. Government Printing Office.

U.S. National Center for Health Statistics. 1982. Monthly Vital Statistics Report 30:13 (December 20).

Wynder, E. L. and N. Mantel. 1966. "Some Epidemiological Features of Lung Cancer among Jewish Males." Cancer 19: 191-195.

12 Exploring Possibilities for Followup Studies of Jewish Communal Surveys

Bruce A. Phillips

Allocation of funds and long-range planning are two separate (and sometimes independent) aspects of federation planning. Although a Jewish population study provides data for both, it is better suited to allocations because of its cross-sectional ("one-shot" survey) design. It can estimate the size of and collect information about key planning populations (such as single parents or the elderly); and, in general, it provides information about specific populations currently served as well as the community as a whole at the time of the survey. Because it does not collect information about change, it is less useful for long-range planning. Since the scope of federation planning has largely been short-range, this has not been a problem so far. As federation planning moves more toward a long-range perspective, information about population dynamics will take on greater importance.

Surveys can measure change in two ways: through retrospective questions about prior change and through prospective questions about future behavior. Retrospective questions ask about past marriages, previous moves, prior synagogue membership, and other changes that the respondent or the family has experienced. Prospective questions concern intentions and expectations about such things as moving, having more children, or enrolling youngsters in a religious school.

Both sorts of questions have their limitations. Retrospective questions can help us understand the scope and effect of social change that has already occurred, but they cannot predict it. Prospective questions are limited to what people say they will do, which is not necessarily what they will do in fact. Cross-sectional studies are limited in other ways. For example, Sunbelt communities are affected by growth, but Jews planning to move there can be studied only in the communities they are planning to leave.

Longitudinal studies, because they are repeated over time, do not have these limitations. There are but a few examples of longitudinal Jewish research, and only one was actually designed to be longitudinal. In 1975 Floyd Fowler replicated the Boston study conducted ten years earlier. The sample design and question wording of the 1975 study were constructed so as to insure comparability with the 1965 study. The focus of the discussion in the 1975 report is on the changes that had taken place during the previous decade. The series of cross-sectional studies conducted in Los Angeles by Fred Massarik in 1951, 1959, and 1968 (and supplemented by the author in 1979) were not primarily intended to be longitudinal. Taken together, however, they dramatically demonstrate the overall growth of Jewish population, the move to the suburbs, increases in divorce and intermarriage, and changes in the structure of the Jewish family. Peter Friedman, who directed the 1981 Chicago study, is using the 1972 Chicago sample of the National Jewish Population Study as baseline data for comparison, taking into account differences in sample and questionnaire design.

One reason for the limited number of longitudinal studies is the cost of repeating a large-scale community survey. An economical alternative to the replication study is a followup study. A followup study may use the respondents from the original sample in a second study or it may use information from the original study to locate new respondents.

Followup studies should not be considered a substitute for serious longitudinal research. Rather, they are a step toward such research. A good followup study can create a greater interest in full replication studies by demonstrating the possibilities for social change research. This paper explores three possible models for followup studies along with examples of planning questions that they can address.

PANEL STUDIES

Respondents in a panel study are interviewed two or more times over a period of time. Using the original sample in a Jewish community survey as a panel has economic as well as scientific advantages. Once the sample has been drawn and the background data collected in the first interview, the followup interview costs only as much as the new data collected. The overhead, so to speak, has been greatly reduced. More important than its relatively lower cost, the panel study can be used to test predictive questions, measure life cycle changes, and to go into greater depth in specific areas. (See Hans Zeisel, Say it with Figures [New York: Harper and Row, 1957], pp. 215-219.)

Testing Predictability

Three examples of predictive questions have already been cited: plans to move, plans to have children, and plans to give children a Jewish education. These questions have potential bias in that respondents might prefer to give what they perceive to be the "socially desirable" answer. For example, parents might tend to answer that they plan to enroll their children in a religious school when, in fact, they do not. Contacting the same respondents two to five years later would evaluate the predictive validity of these questions by finding out how many people who said they would move (or have children or send them to religious school) actually did so, and, conversely, how many who said they would not actually did, despite their announced expectations or intentions. Comparing the intended with the actual behavior could be used to estimate the degree of predictive validity for these and similar questions about future behavior. This refinement would add to the planning utility of these types of questions in future studies. The value of this model for followup studies goes beyond the refinement of predictive questions. Asking people why they did what they did and analyzing differences between true and false predictions helps us understand why some families follow through with their stated intentions while others do not.

Changes in the Life Cycle

Differences among age groups in cross-sectional studies can be attributed either to a maturation process or to different historical contexts of socialization. Age (or life cycle) effects means, for example, that the twenty-five-year-old in the sample who is not now married will probably be married ten years from now, and will probably act and think differently then as a result. The presence of cohort effects, on the other hand, would mean that today's twenty-five-year-old is deeply influenced by when he or she was born and lived, and will not be expected to act or think, ten years from now, like the thirty-five-year-old of today. The ten-year difference in age also includes ten years of potential social change. The only way to disentangle cohort from age effects is to study the cohorts over time. An understanding of cohort effects is the first step to a better anticipation of long-range social change.

A variety of changes are already known to occur throughout the family and life cycles. The following questions might be addressed by a panel study of the original respondents conducted five years later:

1. What proportion of the singles have married or remarried? Have they married Jews or non-Jews?
2. Conversely, what proportion of the current marriages have dissolved?
3. How many women have left or reentered the labor force? At what age? How old were their children (if any) at the time?
4. What sorts of changes in affiliation take place when children are born, and what sorts occur when grown children leave the household?
5. What changes in affiliation and Jewish giving occur as the respondents progress in their careers?
6. What proportion of the elderly are no longer living in the community?

Investigating Specific Issues in Greater Depth

At the conclusion of a study it is not uncommon for researchers to discover that a key question was not included or that some of the findings raise other questions. Similarly, some area has not been explored because of time limitations and cost considerations. These frustrations can be addressed by a panel study because it allows the researcher to ask additional questions of the original respondents. The recently completed Denver study, for example, has raised further questions. As a case in point, Denver has an intermarriage rate higher than any community studied to date. Both parties in an intermarriage were more likely to have been born outside of Denver than the parties in an in-marriage. It appeared that the intermarriages in Denver may have taken place outside of the community, suggesting that intermarrieds were moving to Denver to get away from their home communities. A followup study could include a question on where the couple was married as well as other questions for intermarrieds. The intermarrieds were also found to have lower fertility than in-marrieds of the same age. The opportunity to talk to both sets of respondents again would make it possible to explore some of the reasons why.

Followup studies could be especially valuable to social researchers with a special interest in American Jewry. Since Jewish community surveys are designed as planning tools, more basic research areas such as Jewish identity tend to be neglected. A second study using the original sample could provide scholars with an opportunity to explore the kinds of substantive areas usually excluded from community surveys because sponsors see them as more "basic" than "applied."

AUGMENTED SAMPLES

One sure complication in a panel study are dropouts from the sample. At least some proportion of the households can be expected to have moved by the time the original sample is contacted for a second time. In addition, households that have moved into the community since the study was completed would not have been part of the original sample. While it may be possible to trace dropout households still in the community if they have left a new phone number or if other identifying information such as name and address is available, the followup researcher needs to consider ways to augment the original sample. There are two reasons to augment a sample: to add to or replace dropout cases of special populations, and to find out about changes that have taken place since the original study. In both cases the original sample is augmented by drawing a smaller second sample from the same strata as in the original sample frame. In a list sample the lists are the strata. In a Random Digit Dialing (RDD) screening sample the prefixes are the strata. (The differences between list and screening samples are explained in depth in "Sampling Strategies in Jewish Community Surveys" in this volume.)

How the sample is augmented depends on the purpose of the augmentation. If the intent is to replace dropout cases, or to add to the size of the subsamples (such as intermarrieds, single parents, the elderly, Jews in new areas), then the second sampling should include only those strata from which the dropout respondents originally came. If the purpose is to update the original study by observing changes that have taken place in the community, then a smaller version of the entire original sample should be drawn. To augment a list sample, the original lists should be updated. An RDD screening sample can be augmented simply by drawing a new sample stratified in the same way as the original. A better approach is to use the information gained in the first study to draw a more efficient and therefore less expensive second sample. This can be accomplished by eliminating all prefixes where no Jewish households were located and reducing the size of the sample from those where Jewish households were scarce.

COMBINING STUDIES

As many as fifteen Jewish community surveys will have been conducted by mid-decade. Either of the two techniques above could be used to create a national study out of local ones. A sample of respondents from the studies conducted to date could be interviewed to create a much smaller version of the National Jewish Population Study. While the validity of national projections from such a study would be problematic (because of inadequate geographic coverage), it would be particularly valuable for collecting a national sample of special populations (such as intermarrieds).

A national sample made up of cases from local studies would add a new dimension to the comparative analysis of Jewish community surveys. Various sociologists have incorporated comparisons of the findings of local surveys as part of a larger analysis. Marshall Sklare, in America's Jews (1971) and in his article "Intermarriage and the Jewish Future" (Commentary, April 1964), Sidney Goldstein, in his American Jewish Year Book articles, and most recently, Gary A. Tobin and Julie A. Lipsman in this volume (see next article) have done extensive comparisons of Jewish community surveys. They were, however, limited by the published tables. Even if they had access to all the data of all the studies they would still have been limited to the questions included in the studies. Then too, the differences in the formulations of the various surveys introduce a further variable. A national survey using comparably worded questions would greatly increase the reliability of the analysis. It would also add new dimensions to the kind of analysis that could be done. For example, there is a commonly held assumption that Jews with weaker Jewish and family roots are more likely to migrate to the west than those with stronger roots. A national sample made up of local respondents would make possible comparisons between Chicago, New York, St. Louis, Philadelphia, Boston, Milwaukee, and Cleveland Jews who have remained in their home communities with their counterparts who have migrated to Denver, Las Vegas, Phoenix, Los Angeles, Miami, and Washington, D.C.

In sum, we have little experience as of yet in the conduct of followup, trend, or longitudinal studies, critical as such efforts might be. Such experience will undoubtedly permit us to assess the value of alternative techniques in the future. In this paper we have tried to outline some of the most promising possibilities for followup studies, fully cognizant of the very limited undertakings in this area of Jewish population studies thus far.

PART THREE

Resources for Questionnaire Design and Interpretation of Findings

The two articles in this section should be extremely useful to both planners and researchers in the design of a survey instrument and in the ultimate interpretation of the results.

Both papers--the overview of research findings and the "Annotated Inventory of Questions"--are the product of careful review of several recent Jewish community studies. Gary A. Tobin and Julie A. Lipsman read through and organized several dozen recent studies. From these they selected a representative sample of studies the results of which illustrate the intercommunal diversity in research findings. They have arranged the findings by variable or subject and presented the results from several studies side by side (or, more accurately, in vertical columns) so that the reader may immediately discern both the range of results as well as their patterns. Tobin and Lipsman go well beyond a simple presentation of results to offer some helpful comments on question wording as well as some useful interpretation of differences in communities by size and region. Their observations alert questionnaire designers to nuances in wording and also help designers situate their findings in a context that will make them more plausible and understandable.

Steven M. Cohen's "Annotated Inventory of Questions" offers a complete illustration of a comprehensive survey instrument. Drawing upon questionnaires from several recent Jewish population studies, Cohen not only provides the questions (worded for administration by telephone), but also suggests a priority ranking for each question. The annotation section provides a rationale for each question or set of items. While in no way meant to be definitive or conclusive, the inventory does aspire to provide researchers and planners with a useful jumping-off point in designing questionnaires tailored to their local needs and resources.

13 A Compendium of Jewish Demographic Studies

Gary A. Tobin and Julie A. Lipsman

The National Jewish Population Study, completed over a decade ago, provides baseline data from which to compare current population trends and characteristics. It is unlikely that another such national survey will be undertaken again in the near future. In the absence of a national study, any profile of the Jewish community in 1983 must come from comparing data obtained in the individual community studies. This compendium represents the first attempt to juxtapose the findings of a variety of local studies and to compare different cities with the national data collected in 1971. Because of the limitations of time and space, it does not provide detailed analysis of the data. We hope this work will be continued and more sophisticated analysis will be done. The purpose of this report is primarily to present the data to the reader.

The task has not been simple. Communities use different sampling techniques and interviewing methods; they ask different questions in varied forms and report the findings in different formats (or not at all). Comparability is difficult to achieve, and the tables that are presented in the compendium are a distillation and reconstruction of very different originals. In some cases the differences were so great as to be irreconcilable. For example, no meaningful table could be distilled from the data on attitude toward intermarriage. The questions were asked in various ways in several studies and results were aggregated and presented differently. Comparability in this area simply could not be achieved, and this was the case with some other variables as well. The best we could do in such situations was to discuss and summarize the communities' findings; the unruly data could not be reduced to a table.

In all, we surveyed and analyzed thirty-seven Jewish demographic studies conducted between 1967 and 1982, including studies from twenty-three different states and one community in Canada, as shown in Table 13.1. Table 13.2 shows the issues that are included in these studies. Not all of them, however, could be summarized in this compendium.

Of the thirty-seven surveys examined, only the thirteen listed in Table 13.3 are presented here. The remainder were excluded for a variety of reasons, as mentioned above. The tables in this report represent the best possible compromise between comprehensiveness and accuracy. All studies chosen were completed between 1979 and 1982. This will allow for maximum comparability between the studies, since all were completed within a relatively short period of time.

TABLE 13.1
Jewish Community Surveys

California	
Los Angeles	1979
Oakland	1970
San Diego	1979
San Francisco	1979
Colorado	
Denver	1981
Florida	
Miami	1982
Sarasota	1982
Illinois	
Chicago	1982
Indiana	
Fort Wayne	1982
Louisiana	
New Orleans	1973
Shreveport	1978
Maryland	
Baltimore	1975
Massachusetts	
Boston	1975
Michigan	
Flint	1967
Minnesota	
Minneapolis	1981
St. Paul	1981
Missouri/Kansas	
Kansas City	1977
St. Louis	1982
Nebraska	
Omaha	1976
New Jersey	
North Jersey	1981
Raritan Valley	1980
Vineland	1976
New York	
New York	1981
Rochester	1980
Ohio	
Akron	1975
Cincinnati	1980
Cleveland	1981
Columbus	1969
Oklahoma	
Oklahoma City	1982
Oregon	
Portland	1978-1982
Pennsylvania	
Pittsburgh	1975-1977
Tennessee	
Nashville	1982
Texas	
Dallas	1974
Houston	1976
Utah	
Salt Lake City	1976-1977
Washington	
Seattle	1979
Canada	
Hamilton, Ontario	1978

Enough variables were compiled, however, to make the compendium a useful reference tool for all Jewish communities. Tables were reconstructed wherever possible. Data were recomputed, categories redefined, and the data presented in tables that summarize the results. The tables form the heart of this report. For the first time in over a decade, we have some benchmarks from which to compare population components. This summary can serve to identify trends, regional differences, and potential areas of further inquiry. It should be noted that data are scarce for small cities and cities in the South and Southwest. Wherever new computations were necessary we have noted it. In some cases complete comparability was not possible, so wider categories are shown next to the general delineations. In some cases cities were left out of a table because comparability simply was not possible. Therefore, some tables may compare five cities, while others may compare ten or more cities.

In order to insure maximum accuracy, each of the tables we prepared was sent to the appropriate Jewish federation for review and approval. Each federation was asked to supply, when possible, any additional data that were not provided in the published demographic study, and to correct any errors. San Diego expressed doubts about the accuracy of some of the data in its study, and this concern is noted here. All other studies were reviewed and corrections made by the federations of Chicago, Cleveland, Los Angeles, and New York.

The diversity of the studies, and the resultant difficulties in comparing them, underscore the need for standardized questions and formats of presentation. (See, for example, the "Annotated Inventory of Questions" by Steven M. Cohen elsewhere in this volume.) Any community contemplating a study should carefully consider participating in existing networks of planners and scholars who are involved in Jewish demographic research. Standardization can be furthered by a number of processes. Wherever possible, questions should be comparable to the U.S. Census and to other Jewish population studies. This will allow for comparison with the general population and, ultimately, between Jewish communities.

The compendium is designed so that it can be updated in the future. Demographic surveys have just recently been completed or are under way in Kansas City, Milwaukee, central New Jersey, New Orleans, Philadelphia, Phoenix, and Washington. These are major centers of Jewish population and will be important additions to the compendium.

The idea of this compendium originated at the Workshop in Jewish Population Studies sponsored by the Center for Modern Jewish Studies at Brandeis University. Funds for research assistance were provided by the Center for Modern Jewish Studies at Brandeis University. The authors gratefully acknowledge the support of the Center, and particularly of Professor Steven M. Cohen and Professor Marshall Sklare. We would also like to thank Vicki Ibera, who typed the manuscript a number times.

TABLE 13.2
Variable Data

	Jewish Population	Household Size	Age	Sex	Marital status	Childern	Place of birth
Akron 1975	x	x	x	x	x	x	x
Baltimore 1975	x	x	x	x	x		
Boston 1975	x	x	x	x	x	x	x
Chicago 1982	x	x	x	x	x	x	x
Cincinnati 1980	x	x	x		x	x	
Cleveland 1981	x	x	x	x	x	x	x
Columbus 1969	x	x	x	x	x	x	x
Dallas 1974	x	x	x	x	x	x	x
Denver 1981	x	x	x	x	x	x	x
Flint 1967	x	x	x	x	x	x	x
Fort Wayne 1982			x	x	x		x
Hamilton, Ontario 1978	x	x	x			x	
Houston 1976	x	x	x	x	x	x	x
Kansas City 1977	x	x	x	x	x	x	x
Los Angeles 1979	x	x	x		x	x	
Miami 1982	x	x		x	x	x	x
Minneapolis 1981	x	x	x	x	x	x	x
Nashville 1982	x	x	x	x	x	x	x
New Orleans 1973	x	x	x	x	x		
New York 1981		x	x	x	x	x	x
North Jersey 1981	x	x	x	x	x	x	x
Oakland 1970	x	x	x	x	x	x	x
Oklahoma City 1982	x	x	x	x	x	x	x
Omaha 1976	x	x	x	x	x	x	x
Pittsburgh 1975-1977	x	x	x	x	x	x	
Portland 1978-1982	x	x	x	x	x	x	
Raritan Valley 1980			x		x		
Rochester 1980	x	x	x	x	x	x	x
Salt Lake City 1976-1977	x		x	x	x	x	x
San Diego 1979	x	x	x	x	x	x	
San Francisco 1979	x	x	x		x	x	
Sarasota 1982	x		x	x	x		
Seattle 1979	x		x	x	x	x	x
Shreveport 1978	x	x	x	x	x		
St. Louis 1982	x	x	x	x	x	x	x
St. Paul 1981	x	x	x	x	x		x
Vineland 1976	x	x	x	x	x	x	x

TABLE 13.2 (continued)
Variable Data

	Education	Ocupation	Income	Home ownership	Years in home/area	Moving plans
Akron 1975	x	x	x	x	x	x
Baltimore 1975	x					
Boston 1975	x	x	x	x	x	x
Chicago 1982	x	x	x	x	x	x
Cincinnati 1980	x	x	x			
Cleveland 1981		x			x	x
Columbus 1969	x	x	x	x	x	x
Dallas 1974	x	x	x	x	x	x
Denver 1981	x	x			x	x
Flint 1967	x	x	x			
Fort Wayne 1982	x					x
Hamilton, Ontario 1978		x			x	x
Houston 1976	x	x	x	x	x	x
Kansas City 1977	x	x	x		x	
Los Angeles 1979						x
Miami 1982	x	x	x	x	x	x
Minneapolis 1981	x	x	x	x	x	x
Nashville 1982	x	x	x		x	
New Orleans 1973	x	x	x		x	x
New York 1981	x	x	x	x	x	x
North Jersey 1981	x	x		x		x
Oakland 1970	x	x	x	x	x	x
Oklahoma City 1982	x	x	x		x	x
Omaha 1976	x	x	x	x	x	x
Pittsburgh 1975-1977	x	x			x	x
Portland 1978-1982	x	x	x		x	x
Raritan Valley 1980				x	x	
Rochester 1980	x	x	x	x	x	x
Salt Lake City 1976-1977	x	x			x	x
San Diego 1979		x			x	
San Francisco 1979		x	x		x	x
Sarasota 1982		x	x	x	x	
Seattle 1979	x	x	x		x	
Shreveport 1978	x	x			x	
St. Louis 1982	x	x	x	x	x	x
St. Paul 1981	x	x	x	x	x	x
Vineland 1976	x	x				

TABLE 13.2 (continued)
Variable Data

	Preference for Jewish neighborhood	Jewish federation/ council: Attitudes	Jewish Community Center	Jewish agencies: attitudes/usage	Aged housing
Akron 1975			x	x	x
Baltimore 1975					
Boston 1975	x	x	x	x	
Chicago 1982		x	x	x	x
Cincinnati 1980					
Cleveland 1981					
Columbus 1969	x	x	x	x	x
Dallas 1974		x	x	x	x
Denver 1981					
Flint 1967			x	x	
Fort Wayne 1982		x		x	
Hamilton, Ontario 1978			x	x	
Houston 1976			x	x	x
Kansas City 1977					
Los Angeles 1979					x
Miami 1982	x	x	x	x	x
Minneapolis 1981			x	x	x
Nashville 1982					
New Orleans 1973	x		x	x	x
New York 1981	x		x	x	
North Jersey 1981	x	x		x	
Oakland 1970		x	x	x	x
Oklahoma City 1982			x	x	x
Omaha 1976			x	x	x
Pittsburgh 1975-1977				x	x
Portland 1978-1982		x	x	x	x
Raritan Valley 1980			x	x	
Rochester 1980	x	x	x	x	x
Salt Lake City 1976-1977		x	x	x	x
San Diego 1979		x	x	x	
San Francisco 1979	x		x	x	
Sarasota 1982			x	x	x
Seattle 1979		x	x	x	x
Shreveport 1978					
St. Louis 1982	x	x	x	x	x
St. Paul 1981			x	x	x
Vineland 1976			x	x	x

TABLE 13.2 (continued)
Variable Data

	Jewish publications	Jewish federation contributions	Preference for usage of federation funds	General organizational membership	Jewish organizational membership
Akron 1975				x	x
Baltimore 1975					
Boston 1975	x	x	x	x	x
Chicago 1982	x	x		x	
Cincinnati 1980					
Cleveland 1981					x
Columbus 1969		x	x	x	x
Dallas 1974	x	x	x	x	x
Denver 1981					
Flint 1967				x	x
Fort Wayne 1982			x		
Hamilton, Ontario 1978				x	x
Houston 1976	x			x	x
Kansas City 1977					
Los Angeles 1979					
Miami 1982		x	x	x	x
Minneapolis 1981	x	x	x		
Nashville 1982					
New Orleans 1973	x		x		x
New York 1981	x	x	x		x
North Jersey 1981	x	x	x	x	x
Oakland 1970	x	x	x	x	x
Oklahoma City 1982				x	x
Omaha 1976	x				x
Pittsburgh 1975-1977					
Portland 1978-1982	x	x	x		
Raritan Valley 1980	x	x	x	x	x
Rochester 1980		x		x	x
Salt Lake City 1976-1977		x	x	x	x
San Diego 1979	x		x		
San Francisco 1979		x			x
Sarasota 1982		x		x	x
Seattle 1979		x	x	x	x
Shreveport 1978					
St. Louis 1982	x	x	x	x	x
St. Paul 1981		x	x		x
Vineland 1976	x	x	x	x	x

TABLE 13.2 (continued)
Variable Data

	Religion at birth	Current religious identification	Synagogue/temple membership	Religious service attendance	Jewish ritual observances
Akron 1975	x	x	x	x	x
Baltimore 1975	x				
Boston 1975	x	x	x	x	x
Chicago 1982	x	x	x	x	x
Cincinnati 1980	x	x			
Cleveland 1981		x	x		
Columbus 1969		x	x	x	x
Dallas 1974	x	x	x	x	x
Denver 1981	x	x			
Flint 1967		x	x	x	x
Fort Wayne 1982	x		x		
Hamilton, Ontario 1978			x		
Houston 1976	x	x	x	x	x
Kansas City 1977		x	x	x	x
Los Angeles 1979					
Miami 1982	x	x	x	x	x
Minneapolis 1981		x	x		
Nashville 1982		x	x		
New Orleans 1973		x			x
New York 1981	x	x	x	x	x
North Jersey 1981			x	x	x
Oakland 1970	x	x	x	x	x
Oklahoma City 1982	x	x	x		x
Omaha 1976	x	x	x		
Pittsburgh 1975-1977		x	x	x	x
Portland 1978-1982		x	x		
Raritan Valley 1980		x	x		
Rochester 1980		x	x	x	x
Salt Lake City 1976-1977					x
San Diego 1979			x		
San Francisco 1979			x		
Sarasota 1982		x	x		
Seattle 1979	x	x	x	x	x
Shreveport 1978		x	x		
St. Louis 1982	x	x	x	x	x
St. Paul 1981		x	x		
Vineland 1976		x	x	x	x

TABLE 13.2 (continued)
Variable Data

	Respondent Jewish education	Children's Jewish education	Adult Jewish Education	Intermarriage	Anti-Semitism	Israel Attitudes
Akron 1975	x	x		x		
Baltimore 1975				x		
Boston 1975	x	x	x	x	x	x
Chicago 1982	x	x	x	x		
Cincinnati 1980						
Cleveland 1981		x		x		
Columbus 1969	x	x		x	x	
Dallas 1974	x	x			x	
Denver 1981				x		
Flint 1967	x	x				
Fort Wayne 1982	x			x		x
Hamilton, Ontario 1978		x				
Houston 1976	x	x	x	x	x	x
Kansas City 1977	x	x		x		
Los Angeles 1979		x				
Miami 1982	x	x	x	x	x	x
Minneapolis 1981	x	x	x	x	x	x
Nashville 1982					x	x
New Orleans 1973	x	x		x		
New York 1981	x	x	x	x		x
North Jersey 1981	x	x	x	x	x	x
Oakland 1970	x	x	x		x	
Oklahoma City 1982	x	x	x		x	x
Omaha 1976	x	x	x	x		
Pittsburgh 1975-1977		x				x
Portland 1978-1982	x	x	x	x		x
Raritan Valley 1980		x				x
Rochester 1980	x	x			x	x
Salt Lake City 1976-1977		x		x	x	x
San Diego 1979		x				
San Francisco 1979		x	x			
Sarasota 1982						
Seattle 1979		x				
Shreveport 1978						
St. Louis 1982	x	x	x	x	x	x
St. Paul 1981	x	x	x	x		
Vineland 1976	x	x	x			x

TABLE 13.3
Cities Included in Compendium

Chicago	1982
Cleveland	1981
Denver	1981
Los Angeles	1979
Miami	1982
Minneapolis	1981
Nashville	1982
New York	1981
Rochester	1980
St. Louis	1982
St. Paul	1981
San Diego	1979
Seattle	1979

VARIABLES INCLUDED IN COMPENDIUM

Social and Demographic Characteristics

13.4 Mean household size*
13.5 Household size*
13.6 Age*
13.7 Sex*
13.8 Current marital status*
13.9 Secular education*
13.10 Occupation*
13.11 Annual household income*
13.12 Nativity*
13.13 Moving plans*

Religion

13.14 Denominational identification*
13.15 Synagogue/temple membership*
13.16 Religious service attendance
13.17 Ritual observances*

Community Involvement

13.18 Membership in JCC
13.19 Membership in Jewish organizations
13.20 Jewish newspapers
13.21 Jewish charitable contributions
13.22 Visited Israel*

Special Issues

Anti-Semitism (no table)
Intermarriage* (no table)

*Includes comparison with data from 1971 NJPS.

DATA HIGHLIGHTS

Methodology

1. A great need exists for some measure of standardization of surveys, in terms of format and reporting. Wherever possible, comparability to the U.S. Census and to other Jewish population studies should be sought.
2. Data are scarce for small cities as well as southwestern and southern cities. It is difficult to assess the comparability of the data in this compendium to cities of smaller size.
3. Data on certain topics are not available in sufficient detail for many studies. These topics include unemployment and service usage.

Findings

1. Average household size has decreased substantially since 1971, with most cities reporting average Jewish household size between 2.2 and 2.6 persons per household as compared to about 2.8 in the 1971 National Jewish Population Study (NJPS).
2. There has been a sharp increase in single-person households since 1971, and also of 2-person households. Households with 4 or 5 persons have decreased sharply.
3. The population is an aging one, with higher proportions of the population in the 70+ category in every city than was found nationally in the NJPS, with the exception of Denver and Los Angeles.
4. Each city has a significantly higher proportion of women than men, particularly in Sunbelt cities, such as Miami and San Diego.
5. The proportion of currently divorced/separated households has not increased dramatically from the 1971 national figure, except for Denver, New York, and Los Angeles. Thus, if the divorce rates are rising, so are remarriage rates. The proportion of single and widowed households has increased dramatically, signifying the growing propensity of single Jews to marry later or not at all, and of all Jews to live longer.
6. Most cities show higher education levels than in 1971. However, cities with large elderly populations, such as Miami, still show high proportions of the population with a high school diploma or less.
7. Mobility and nativity data reveal the movement of Jews to cities such as Denver, Los Angeles, and Miami, and the general decrease in the proportion of foreign-born, except in those cities with older populations.
8. About 25 percent of the households, except in New York, belong to a Jewish Community Center. A greater proportion, of course, may belong to a JCC at different times throughout their lives.
9. Larger cities tend to have smaller proportions of their populations belonging to Jewish organizations.
10. A significant proportion of the households--22 to 38 percent--make no contributions to any Jewish organization. In larger cities, more households make no contributions.

11. The biggest shift in religious identification since 1971 has been to the "no preference/other" category, with most communities having a larger proportion of Jews identifying themselves as "no preference" than identifying themselves as Orthodox.
12. Synagogue membership seems to be substantially higher than in 1971. Large cities and cities with older populations tend to have lower synagogue affiliation rates.
13. A significant proportion of households--18 to 30 percent--never attend religious services at all.
14. The lighting of Chanukah candles and a Passover Seder are the two most observed rituals in all cities. Kashrut is most heavily observed in Miami and New York.
15. The number of people who have visited Israel has increased significantly since 1971 in all cities in the United States, up from 16 percent nationally to roughly the high 30s in most cities, ranging from 27 percent (in St. Louis) to 45 percent (in Miami).
16. Rates of intermarriage are significantly higher than in 1971, from a low of 8 percent in Miami to a high of 37 percent in Denver.
17. Depending on the city, between 13 and 25 percent of respondents said that they had had experience with anti-Semitism in a twelve-month period.

SOCIAL AND DEMOGRAPHIC CHARACTERISTICS

Mean Household Size

Mean household sizes vary from a low of 2.2 persons per household in Los Angeles to a high of 2.8 in Cleveland. There is a clear tendency for lower household size in large cities such as Los Angeles, retirement cities such as Miami, and growing cities such as Denver. Further, while the mean reported here for the New York metropolitan area is 2.4, the mean for New York City is 2.2. Conversely, medium-sized midwestern cities have a larger mean household size, with Cleveland the highest at 2.8, followed by 2.6 in St. Louis, Minneapolis, and Chicago.

There is a clear decline in household size over the past decade, evidenced by the 1971 National Jewish Population Survey (NJPS) mean of 2.8, indicating the general drift toward smaller families, higher proportions of singles, and so on.

Household Size

In every city, the largest portion of the population resides in two-person households, ranging from 34 percent in Cleveland and Nashville to 39 percent in St. Paul. Two-person households were only 31 percent in the 1971 NJPS study. One-person households are the second most common, with a low of 19 percent residing alone in Cleveland and a high of 33 percent in Los Angeles; this follows the same pattern of lower household sizes in major metropolises such as Los Angeles, and larger households in communities the size and location of Cleveland. Only 18 percent lived alone in 1971.

TABLE 13.4
Mean Household Size*

	Members of Jewish households
Chicago 1982	2.6
Cleveland 1981	2.8
Denver 1981	2.2
Los Angeles 1979	2.2
Miami 1982	2.2
Minneapolis 1981	2.6
Nashville 1982	2.6
New York 1981	2.4
Rochester 1980	2.5
St. Louis 1982	2.6
St. Paul 1981	2.3
San Diego 1979	2.3
NJPS 1971	2.8

* Household size will vary depending on whether or not children of college age who attend school out of town are used to compute the figure, as they were in Cleveland.

TABLE 13.5
Household Size

	% 1 person	% 2 persons	% 3 persons	% 4 persons	% 5 persons	% 6+ persons
Chicago 1982	21	36	21	12	8	2
Cleveland 1981	19	34	16	17	9	5
Denver 1981	30	37	16	13	3	1
Los Angeles 1979	33	36	12	13	5	1
Minneapolis 1981	22	37	16	15	8	2
Nashville 1982	24	34	16	16	8	2
New York 1981	30	35	16	13	5	1
Rochester 1980	24	37	15	16	7	1
St. Louis 1982	22	37	17	15	7	2
St. Paul 1981	27	39	15	12	5	2
NJPS 1971	18	31	14	21	10	4

Large households are the least common, no city having more than 5 percent of its households with six or more members, and no city having more than 10 percent of its households reporting five members. Cleveland reports the highest in each of these categories with 5 percent of its households having six or more members and 9 percent having five members. Other cities with a notable proportion of large households include Minneapolis, Nashville, and Chicago (8 percent having five persons) and Rochester and St. Louis (7 percent having five persons). The 1971 NJPS was somewhat higher than most of the recent studies, with 10 percent having five members and 4 percent having six or more.

Percentages for medium-sized families (three or four persons) range between 12 percent and 21 percent in all cities, while the NJPS figures were 14 percent (three-person) and 21 percent (four-person).

Age

One of the most definitive trends shown in this study is that the American Jewish population is aging. Designated age ranges varied too much from community to community to allow for exact comparisons, but it is possible to identify trends among the youth, middleaged, and elderly populations. Specific comparisons are made using only those communities which fit into designated categories.

Compared to the National Jewish Population Study, which measured 32 percent of the population as being between 0 and 19 years old in 1971, recent surveys report fewer youngsters, ranging from 20 percent (Miami) to 30 percent (San Diego), with most communities much closer to the low end of the range.

Percentages for the twenties age group went as low as 8 percent in Miami and as high as 22 percent in Denver, while for the thirties the range is from 11 percent (Miami) to 21 percent (Denver). These figures, to some degree, reflect differences of various geographical locations: Miami is a retirement community and Denver is a growing employment center. This compares to 1971 NJPS figures of 14 percent 20- to 29-year-olds and 11 percent 30- to 39-year-olds, illustrating a growing proportion in these age groups.

Percentages in the forties age range are comparable to the NJPS figure of 13 percent, ranging from a high of 12 percent in several communities to a low of 7 percent, again in Miami.

A very clear trend toward an aging population is seen in the 50 to 70 age brackets. While the NJPS reported 22 percent in this age range, recent surveys report between 18 percent (Denver) and 32 percent (St. Paul). This is further substantiated by the "over seventies" where an NJPS proportion of 7 percent is updated by a preponderance of communities with more than 10 percent in this bracket, going as high as 26 percent in Miami.

Sex

Invariably, females outnumber males in Jewish communities, as in the American population as a whole. The ratios are closest to equal in Minneapolis, Nashville, and Rochester, which all have 51:49 ratios. San Diego and Miami both show a considerable imbalance, with 56 percent females and 44 percent males. These figures compare to a 1971 NJPS report of 51 percent females and 48 percent males nationwide (1 percent lacking due to inclusion of "no response" category).

TABLE 13.6
Age

	% 0-9	% 10-19	% 20-29	% 30-39	% 40-49	% 50-59	% 60-69	% 70+
Chicago 1982	21			35		30		14
Cleveland 1981	22		11	33			20	14
Denver* 1981	12	9	22	21	11	10	8	7
Los Angeles 1979	16	13	19	13	14	13	8	4
Miami 1982	9	11	8	11	7	10	18	26
Minneapolis 1981	12	15	12	15	12	12	11	10
Nashville 1982	21	7	11		41			20
New York 1981	9	12	16	13	12	14	13	10
Rochester 1980	12	8	14	17		29		20
St. Louis* 1982	11	14	14	14	12	13	11	11
St. Paul 1981	10	12	11	13	8	16	16	14
San Diego 1979	14	16	9	21		24		16
Seattle 1979	20		12	23	10	22		13
NJPS 1971	12	20	14	11	13	13	9	7

* One or more age categories will vary 1-2 years from the designated range.
For Denver, the categories are 0-9; 10-17; 18-29; 30-39; 40-49; 50-59; 60-69. 70-94.
For St. Louis, the categories are 0-10; 11-20; 21-30; 31-40; 41-50; 61-70; 71+.

TABLE 13.7
Sex

	% Male	% Female
Cleveland 1981	47	53
Los Angeles 1979	48	52
Miami 1982	44	56
Minneapolis 1981	49	51
Nashville 1982	49	51
Rochester 1980	49	51
St. Louis 1982	47	53
St. Paul 1981	47	53
San Diego[a] 1979	44	56
NJPS[b] 1971	48	51

[a] Represents the sum of two tables (sex of all adults, sex of all children), using sample sizes.

[b] Figures have been rounded.

Current Marital Status

Most households consist of married partners, although the proportions vary widely from survey to survey. Los Angeles reports the lowest proportion of married respondents, with 57 percent, and Rochester the highest, with 71 percent. That almost all communities fall below the 1971 figure illustrates the point that Jewish families reflect trends common all across America: later marriages, more broken families, and more single elderly individuals, especially women.

The second largest category in most communities was "single" (never married), ranging from 7 percent in Miami to 23 percent in Chicago and Denver. Part of the disparity in this category can be explained by definitions of the samples; in Chicago, for example, the marital status table included everyone in the population over eighteen years old.

The number of respondents who are widowed reflects proportions of elderly. They ranged from a low of 4 percent in Denver to highs of 17 percent in St. Louis and 23 percent in Miami. Finally, the rate of divorced/separated is significantly higher in Los Angeles (14 percent) than in all other communities, followed by 9 percent in New York and Denver and 8 percent in Miami. All other communities reported between 3 and 6 percent of the population currently divorced or separated, which corresponds to the earlier NJPS figure (5 percent).

Secular Education

In examining the secular education received by respondents, it is important to note that most of those within the category "high school or

TABLE 13.8
Current Marital Status

	% Married	% Single	% Widowed	% Divorced/ separated
Chicago[a] 1982	65	23	6	6
Cleveland 1981	69	11	13	8
Denver[b] 1981	64	23	4	9
Los Angeles[b] 1979	57	17	12	14
Miami 1982	61	7	23	8
Minneapolis 1981	66	22	7	5
Nashville 1982	70	17	8	5
New York 1981	65	15	11	9
Rochester 1980	71	18	8	3
St. Louis 1982	68	9	17	6
St. Paul 1981	66	20	11	3
San Diego 1979	77	9	← 14 →	
NJPS 1971	78	6	10	5

[a] Chicago data for marital status of adults, 18 and over.

[b] Tables reconstituted. Figures are approximate.
For two of the cities, the statistics on marital status were given only as a cross-tabulation with age groups. For Los Angeles, the figures shown were calculated using a weighted average from the sample sizes in each age group. For Denver, the same process was used, but sample sizes were unavailable so percentages were used.

less" in fact had a high school diploma. Because the specific level was not isolated in many of the surveys, they have been grouped with those who had less than a high school diploma.

The Jewish population is more educated than it was ten years ago. While the NJPS reported 46 percent with a high school diploma in 1971, more recent studies place this figure between 22 percent (Chicago) and 43 percent (St. Paul), with most communities toward the lower end. This means that a greater proportion have had at least some college education.

While only 15 percent reported college degrees in 1971, almost all recent studies report at least 24 percent with college degrees, ranging as high as 28 percent in Minneapolis and Nashville and 31 percent in New York. There is also an increase in advanced degrees, although not quite as marked. Compared to an NJPS total of 19 percent with advanced degrees, recent reports range from 12 percent in Miami and 15 percent in St. Paul to 26 percent in Chicago and 27 percent in Seattle.

TABLE 13.9
Secular Education

	% High school or less	% Some college	% College degree[a]	% Advanced degree
Chicago[b] 1982	22	27	25	26
Los Angeles 1979	32	25	26	18
Miami 1982	41	23	24	12
Minneapolis 1981	25	29	28	19
Nashville 1982	← 52 →		28	22
New York 1981	31	18	31	20
Rochester 1980	36	15	24	25
St. Louis[c] 1982	33	22	27	18
St. Paul 1981	43	23	20	15
Seattle 1979	29	18	26	27
NJPS 1971	46	20	15	19

[a] "College degree" includes completed bachelor's degrees and incomplete advanced degrees.
[b] Respondent and spouse.
[c] "Other education" excluded and percentages recomputed.

TABLE 13.10
Occupation[a]

	% Professional	% Managers/ proprietors	% Sales	% Clerical	% Blue collar
Chicago[b] 1982	33	21	21	15	10
Cleveland 1981	39	22	17	12	10
Los Angeles 1979	34	16	20	19	11
Miami 1982	31	27	17	17	9
Minneapolis 1981	23	42	← 25 →		10
Nashville 1982	43	34	9	10	4
Rochester 1980	45	19	← 26 →		10
St. Louis 1982	29	20	33	12	6
St. Paul 1981	27	38	← 26 →		9
Seattle 1979	40	29	20	← 11 →	
NJPS 1971	28	34	12	16	10

[a] Housewives, students, retired, unemployed, and unknown excluded from figures; percentages recomputed to include only those employed for wages.

[b] Respondent and spouse.

Occupation

Occupational types indicate varied patterns, with the only marked trend being a very small percentage of blue collar workers in all communities. About half of the communities still report 10 percent in this category, as the NJPS did in 1971, with the remaining reporting less; the lowest proportion (4 percent) is reported in Nashville.

Conversely, professional workers represent a significant proportion of the population in all communities. Percentages here range widely from a high of 45 percent in Rochester to a low of 23 percent in Minneapolis. Most cities are higher than the 1971 NJPS proportion of 28 percent and this identifies a significant trend in the American Jewish community toward the professions.

Managers and proprietors are also common occupations, ranging from a low of 16 percent in Los Angeles to a high of 42 percent in Minneapolis. This is a very wide range, but most communities fall between 20 and 38 percent, a somewhat smaller range, which also includes the 1971 figure of 34 percent. Finally, sales workers and clerical workers represent a more uniform ratio, ranging between 25 and 36 percent, except for Nashville's low (19 percent) and St. Louis's high (45 percent).

Annual Household Income

Annual household incomes are relatively uniform among Jewish communities, allowing for variations due to geographical location and slight time differences of the surveys (all completed within the three-year period 1980-1982).

All communities report no more than one-fifth of their households in the lowest income bracket, 0-$9,999, with Nashville (10 percent) having the lowest proportion in this range and Los Angeles (21 percent) and St. Paul (20 percent) having the highest. The NJPS measured 33 percent in this range about ten years earlier, when the Consumer Price Index was about half of what it would be in the early 1980s.

A somewhat larger proportion of households are found in the next two brackets; combining these two proportions gives all communities between 36 and 48 percent in the $10,000-$29,999 range. Nashville again has the lowest proportion followed Denver and New York, each with 37 percent. Rochester represents the high end of the scale, followed by Chicago (44 percent). This compares to the NJPS figure of 35 percent for only one-half of this range, $10,000-$19,999. Between 12 percent (Los Angeles) and 19 percent (Denver) report incomes between $30,000-$39,999.

Finally, in the range for highest earners, St. Louis reports the highest percentage (43 percent) while Rochester and St. Paul are lowest (each 25 percent). Other communities are between 27 percent and 33 percent in this bracket. This cannot even be compared to the NJPS because at that time the maximum range was $20,000+ (32 percent), a telling indicator of how inflationary the past decade has been.

Nativity

The vast majority of American Jews today were born in America, with numbers of foreign-born ranging from a low of 11 percent in Denver to highs

TABLE 13.11
Annual Household Income*

	0-$9,999	$10,000- $19,999	$20,000- $29,999	$30,000- $39,999	$40,000+
Chicago 1982	13	19	25	14	29
Denver 1981	16	21	16	19	28
Los Angeles 1979	21	21	20	12	27
Miami 1982	← 36	→ ← 19 →	← 15 →	← 31	→
Minneapolis 1981	13	20	23	13	31
Nashville 1982	10	16	20	← 54	→
New York 1981	12	16	21	18	33
Rochester 1980	14	26	22	13	25
St. Louis 1982	13	16	13	15	43
St. Paul 1981	20	18	23	14	25
NJPS 1971	33	35	←	32	→

* Refusals excluded from figures.

* Data are not truly comparable, because of changes in cost of living over four-year period and because of variance in cost of living between metropolitan areas.

TABLE 13.12
Nativity

	% Locally born	% U.S.-born[a]	% Foreign-born
Chicago[b] 1982	66	22	12
Cleveland 1981	58	27[c]	15
Denver 1981	22	67	11
Los Angeles 1979	16	60	24
Miami 1982	4	69	27
Minneapolis 1981	47	40	13
New York 1981	← 83	→	17
Rochester 1980	← 85	→	15
St. Louis 1982	50	34	16
St. Paul 1981	46	36	18
Seattle 1979	← 77	→	23
NJPS 1971	← 77	→	23

[a] Other than locally born.

[b] Respondent and spouse.

[c] Includes Canada.

TABLE 13.13
Moving Plans

	% Moving within metro area	% Moving out of metro area	% Don't know	% No plans to move
Chicago[a] 1982	16	8	16	60
Cleveland 1981	9	7	0	84
Los Angeles 1979	26	12	5	56
Miami 1982	7	5	18	70
Minneapolis 1981	11	5	0	84
Rochester 1980	10	5	15	70
St. Louis 1982	11	5	5	80
St. Paul 1981	7	7	0	86
San Diego 1979	--[b]	4	4	92
NJPS 1971	5[c]	10	2	83

[a] Moving within next 3 years.

[b] Not asked.

[c] Moving within same city.

of 23 percent in Seattle (where a special effort was made to include immigrants in the sample base) and 27 percent in Miami (where a large percentage of the population is elderly). In 1971, 23 percent of all American Jews were foreign-born; this rate has been steadily declining.

Of those born in America, a large percentage were also born in the community where they now reside. Excluding the communities which did not separate locally born and U.S.-born, the community with the greatest proportion of Jews locally born is Chicago with 66 percent in this category. The low in this category drops to 4 percent in Miami, a popular destination for movers.

Moving Plans

In all cases, the majority of households have no intentions of moving, ranging from a low of 56 percent in Los Angeles to a high of 86 percent in St. Paul (San Diego excluded those planning intracity moves, resulting in its high rate of 92 percent non-movers). In addition, there are potential movers in the "don't know" designation. These proportions are fairly uniform with NJPS proportions of 83 percent with no plans to move and 2 percent who did not know (in 1971).

Of those who are moving, almost all communities report a greater percentage of local moves than moves out of the metropolitan area. Los Angeles reports the greatest amount of local moves (26 percent), while St. Paul and Miami report the least (both 7 percent).

TABLE 13.14
Denominational Identification

	% Orthodox	% Conservative	% Reform	% No preference/ other
Chicago 1982	6	35	39	20
Cleveland 1981	9	39	47	5
Los Angeles 1979	5	33	35	28
Miami 1982	11	35	24	30
Minneapolis 1981	5	53	32	10
New York 1981	13	36	28	23
Rochester 1980	12	36	42	10
St. Louis 1982	8	26	52	14
St. Paul 1981	7	55	27	11
Seattle 1979	15	30	46	9
NJPS 1971	9	56	24	11

RELIGION

Denominational Identification

Although many recent community surveys, including Miami, New York, Rochester, and Seattle, report a somewhat higher proportion of Orthodox Jews than the 1971 NJPS figure of 9 percent, this remains the smallest of denominations, with all communities reporting 15 percent or less considering themselves Orthodox.

The distribution of Conservative and Reform identifiers changes dramatically from community to community. For instance, St. Louis reports 26 percent Conservative and 52 percent Reform, while St. Paul reports almost the opposite: 55 percent Conservative and 27 percent Reform. These figures represent the extreme statistics; the remaining communities fall in between, with Conservative Jews ranging from 30 to 53 percent (the NJPS figure was 56 percent) and Reform Jews from 24 to 47 percent (NJPS was 24 percent). These comparisons suggest a falloff in Conservative and a rise in Reform identification.

The 1971 NJPS found 11 percent expressing no particular preference. This figure has grown in recent studies, particularly in New York (23 percent) and Miami (30 percent), where respondents describe themselves as "just Jews." "No preference" and "other" are not disaggregated in the table, although most studies indicate that the majority of those in this category are classified as "no preference."

Synagogue/Temple Membership

Membership in temples and synagogues varies widely among communities. The highest rate is in St. Paul, where 84 percent of the respondents report membership, followed by Minneapolis (79 percent),

TABLE 13.15
Synagogue/Temple Membership

	% Belonging
Chicago 1982	44
Cleveland 1981	61
Los Angeles 1979	26
Miami 1982	38
Minneapolis 1981	79
Nashville 1982	78
New York 1981	41
Rochester 1980	68
St. Louis 1982	66
St. Paul 1981	84
San Diego 1979	49
Seattle 1979	75
NJPS 1971	47

Nashville (78 percent), and Seattle (75 percent). At the low end are the larger cities: Los Angeles reports only 26 percent, Miami reports 38 percent membership, New York reports 41 percent, and Chicago reports 44 percent. Remaining communities have mainly around 60 to 70 percent membership. This compares to the NJPS 1971 proportion of 47 percent membership nationwide.

Religious Service Attendance

Frequent attendance at religious services is uncommon, with only 14 percent (St. Louis) to 21 percent (New York) attending often. "Occasional" service attendance varies widely among communities, partly because of the different definitions of the term, particularly in St. Louis where a high of 38 percent is reported. Other communities vary from a low of 9 percent in Rochester to a range of 22 to 30 percent who attend occasionaly in all other communities. Approximately one-half of all respondents are included when occasional and frequent attendance are combined.

The oft-cited phenomenon of "three-day Jews" is only partly borne out by statistics of 27 percent (New York) to 45 percent (Rochester) attending on high holidays only. All other communities report 30 percent attending on high holidays only. Finally, the range of those who never attend is 18 percent (St. Louis) to 30 percent (New York).

Ritual Observances

Many rituals are widely practiced. The most commonly reported is the ritual of Passover Seders, with 85 to 95 percent of all homes involved. Chanukah candles are also very common, with 75 to 86 percent observance in all communities. Another frequent observance is lighting of Sabbath candles ranging from 39 percent (New York) to 65 percent (Rochester). Finally, a

TABLE 13.16
Religious Service Attendance[a]

	% Never	% High holidays only	% Occasionally	% Often
Miami 1982	24	30	29	17
New York 1981	30	27	22	21
Rochester 1980	29	45	9	17
St. Louis[b] 1982	18	30	38	14
Seattle[c] 1979	20	30	30	20

[a] Categories as designated, except as follows:
For Miami, occasionally = several times per year; often = more than one per month or more.
For New York, often = more than once per month.
For Rochester, occasionally = less than once per month, but more than high holidays; often = more than once per month.

[b] Figures approximate; multiple answers were given to nine different response choices and have been roughly divided into the four categories as shown.

[c] Figures approximate; taken from general statements in text.

TABLE 13.17
Ritual Observances

	Kashrut					
	2 sets of dishes	Kosher meats	Sabbath candles	Passover Seder	Chanukah candles	Mezuzah
Chicago[a] 1982	11	--	--	85	75	61
Miami 1982	24	45	51	89	77	81
New York 1981	26	36	39	87	78	66
Rochester 1980	34		64	95	86	79
St. Louis 1982	17	--	47	58/79[b]	75	76
Seattle 1979	21		63	90	86	--
NJPS 1971	28		--	--	--	--

[a] Anyone in household.

[b] Seder in home/Seder in or out of home.

high percentage of Jewish homes have mezuzahs on the door between 61 percent (Chicago) and 81 percent (Miami).

Kashrut is observed in a considerable number of homes, although less than other rituals. Seattle and Rochester reported 21 percent and 34 percent general Kashrut observance respectively. Of those communities that reported practices more specifically, between 11 percent (Chicago) and 26 percent (New York) have two sets of dishes and between 36 percent (New York) and 45 percent (Miami) buy only kosher meat.

COMMUNITY INVOLVEMENT

Membership in JCC

Jewish Community Center membership was surveyed in only six communities, but the uniformity of responses suggests an accurate sampling. Excepting a low of 12 percent in the New York metropolitan area, the proportion of respondents who belong to their local JCC range from 23 percent in Minneapolis and Miami to 31 percent in Rochester, giving an average of almost one-third of community members.

Membership in Jewish Organizations

A sizable proportion of respondents belong to at least one Jewish organization, although the disparities in the wording for this question prohibit specific analysis. The three largest communities, Los Angeles (27 percent), New York (33 percent), and Chicago (37 percent), were the only ones surveyed in which only a minority of respondents belonged to any Jewish organizations. Of the remaining communities, membership ranged from 61 percent (Miami) and 62 percent (Cleveland) to 82 percent (Rochester).

TABLE 13.18
Membership in JCC

	% Belonging
Miami* 1982	23
Minneapolis 1981	23
New York 1981	12
Rochester 1980	31
St. Louis 1982	30
San Diego 1979	25

* Response based on participation/nonparticipation, rather than membership/nonmembership.

TABLE 13.19
Membership in Jewish Organizations

	% Belonging
Chicago[a] 1982	37
Cleveland 1981	62
Los Angeles 1979	27
Miami 1982	61
New York 1981	33
Rochester 1980	82
St. Louis[b] 1982	75

[a] Respondent and spouse.

[b] Includes synagogue and temple membership.

TABLE 13.20
Jewish Newspapers

	% Reading/receiving
Chicago 1982	33
Cleveland 1981	75
Los Angeles 1979	36
Minneapolis 1981	70
New York 1981	33
St. Louis 1982	83
San Diego 1979	54/33*

* Synagogue newsletters/"other Jewish Publications."

Jewish Newspapers

Readership of Jewish publications was only infrequently asked, and it was asked in very varied forms. Thus, the figures presented here should be viewed only as a rough indicator. Of those reporting, there is a low proportional distribution of Jewish newspapers in New York (33 percent), Chicago (33 percent), and Los Angeles (36 percent), and a high distribution in Minneapolis (70 percent), Cleveland (75 percent), and St. Louis (83 percent).

Jewish Charitable Contributions

American Jews claim they contribute to Jewish causes in significant proportions. Of the communities surveyed, the lowest proportions reporting

TABLE 13.21
Jewish Charitable Contributions[a]

	% Yes	% No	Dollar amounts % $0-$99	% $100-$499	% $500-$1,000	$1,000+
Chicago[b] 1982	69	31	56	23	8	13
Los Angeles[d] 1979	65	35	--	--	--	--
Miami[c] 1982	63	27	34	30	16	20
Minneapolis 1981	73	27	49	26	10	15
New York 1981	68	32	52	30	7	10
Rochester[d] 1980	79	21	--	--	--	--
St. Louis 1982	78	22	32	30	17	21
St. Paul 1981	75	25	51	24	8	17

a Refusals and "don't knows" excluded from figures.

b Without any corrections after validating JUF givers.

c Dollar amounts refer to contributions for all charitable contributions, both Jewish and nonsectarian.

d Dollar amounts not asked.

TABLE 13.22
Visited Israel

	% Who have visited Israel
Chicago 1982	30
Cleveland 1981	38
Miami 1982	45
Nashville 1980	41
New York 1981	37
Rochester 1980	28
St. Louis 1982	27
NJPS 1971	16

contributions were the larger communities, Chicago (69 percent), New York (68 percent), Miami (63 percent), and Los Angeles (65 percent), which are still sizable percentages. All the other communities reported between 73 and 79 percent, with Rochester reporting the highest proportion.

In dollar amounts, the largest portion of contributions fall in the "less than $100" range, from 32 percent in St. Louis to 56 percent in Chicago. In all cities about a quarter contributed $100-$499. For the larger givers, St. Louis leads both in the proportion of $500-$1,000 (17 percent) contributions and in $1,000+ contributions (21 percent).

Visited Israel

Varying numbers of respondents reported having visited Israel, but all communities polled much higher than the 1971 NJPS figure of 16 percent. The lows were St. Louis with 27 percent and Rochester with 28 percent, while Miami was high with 45 percent of its households including someone who had visited Israel. Most communities ranged between 37 percent and 45 percent.

SPECIAL ISSUES

Anti-Semitism (no table)

Anti-Semitism is still perceived by many American Jews to be a serious problem. Attitudes and experiences of this phenomenon are varied, and a comparative table was not feasible, but there are several statistics available that provide a general measurement of the perception of anti-Semitism today.

In St. Louis this issue was polled in several different ways. With respect to perceptions, approximately 37 percent saw little or no anti-Semitism in their community, while about 57 percent felt there was a moderate amount or a great deal, and 6 percent did not know. About 56 percent have personally experienced little or no anti-Semitism in their lifetimes, while 44 percent have experienced a moderate amount or a great deal. About 25 percent of the respondents had personally experienced anti-Semitism within the past twelve months. Finally respondents were asked, "In what ways does the anti-Semitism which you have perceived manifest itself?" They gave the following responses: social clubs, 60 percent; business, 54 percent; informal relations, 52 percent; employment, 49 percent; schools, 44 percent; politics, 42 percent; and housing, 32 percent.

Cleveland reported 19 percent having had direct experience of anti-Semitism, but this was from a sample of 18- to 29-year-olds. In Miami, 19 percent see anti-Semitism as extremely or fairly serious in the region, 40 percent see it as a moderate problem, and 37 percent see very little anti-Semitism or none at all in the community. Perceptions of anti-Semitism are highest in the regions of Miami with the most Jews, and it is viewed as a more serious problem as age increases.

Nashville's community survey polled respondents' attitudes toward anti-Semitism in the nation rather than just in the local community. Of the respondents, 70 percent agreed that anti-Semitism is increasing in the nation, 11 percent had no opinion on the subject, and 19 percent felt that it is not increasing. In Minneapolis, a special survey was conducted of unaffiliated households which had been located and included in the sample. Of 96 households in this category, 12 households (13 percent) reported incidents of anti-Semitism within the past year, ranging from work problems to sorority blackballing.

Intermarriage (no table)

There are statistics available for proportions of Jewish households which are intermarried in many of the communities surveyed, but these figures must be approached with caution. First, it is possible to measure this proportion in many different ways (e.g., does one include converted Jews or not; or if measuring as a percentage of respondents rather than households, does one count both members of a household as intermarried or only the originally Jewish partner?). Second, the survey methodologies are varied; communities that rely primarily on federation lists may omit many intermarried households (which are more likely to be unaffiliated) from the sample, while more extensive list-merging or Random Digit Dialing will include more of these households. Communities that rely on lists of distinctive Jewish surnames to find their samples will undercount women who intermarried.

With these limitations in mind, the following proportions of intermarried households are reported, from highest to lowest: Denver, 37 percent of all marriages involving one or two Jews; Seattle, 28 percent; Minneapolis, 25 percent; St. Paul, 21 percent; Cleveland, 18 percent; Chicago, 17 percent; St. Louis, 16 percent; New York, 10 percent; and Miami, 8 percent. As a point of comparison, the 1971 National Jewish Population Study reported that 9.2 percent of all marriages involving a Jew were intermarriages.

Many surveys also examined attitudes toward intermarriage. This issue is explored at length in the contemporary literature, so only a sampling of findings is presented here. Miami's survey asked, "What are your feelings about intermarriage?" and found only 9 percent expressing favorable feelings toward it, while 29 percent were neutral, and 62 percent had negative feelings. Negative feelings increased with the age of the respondent, and more Orthodox Jews and synagogue members had negative feelings than other Jews.

Analyzing intermarriage from a different viewpoint, Minneapolis and St. Paul both included sections in their survey instrument designed exclusively for intermarried respondents, in an attempt to locate the breadth and depth of problems faced by intermarried couples. Responses for the two cities were combined and presented in both surveys as results for the Twin Cities.

Perhaps the question of greatest concern is "In what faith will the children be raised?" In this survey, the following responses were obtained: Jewish, 56 percent; Unitarian, 14 percent; unknown, 10 percent; Catholic, 3 percent; Lutheran, 3 percent; no children, 3 percent; all other answers combined, 12 percent.

In response to questions about problems faced in social interaction as a result of the intermarriage, the majority faced very few problems in this regard. The greatest percentages reported where 10 percent who were sometimes or always excluded by Jewish acquaintances and 8 percent who were excluded by non-Jewish relatives.

More problems were reported concerning relations with synagogues or other Jewish organizations--23 percent reported uncomfortable feelings in synagogues, 4 percent in JCCs (but 22 percent had never joined), and 7 percent in organizations (with another 7 percent never having joined).

Finally, results were reported for singles' views on intermarriage: 76 percent said they preferred to marry someone who is Jewish, 3 percent preferred to marry a non-Jew, 18 percent said it doesn't matter, and 4 percent didn't know.

Bibliography

Allied Jewish Federation of Denver. 1981. The Denver Jewish Population Study. Denver: Allied Jewish Federation of Denver.

Geer, Lois. 1981. 1981 Population Study of the St. Paul Jewish Community. St. Paul: United Jewish Fund and Council.

______. 1981. The Jewish Community of Greater Minneapolis 1981 Population Study. Minneapolis: Minneapolis Federation for Jewish Service.

Hendrix, Nancy. 1982. A Demographic Study of the Jewish Community of Nashville and Middle Tennessee. Nashville: The Jewish Federation of Nashville and Middle Tennessee.

McCann, James and Debra Friedman. 1979. A Study of the Jewish Community in the Greater Seattle Area. Seattle: Jewish Federation of Greater Seattle.

Maynard, Betty J. 1974. The Dallas Jewish Community Study. Dallas: Jewish Federation of Greater Dallas.

Phillips, Bruce A. 1980. Los Angeles Jewish Community Survey Overview for Regional Planning. Los Angeles: Jewish Federation Council of Greater Los Angeles.

Policy Research Corporation. 1982. Chicago Jewish Population Study. Chicago: Jewish Federation of Metropolitan Chicago.

Population Research Committee. 1981. Survey of Cleveland's Jewish Population, 1981, Report No. 3. Cleveland: The Jewish Community Federation of Cleveland.

Regenstreif, Peter. 1981. The Jewish Population of Rochester, New York. Rochester: Jewish Community Federation of Rochester, Inc.

Ritterband, Paul and Steven M. Cohen. 1981. The 1981 Greater New York Jewish Population Survey. New York: Center Jewish Studies, Graduate School and University Center of the City University of New York.

Rosen, Donna B. and Associates. 1980. 1979 Long-Range Planning Report: Studies of the Jewish Communities in the San Diego County and the North City Area of San Diego. San Diego: United Jewish Federation of San Diego.

Sheskin, Ira M. 1982. Population Study of the Greater Miami Jewish Community. Miami: The Greater Miami Jewish Federation.

Tobin, Gary A. 1982. A Demographic and Attitudinal Study of the Jewish Community of St. Louis. St. Louis: The Jewish Federation of St. Louis.

14
An Annotated Inventory of Questions for Local Jewish Population Studies

Steven M. Cohen

Researchers and planners embarking upon the design of a questionnaire for a local Jewish population study need to address several issues. First, they need to decide upon the areas to be investigated and, as a corollary, the amount of interview time and space to devote to each area. Second, they need to develop the exact wording of the questions that will constitute the instrument.

This Annotated Inventory aims, among other things, to facilitate these tasks. The illustrative questionnaire is actually in large measure a composite of instruments from several recent Jewish population studies conducted in the United States. (A few questions appear here for the first time. These are largely extensions of previously asked questions to new conceptual areas--e.g., ritual practice at age 25.) Since almost all such studies are being conducted via the telephone, this questionnaire is written for use by telephone interviewers. Those who will collect data in face-to-face interviews or mail-back questionnaires will need to make some minor adjustments.

In the last few years, social scientists have acquired a considerable amount of experience in the conduct of Jewish population studies. While there is certainly much more to learn, many of us now share a consensus as to which questions should be asked and how they should be phrased. Where it is possible, therefore, the Annotated Inventory, in addition to making the task of designing and writing a local Jewish population study questionnaire somewhat easier, also reflects that consensus. The model questionnaire benefited from consultation with several colleagues who have conducted Jewish population studies. In addition, almost all the questions were drawn from the recent major American Jewish population studies: New York (1981), Chicago (1981), Los Angeles (1980), St. Louis (1981), Phoenix (1983), Washington (1983), and two national surveys of American Jews (1981, 1983). Thus most of the question wordings have been previously tested. We hope the movement toward a consensus on questionnaire design will facilitate

----

This inventory draws upon questionnaires designed by several social scientists including, most substantially, Sergio DellaPergola (Hebrew University), Peter Friedman (Chicago), Bruce Phillips (Hebrew Union College, Los Angeles), Paul Ritterband (City University of New York), Gary Tobin (Brandeis University), and Eve Weinberg (Chicago). Daniel Elazar (Bar Ilan University) offered useful comments and suggestions.

comparability across local and national Jewish communities. Researchers adopting the question wordings contained herein will be able to examine their results in the light of other recently conducted studies and thereby understand both the distinctive and typical characteristics of their own research population.

I have marked each question according to a three-tiered estimate of relative essentiality. Some questions occur in almost every local Jewish community survey, suggesting that federations and researchers generally see these areas as "indispensable." Others are found in only some studies, or else they cover important topics which have however not yet worked their way into most community surveys. These may be called "desirable." Still others may have lower priority for planners and research scientists and may be regarded as "optional." "Indispensable" questions are marked with two asterisks next to the question number (**); "desirable" questions are marked by one asterisk next to the question number(*); and "optional" question numbers are unmarked. The entire questionnaire, if adopted in total, would require forty-five minutes to complete.

This Annotated Inventory of Questions can do no better than represent the thinking of researchers and planners as of a particular moment. Surely our thinking will advance even further as we accumulate more experience in conducting Jewish population studies. Nevertheless, we believe it is still helpful and useful to make available to a wider public of potential users the understandings we have gleaned from our work up to now, fully cognizant that developments will undoubtedly modify those understandings in the years to come.

**1. First, I would like to know how many people all together live in your household, including yourself?

Number of persons in household: ____

<u>IF RESPONDENT ONLY PERSON IN HOUSEHOLD, ENTER 01 IN BLANKS WITHOUT ASKING.</u>

**2. How many of them are Jewish?

Jewish persons in household: _____

**3. I would like to find out a little about (you/each member of your household).

(First, let me ask about you.) You are (male/female), right? CODE SEX IN COL. B ON LINE 1 IN ENUMERATION CHART.

And, are you currently married, widowed, divorced, separated, or never married? CODE IN COL. C.

How old were you on your last birthday? ENTER IN COL. D.

<u>IF MORE THAN ONE PERSON IN HOUSEHOLD, CONTINUE</u>: Now, I would like to get that same information for (the other person/all the other people) in your household. (Let's start with the oldest.) ASK A-D FOR EACH PERSON IN HOUSEHOLD. ASK E ("Is person Jewish?") ONLY IF Q. 2 IS LESS THAN THE ANSWER TO Q. 1. IF Q. 2 = Q. 1, CODE "YES" IN COL. E FOR EACH WITHOUT ASKING.

A. How is (that/each) person related to you?	B. CODE SEX		C. ASK EACH PERSON OVER 16: Is (person) currently ...					D. How old was (person) on (his/her) last birthday?	E. CODE WITHOUT ASKING IF YOU KNOW: Is (person) Jewish?	
	M	F	married	widowed	divorced	separated	never married		Yes	No
1. RESPONDENT	1	2	1	2	3	4	5		1	2
2.	1	2	1	2	3	4	5		1	2
3.	1	2	1	2	3	4	5		1	2
4.	1	2	1	2	3	4	5		1	2
5.	1	2	1	2	3	4	5		1	2
6.	1	2	1	2	3	4	5		1	2

Total Lines Used in Enumeration Table Should = Answer To Q. #1.

Now I would like to ask you some questions about life in your neighborhood.

4. How satisfied would you say you are with your home or apartment? Would you say you are very satisfied, fairly satisfied, or not at all satisfied with your home or apartment?

Very satisfied	1
Fairly satisfied	2
Not at all satisfied	3

5. How satisfied are you with your neighborhood? Would you say you are very satisfied, fairly satisfied, or not at all satisfied?

Very satisfied	1
Fairly satisfied	2
Not at all satisfied	3

6. And how satisfied are you with safety in the streets in your neighborhood? Are you very, fairly, or not at all satisfied?

Very satisfied	1
Fairly satisfied	2
Not at all satisfied	3

7. And how about the cleanliness of the streets in your neighborhood? Are you very, fairly, or not at all satisfied?

Very satisfied	1
Fairly satisfied	2
Not at all satisfied	3

8. And, finally, what about the type of people in your neighborhood? Are you very, fairly, or not at all satisfied with them?

Very satisfied	1
Fairly satisfied	2
Not at all satisfied	3

9. Do you think that in three years from now your neighborhood will be better, worse, or about the same as it is now?

Better	1
Worse	2
About the same	3
Don't know	8
No answer	9

10. Where do you expect to be living three years from now--just your best estimate?

In the same house or apartment . . . . . 1 (GO TO Q. 13)
In a different place in the same neighborhood . . . . 2 (GO TO Q. 11)
In a different neighborhood within (CITY) . . 3 (ASK A)
In a different city or town outside the (CITY) area . . . . 4 (ASK B)
In a different country . . . . 5 (ASK B)
Don't know 8

A. IF DIFFERENT NEIGHBORHOOD: In which neighborhood would you be likely to live then? PROBE FOR NAME OF NEIGHBORHOOD.

____

B. IF DIFFERENT CITY, TOWN, OR COUNTRY: In which (city and state/foreign country) would you be likely to live then?

____

*11. Are you and your household actively looking for a new place to live?

Yes 1
No 2

**12. Do you have definite plans to move within the year?

Yes 1
No 2

*13. How many times have you moved during the past five years? ___

**14. Just before you moved to the neighborhood where you now live, did you live in another part of the (CITY) metropolitan area, or did you live outside the (CITY) area?

Another part of the (CITY) area . . 1 (ASK A)
Outside the (CITY) area . . . . . . 2 (ASK B)

A. IF ANOTHER PART OF (CITY) AREA: In what part of the (CITY) area did you live? Do you happen to remember the zip code of your old address?

NEIGHBORHOOD:____________________ZIP:________

B. IF OUTSIDE (CITY) AREA: In what city and state or country did you live just before you moved to the neighborhood where you live now? (If U.S.): Do you happen to remember the zip code of your old address?

CITY AND STATE (OR COUNTRY):____________ZIP:_____

*15. Is your home a single-family house, a duplex, a townhouse, an apartment, or something else?

Single-family house	1
Duplex	2
Townhouse	3
Apartment	4
Other	5

*16. What is your zip code? ___

*17. How long have you lived at your current residence? ___ years

*18. How long have you lived in your current neighborhood? ___ years

*19. Do you own or rent your (house/apartment)?

Own	1 (ASK A)
Rent	2 (ASK B)

A. IF OWNS: What are your monthly payments for interest and amortization on your mortgage?

$____.00

B. IF RENTS: What are your monthly payments for rent for your apartment?

$____.00

*20. When did you first move to the (CITY) area, or were you born here?

YEAR FIRST MOVED TO (CITY) AREA	19__
Born in (CITY) area	1 (GO TO Q. 22)

*21. Where were you born? RECORD VERBATIM; THEN CODE.

____

(CITY) (STATE OR COUNTRY)

(CITY) area	1
Same state	2
Other U.S. or Canada	3
Foreign country (ASK A):	
USSR, Russia	4
Other Europe	5
Israel	6
Other Middle East, No. Africa .	7
Other	8

A. IF FOREIGN COUNTRY: In what year did you first come to this country? 19__

ASK Q's 22 and 23 IF MARRIED; OTHERWISE GO TO Q. 24

*22. In what year did your (husband/wife) first move to the (CITY) area, or was (he/she) born here?

YEAR FIRST MOVED TO (CITY) AREA:. . 19___
Born in (CITY) area . . . . 1 (GO TO Q. 24)

*23. Where was (he/she) born? RECORD VERBATIM; THEN CODE.

____
(CITY) (STATE OR COUNTRY)

(CITY) area	1
Same state	2
Other U.S. or Canada	3
Foreign country (ASK A):	
USSR, Russia	4
Other Europe	5
Israel	6
Other Middle East, No. Africa . .	7
Other	8

A. IF FOREIGN COUNTRY: In what year did (he/she) first come to this country? 19___

*24. A. Where was your father born? RECORD VERBATIM; THEN CODE.

B. Where was your mother born? RECORD VERBATIM; THEN CODE.

FATHER: ______________ MOTHER: ______________

	Father	Mother
(CITY) area	1	1
Same state	2	2
Other U.S. or Canada	3	3
Foreign country (ASK A):		
USSR, Russia	4	4
Other Europe	5	5
Israel	6	6
Other Middle East, No. Africa	7	7
Other	8	8

IF FOREIGN COUNTRY: In what year(s) did they first come to this country? MOTHER: 19____ FATHER: 19____

25. IF MARRIED: And where were your (husband's/wife's) parents born?
FATHER: ________________ MOTHER: __________________

	Father	Mother
(CITY) area	1	1
Same state	2	2
Other U.S. or Canada	3	3
Foreign country (ASK A):		
USSR, Russia	4	4
Other Europe	5	5
Israel	6	6
Other Middle East, No. Africa .	7	7
Other	8	8

A. IF FOREIGN COUNTRY: In what year(s) did they first come to this country?
MOTHER: 19___ FATHER: 19___

**26. A. How many of your grandparents were born in the United States?

B. IF MARRIED: And how many of your (husband's/wife's) grandparents were born in the United States?

	Respondent	Spouse
None	0	0
One	1	1
Two	2	2
Three	3	3
Four	4	4
Don't know	8	8
No spouse	-	9

*27. Are both your parents living? (IF NO, ASK:) Which one is living?

Both living	1 (ASK A)
Father living	2 (ASK A)
Mother living	3 (ASK A)
Neither living	4 (GO TO Q. 28)

A. IF EITHER LIVING: How old (is/are) (he/she/they)?

FATHER: __________
MOTHER: __________

Do(es) (he/she/they) live in (CITY)?

Yes, both do	1
Yes, one does	2
No, neither does	3

(27. A. continued)

Do(es) (he/she/they) live in a nursing home or home for the aged?

Yes, both 1
Yes, father only 2
Yes, mother only 3
No, neither 4

During the past year did you provide any financial assistance to your (father/mother/parents) for rent, utility bills, medical bills, or any other purpose?

Yes 1
No 2

During the past year did you (IF MARRIED: or your husband/wife) regularly provide any personal assistance to your (father/mother/parents) with cooking, housecleaning, shopping, or anything else?

Yes 1
No 2

28. IF MARRIED: Are both your (husband's/wife's) parents living? (IF NO, ASK:) Which one is living?

Both living . . . . 1 (ASK A)
Father living . . . . 2 (ASK A)
Mother living . . . . 3 (ASK A)
Neither living . . . . 4 (GO TO Q. 29)

A. IF EITHER LIVING: How old (is/are) (he/she/they)?

FATHER: ____
MOTHER: ____

Do(es) (he/she/they) live in (CITY)?

Yes, both do 1
Yes, one does 2
No, neither does 3

Do(es) (he/she/they) live in a nursing home or home for the aged?

Yes, both 1
Yes, father only 2
Yes, mother only 3
No, neither 4

During the past year did you provide any financial assistance to (his/her) (father/mother/parents) for rent, utility bills, medical bills, or for any other purpose?

Yes 1
No 2

(28. A. continued)

During the past year, did you or your (husband/wife) regularly provide any personal assistance to (his/her) (father/mother/parents) with cooking, housecleaning, shopping, or anything else?

Yes 1
No 2

**29. Were (are) both your parents Jewish?

Yes . . . . 1 (GO TO Q. 30)
No . . . . 2 (ASK A)

A. IF NO: Which one was (is) not Jewish?

Father 1
Mother 2
Neither parent 3

**30. Were you brought up Jewish?

Yes . . . . 1 (GO TO Q. 31)
No . . . . 2 (ASK A & B)

A. IF NO: In what religion were you brought up, or weren't you brought up in any religion?

Protestant 1
Catholic 2
Other 3
No Religion 4

B. Did you formally convert to Judaism?

Yes 1
No 2

**31. IF MARRIED: Were (are) (both/either) of your (husband's/wife's) parents Jewish?

Yes . . . . 1 (GO TO Q. 32)
No . . . . 2 (ASK A)

A. IF NO: Which one was (is) not Jewish?

Father 1
Mother 2
Neither 3
Don't know 8

*32. IF MARRIED: Was your (husband/wife) brought up Jewish?

Yes	1 (GO TO Q. 33)
No	2 (ASK A)

A. IF NO: In what religion was (he/she) brought up, or wasn't (he/she) brought up in any religion?

None	1
Protestant	2
Catholic	3
Other (SPECIFY)	________
Don't know	8

IF SPOUSE JEWISH NOW (REFER TO Q. 3), ASK B; OTHERWISE ASK C.

B. IF SPOUSE JEWISH NOW: Did your (husband/wife) formally convert to Judaism?

Yes	1
No	2

C. IF SPOUSE NOT JEWISH NOW: What is your (husband's/wife's) religion now?

None	1
Protestant	2
Catholic	3
Other (SPECIFY)	________
Don't know	8

IF NEVER MARRIED, GO TO Q. 41.

*33. IF MARRIED: You said that you are currently married.

A. Were you ever widowed?

Yes	1
No	2

B. Were you ever divorced?

Yes	1
No	2

C. IF EVER WIDOWED OR DIVORCED: How many times you have been married including your (present/last) marriage? ________

*34. IF CURRENTLY OR PREVIOUSLY DIVORCED OR WIDOWED: Was your (former) (husband/wife) Jewish? (IF MORE THAN ONE FORMER SPOUSE, ASK ABOUT MOST RECENT.)

Yes 1
No 2

**35. IF EVER MARRIED: How old were you when you (first) married?

___ years old

36. IF MARRIED:

	Yes	No	DK
A. Was your (husband/wife) ever widowed?	1	2	7
B. Was your (husband/wife) ever divorced?	1	2	7

C. IF EVER WIDOWED OR DIVORCED: How many times has (he/she) been married including your present marriage? ___

D. IF SPOUSE PREVIOUSLY DIVORCED OR WIDOWED: Was your (husband's/wife's) former (wife/husband) Jewish? (IF MORE THAN ONE FORMER SPOUSE, ASK ABOUT MOST RECENT.)

Yes	No	DK
1	2	7

E. How old was your (husband/wife) when (he/she) (first) married? ___ years old

**37. How many babies have (you fathered/been born to you) all together, counting any who may not be living now (and any by a previous marriage)? ___

A. IF PARENT: How old were you when you had your first child? ___

38. IF MARRIED: And how many babies (has your wife had/has your husband fathered) all together, counting any who may not be living now (and any by a previous marriage)? ___

A. IF MARRIED AND SPOUSE IS A PARENT: How old was (he/she) when (he/she) had (his/her) first child? ___

*39. IF MALE RESPONDENT OR IF WOMAN OF THE HOUSE IS UNDER 45: How many (more) children do you expect to have (in addition to those you already have)? ___

Don't know 8

*40. IF EVER MARRIED: Do you have any living children or stepchildren who are away at school, live in their own household, are in the military, or live elsewhere for some other reason?

Yes . . . . 1 (ASK A)
No 2

A. IF YES: How many? ___
IF YES: (Does [he/she]/Do any of them) live in the (CITY) area?

Yes 1
No 2

IF YES: During the past year did you receive any financial assistance from (him/her/them) for rent, utility bills, medical bills, or for any other purpose?

Yes 1
No 2

IF YES: During the past year did you regularly receive any personal assistance from (him/her/them) with cooking, house-cleaning, shopping, or anything else?

Yes 1
No 2

Now I'd like to ask you a few questions about your Jewish practices and beliefs.

*41. Do you think of yourself as Orthodox, Conservative, Reform, or something else?

A. IF MARRIED AND SPOUSE JEWISH: And does your (husband/wife) think of (him/herself) as Orthodox, Conservative, Reform, or something else?

B. IF 30 OR OLDER: When you were 25, what did you think of yourself as--Orthodox, Conservative, Reform, or something else?

	Respondent	Spouse	Age 25
Orthodox	1	1	1
Conservative	2	2	2
Reform	3	3	3
Something else	4	4	4
Don't know	8	8	8
Spouse not Jewish . . .	-	9	-

*42. Do you or does anyone in your household belong to a synagogue or temple?

Yes	1 (ASK A)
No	2 (ASK B)

A. IF YES: Is it Orthodox, Conservative, Reform, or something else?

Orthodox	1
Conservative	2
Reform	3
Reconstructionist	4
Havurah	5
Other	6
Don't know	8

IF YES: When did you first join this synagogue? 19 ___

B. IF NO: Have you ever been a member of a synagogue or temple?

Yes	1 (ASK B-1)
No	2

B-1. IF YES, WAS MEMBER: How old were you when you were last a member of a synagogue or temple? ___

*43. How often do you (IF MARRIED, ALSO ASK: does your husband/wife) attend synagogue or temple services? (READ CHOICES.)

A. IF 30 OR OLDER: When you were 25, how often did you attend synagogue or temple services?

	Respondent	Spouse	Age 25
Never	1	1	1
Only for weddings or Bar/Bat Mitzvahs	2	2	2
High Holidays (Rosh Hashana or Yom Kippur	3	3	3
High Holidays & a few other times a year	4	4	4
About once a month	5	5	5
Two or three times a month. .	6	6	6
Weekly	7	7	7
More often than weekly . . .	8	8	8
No spouse	-	9	-

*44. Do you (IF MARRIED, ALSO ASK: or does your husband/wife) belong to these Jewish organizations? (READ CHOICES; IF MARRIED, SPECIFY RESPONDENT/SPOUSE)

	Respondent		Spouse		
	Yes	No	Yes	No	DK
A synagogue-related group such as a sisterhood or men's club	1	2	1	2	8
A Jewish Community Center or YMHA	1	2	1	2	8
An adult education class or text study circle . .	1	2	1	2	8
B'nai B'rith	1	2	1	2	8
Hadassah	1	2	1	2	8
Any other Zionist group . .	1	2	1	2	8
Any other Jewish group . .	1	2	1	2	8

A. IF YES TO ANY GROUPS LISTED: Would you regard yourself (your husband/wife) as an active member of (EACH GROUP LISTED)?

	Respondent		Spouse		
	Yes	No	Yes	No	DK
A synagogue-related group such as a sisterhood or men's club	1	2	1	2	8
A Jewish Community Center or YMHA	1	2	1	2	8
An adult education class or text study circle	1	2	1	2	8
B'nai B'rith	1	2	1	2	8
Hadassah	1	2	1	2	8
Any other Zionist group . .	1	2	1	2	8
Any other Jewish group . .	1	2	1	2	8

*45. Do you (IF MARRIED ALSO ASK: or does your husband/wife) belong to any clubs or organizations that are not Jewish?

	Respondent	Spouse
Yes	1	1
No	2	2
Don't know	8	8
No spouse	-	9

*46. During the past year have you (IF MARRIED ALSO ASK: has your husband/wife) done any kind of volunteer work, whether individually or as part of a group?

	Respondent	Spouse
Yes	1 (ASK A)	1 (ASK A)
No	2	2
Don't know	8	8
No spouse	-	9

A. IF YES: Was that for a Jewish organization or cause, or one that is not specifically Jewish?

	Respondent	Spouse
Jewish organization or cause . .	1	1
Not specifically Jewish	2	2
Both types	3	3
Don't know	8	8
No spouse	-	9

47. Which of the following newspapers or magazines do you regularly read?

	Yes	No
Local paper #1	1	2
Local paper #2 etc.	1	2
Jewish paper #1	1	2
Jewish paper #2	1	2
Jewish periodical #3 etc.	1	2
Jerusalem Post	1	2

*48. Thinking about your close friends, what proportion of them are Jewish--all, nearly all, most, about half, less than half, just a few, or none at all?

All	1
Nearly all	2
Most	3
About half	4
Less than half	5
Just a few	6
None at all	7
No close friends	8
D.K., refused	9

**49. Of your three closest friends, how many are Jewish? ___

*50. Of the people who live in your neighborhood, what proportion of them would you say are Jewish--nearly all, most, about half, less than half, just a few, or almost none?

Nearly all	1
Most	2
About half	3
Less than half	4
Just a few	5
Almost none	6
D.K., refused, not sure	7

51. If you had your choice, would you like to have more Jews in your neighborhood, fewer Jews in your neighborhood, or is it just about right now?

More	1
About the same	2
Fewer	3
Don't care/shouldn't matter	4
Don't know	8

*52. Have you ever been to Israel?

Yes	1 (ASK A)
No	2

A. IF YES:
How many times have you been there? ___
When (what year) were you last there? 19 ___

*53. Do you intend to visit Israel (again) soon?

Yes	1
No	2

*54. Have you ever seriously considered living in Israel?

Yes	1
No	2

*55. Do you have any family living in Israel?

Yes	1
No	2

*56. Do you have any personal friends living in Israel?

Yes	1
No	2

*57. In the last 12 months, have you contributed money to a political candidate because you believed he or she would support Israel?

Yes 1
No 2

*58. In the last 12 months, have you written to a newspaper or elected official in support of Israel?

Yes 1
No 2

*59. Do you often talk about Israel with friends and relatives?

Yes 1
No 2

*60. Do you pay special attention to articles about Israel when you read newspapers or magazines?

Yes 1
No 2

61. Are you registered to vote in the next election?

Yes 1
No 2

**62. Did you vote in the last presidential election, that is, in 198 ___ ?

Yes 1
No 2
No, too young 3
Don't know 8

**63. Do you usually think of yourself as a Democrat, Republican, or Independent?

Democrat 1
Republican 2
Independent 3
Other 4
Don't know 8

**64. Do you usually think of yourself as liberal, conservative, or moderate?

Liberal, left, radical 1
Moderate 2
Conservative 3
Don't know 8

65. In the last 12 months, how much, if anything, would you say you (IF MARRIED: and your husband/wife) donated to political candidates, causes, and parties?

Under $25	1
$25-$49	2
$50-$99	3
$100-$299	4
$300-$499	5
$500-$999	6
$1,000-$1,999	7
$2,000-$4,999	8
$5,000 and over	9

REFER TO HOUSEHOLD ENUMERATION (Q. 3) AND ASK Q. 66 FOR EACH CHILD IN HOUSEHOLD UNDER 18; IF NO CHILDREN UNDER 18 IN HOUSEHOLD, SKIP TO Q. 73.

Now I would like to ask some questions about children in the household under eighteen years of age.

You said you have ___ child(ren) under eighteen. Please tell me (his/her/their) first name(s). WRITE EACH CHILD'S NAME AND AGE IN SEPARATE COLUMN. ASK Q. 66 FOR EACH CHILD LISTED. IF MORE THAN 4 CHILDREN UNDER AGE 18, USE CONTINUATION SHEET FOR CHILD 5, ETC.

*66. In what religion is (CHILD) being raised?		Child 1	Child 2	Child 3	Child 4
	NAME:				
	AGE:				
	Jewish	1	1	1	1
	Protestant	2	2	2	2
	Catholic	3	3	3	3
	Other	4	4	4	4
	(SPECIFY)	______	______	______	______
	None	5	5	5	5

CONTINUE WITH Q. 67 FOR EACH CHILD 6-18.

*67. Is (CHILD) enrolled in a Jewish day school, Yeshiva, or a part-time religious school, or is (he/she) receiving any formal Jewish education?					
	Yes	1 (GO TO Q. 68)	1 (GO TO Q. 68)	1 (GO TO Q. 68)	1 (GO TO Q. 68)
	No	2 (GO TO Q. 69)	2 (GO TO Q. 69)	2 (GO TO Q. 69)	2 (GO TO Q. 69)

		Child 1	Child 2	Child 3	Child 4
*68.	In what kind of school is (CHILD) enrolled, or from whom is (CHILD) receiving Jewish education? CODE ALL THAT APPLY.				
	Sunday or other one-day-a-week school	1	1	1	1
	Weekday afternoon or afternoon and weekend school	2	2	2	2
	Day school or yeshiva	3	3	3	3
	Private tutor	4	4	4	4
	Parents/relatives . . .	5	5	5	5
	Other . . . . (SPECIFY)	6 ______	6 ______	6 ______	6 ______
		(NOW GO TO Q. 71)	(NOW GO TO Q. 71)	(NOW GO TO Q. 71)	(NOW GO TO Q. 71)
69.	Was (CHILD) ever enrolled in a Jewish day school or a religious school? Yes	1	1	1	1
	No	2	2	2	2
	(IF NO, GO TO Q. 71)				
70.	What kind of school was it? CODE ALL THAT APPLY.				
	Sunday or other one-day-a-week school	1	1	1	1
	Weekday afternoon or afternoon and weekend school	2	2	2	2
	Day school	3	3	3	3
	Private tutor	4	4	4	4
	Parents/relatives . . .	5	5	5	5
	Other . . . . (SPECIFY)	6 ______	6 ______	6 ______	6 ______

	Child 1	Child 2	Child 3	Child 4
71. Did (CHILD) go to a day or overnight camp this past summer?				
Yes, day camp	1	1	1	1
Yes, overnight camp . .	2	2	2	2
No, neither	3	3	3	3
(IF NO, GO TO Q. 73)				
72. Did the camp offer any Jewish content or programs?				
Yes	1	1	1	1
No	2	2	2	2
Don't know	7	7	7	7

*73. When you were growing up, did you have any formal Jewish education?

Yes . . . . 1 (ASK A)
No . . . . 2 (GO TO Q. 74)

IF YES:
A. Where or how did you get your formal Jewish education? READ ITEM (1) AND CODE YES OR NO; IF YES, ASK B. THEN ASK ITEMS (2)-(5) IN SAME WAY.

B. For how many years did you study there?

	Yes	No
(1) In Sunday or other one-day-a-week school?	1 ___ years	2
(2) In Hebrew school, Talmud Torah, Torah, or other part-time Hebrew Classes?	1 ___ years	2
(3) In yeshiva, day school, or other full-time Jewish school? . .	1 ___ years	2
(4) From a private tutor?	1 ___ years	2
(5) From someplace or someone else? .	1 ___ years	2

IF YES: Who was that? ____________________

<u>IF MARRIED AND SPOUSE JEWISH, CONTINUE WITH Q. 74.</u>
<u>IF MARRIED AND SPOUSE NOT JEWISH, GO TO Q. 75.</u>

**74. How about your (husband/wife), did (he/she) have any formal Jewish education when (he/she) was growing up?

Yes	1 (ASK A)
No	2 (GO TO Q. 75)
Don't know	7 (GO TO Q. 75)

<u>IF YES</u>:
A. Where or how did (he/she) get (his/her) formal Jewish education? READ ITEM (1) AND CODE YES OR NO; IF YES, ASK B. THEN ASK ITEMS (2)-(5) IN SAME WAY.

B. For how many years did (he/she) study there?

	Yes	No
(1) In Sunday or other one-day-a-week school?	1 ___ years	2
(2) In Hebrew school, Talmud Torah, or other part-time Hebrew classes?	1 ___ years	2
(3) In yeshiva, day school, or or other full-time Jewish school?	1 ___ years	2
(4) From a private tutor?	1 ___ years	2
(5) From someplace or someone else?	1 ___ years	2

<u>IF YES</u>: Who was that? ________________

75. Which of the following Jewish ceremonial objects do you have in your home?

	Yes	No
A haggadah for Passover	1	2
A yarmulke or kippah	1	2
A menorah for Chanukah	1	2
Candlesticks for the Sabbath . . .	1	2
A siddur or Jewish prayer book . . .	1	2
A Hebrew Bible	1	2
A kiddush cup	1	2

		Yes	No
*76.	Last Passover, did you have a Seder in your home or attend one somewhere else?	1	2
*77.	Last Chanukah, did someone in your household light Chanukah candles?	1	2
*78.	Did you fast this past Yom Kippur?	1	2
	IF MARRIED: Did your (husband/wife) fast this past Yom Kippur?	1	2
*79.	Do you have a mezuzah on the door?	1	2
*80.	Did someone in your household light candles this past Friday night?	1	2
*81.	Do you use separate dishes for meat and dairy products in your home?	1	2
*82.	Do you buy meat only from a kosher butcher?	1	2
*83.	Do you refrain from eating fish cooked in nonkosher restaurants?	1	2
*84.	Does someone in your household usually recite the kiddush Friday nights?	1	2
*85.	Do you refrain from turning lights on and off on the Sabbath?	1	2
*86.	Did you fast on the Fast of Esther this year?	1	2
	IF MARRIED: Did your (husband/wife) fast on the Fast of Esther this year?	1	2
*87.	Do you have a tree in your home Christmas time?	1	2

Now I would like to ask you about the practices of your parents when you were growing up in your childhood home.

*88.	Did your parents have a Passover Seder at home or attend one somewhere else?	1	2
*89.	Did someone in their household light Chanukah candles?	1	2
*90.	Did your father fast on Yom Kippur?	1	2
	Did your mother fast on Yom Kippur?	1	2
*91.	Did your parents have a mezuzah on the door?	1	2

		Yes	No
*92.	Did someone in your childhood household light candles Friday night?	1	2
*93.	Did your childhood family use separate dishes for meat and dairy products?	1	2
*94.	Did your parents buy meat only from a kosher butcher?	1	2
*95.	Did either of them refrain from eating fish cooked in a nonkosher restaurant?	1	2
*96.	Did someone in your childhood household usually recite the kiddush Friday nights?	1	2
*97.	Did either of your parents refrain from turning lights on and off on the Sabbath?	1	2
*98.	Did either of them fast on the Fast of Esther?	1	2
*99.	Did you ever have a tree in your childhood home Christmas time?	1	2
*100.	Did your parents belong to a synagogue or temple at any time while you were growing up?	1	2

A. IF YES: Was it Orthodox, Conservative, Reform, or something else? (IF SEVERAL, ASK FOR DENOMINATION OF SYNAGOGUE/TEMPLE PARENTS BELONGED TO FOR GREATEST PERIOD OF TIME.)

Orthodox 1
Conservative 2
Reform 3
Reconstructionist 4
Other 5
Don't know 8

101. Was either your father or your mother a member of any Jewish clubs or organizations at any time when you were growing up?

IF YES: Which parent?

Father only 1
Mother only 2
Both parents 3
Neither parent 4
Don't know 8

102. Did your parents ever buy Israel Bonds or give a contribution to the local Jewish federation or UJA at any time when you were growing up?

Yes	1
No	2
Don't know	8

*103. Did your (father/mother) usually think of (himself/herself) as Orthodox, Conservative, Reform, something else, or not Jewish?

	Father	Mother
Orthodox	1	1
Conservative	2	2
Reform	3	3
Something else	4	4
Not Jewish	7	7
Don't know	8	8

104. Now I have a question about charitable giving. I will read the names of several different types of organizations and I would like you to tell me whether (you/your household) gave money to that type of organization in the past 12 months, that is since (MONTH, YEAR).

(IF VOLUNTEERED: DID NOT CONTRIBUTE TO ANY, CHECK BOX ___ AND GO TO Q. 105.)

		Yes	No	DK
a.	United Way	1	2	8
b.	Any hospitals, health agencies, or disease research funds	1	2	8
c.	Museums, art centers, or performing arts, such as symphony or opera	1	2	8
d.	Political organizations or election campaigns	1	2	8
e.	American colleges or universities	1	2	8
f.	UJA or (LOCAL JEWISH FEDERATION)	1	2	8
g.	Synagogue or temple (dues or contributions)	1	2	8
h.	Any other local Jewish organization, agency, or school in the (CITY) area	1	2	8
i.	Any national Jewish organization or cause	1	2	8
j.	Israel Bonds	1	2	8
k.	Directly to universities, yeshivas, hospitals, or other causes in Israel	1	2	8
l.	Any other Jewish cause or organization I haven't mentioned	1	2	8
m.	Any other nonsectarian cause or organization I haven't mentioned	1	2	8

105. Have you given to UJA/(LOCAL JEWISH FEDERATION) in years prior to this one, that is, before (MONTH, YEAR)?

Yes	1	(ASK A)
No	2	
Don't know	8	

A. IF YES: In what year did you first give to UJA/(LOCAL JEWISH FEDERATION)? 19__

ASK Q's 106-110 ONLY IF RESPONDENT GAVE CHARITABLE CONTRIBUTIONS; OTHERWISE, SKIP TO Q. 111.

ASK Q. 106 ONLY IF RESPONDENT SAID HE/SHE GAVE TO ANY NONSECTARIAN CAUSES (a-e, m in Q. 104).

*106. Over the last 12 months, that is since (MONTH, YEAR), how much did (you/your household) give all together to various nonsectarian charities, and causes such as the United Way, health-related charities, artistic causes, American universities, and political causes? (READ CHOICES)

Under $25	1
$25-$49	2
$50-$99	3
$100-$299	4
$300-$499	5
$500-$999	6
$1,000-$1,999	7
$2,000-$4,999	8
$5,000 and over	9

ASK Q. 107 ONLY IF RESPONDENT SAID HE/SHE GAVE TO SYNAGOGUE OR TEMPLE (g in Q. 104).

*107. Over the last 12 months, that is since (MONTH, YEAR), how much did (you/your household) give all together to your synagogue or temple, including membership dues, building fund contributions, high holiday seats, tuition in the religious school, and other charitable contributions?

Under $25	1
$25-$49	2
$50-$99	3
$100-$299	4
$300-$499	5
$500-$999	6
$1,000-$1,999	7
$2,000-$4,999	8
$5,000 and over	9

ASK Q. 108 ONLY IF RESPONDENT HAS CHILDREN IN RELIGIOUS SCHOOL (SEE Q. 67 OR ASK RESPONDENT TO REMIND YOU IF HE/SHE HAS CHILDREN ATTENDING RELIGIOUS SCHOOL).

*108. Over the last 12 months, how much have you spent on tuition and related expenses and contributions to send your child(ren) to religious school?
(<u>IF RESPONDENT ANSWERED Q. 107</u>: If you already reported these expenditures in the previous answer we can skip this question and move on to the next one.)

Under $25	1
$25-$49	2
$50-$99	3
$100-$299	4
$300-$499	5
$500-$999	6
$1,000-$1,999	7
$2,000-$4,999	8
$5,000 and over	9

ASK Q. 109 ONLY IF RESPONDENT SAID HE/SHE GAVE TO UJA/FEDERATION (f in Q. 104).

*109. Over the last 12 months, that is since (MONTH, YEAR), how much did (you/your household) give to the UJA or (LOCAL JEWISH FEDERATION)?

Under $25	1
$25-$49	2
$50-$99	3
$100-$299	4
$300-$499	5
$500-$999	6
$1,000-$1,999	7
$2,000-$4,999	8
$5,000 and over	9

ASK Q. 110 ONLY IF RESPONDENT SAID HE/SHE GAVE TO JEWISH CAUSES OTHER THAN UJA/FEDERATION, SYNAGOGUE, TEMPLE, OR RELIGIOUS SCHOOL TUITION (h-l in Q. 104).

*110. Over the last 12 months, that is since (MONTH, YEAR), how much did (you/your household) give to Jewish charities other than the UJA, (LOCAL JEWISH FEDERATION), or those connected with your synagogue or temple or religious school tuition? These would include local or national Jewish agencies, direct contributions to various Israeli institutions, Israel Bonds, or other such Jewish charities.

Under $25	1
$25-$49	2
$50-$99	3
$100-$299	4
$300-$499	5
$500-$999	6
$1,000-$1,999	7
$2,000-$4,999	8
$5,000 and over	9

*111. In the past 12 months, did you receive any requests to contribute to (LOCAL JEWISH FEDERATION) whether or not you actually contributed?

Yes	1 (ASK A)
No	2
Don't know	8

A. IF YES: Were these requests by telephone, through the mail, by a one-on-one solicitation where someone you know personally asked you to contribute, at a fund-raising dinner or function, at a small meeting, or in some other way? CODE ALL THAT APPLY.

	Yes	No
Telephone	1	2
Mail	1	2
One-on-one	1	2
Dinner, function	1	2
Small meeting	1	2
Other	1	2

IF YES: During the past 12 months, were you asked to contribute to (LOCAL JEWISH FEDERATION) by ...

	Yes	No
a. friends, relatives, or neighbors?	1	2
b. people from your synagogue or temple?	1	2
c. someone you didn't know before he/she asked you to contribute?	1	2
d. people from where you (IF MARRIED: or where your husband/wife) work(s)?	1	2

Some of the things we are trying to find out in this survey are the needs for certain services that the Federation or other agencies sometimes offer in a community.

I am going to read you a list of such services. I would like you, first, to tell me if anyone in your household has used this service any time within the last three years, and then, tell me if you think anyone in the household will use these services within the next three years.

ASK RESPONDENT BOTH 112A AND 112B.

112A. Has anyone in your household used any services for the elderly in the last 3 years?

Yes	.... 1 (Q. 113A)
No	.... 2 (Q. 112B)
DK	.... 8 (Q. 112B)

112B. Will anyone in your household be using any services for the elderly in the next 3 years?

Yes	... 1 (Q. 113B)
No	... 2 (Q. 114A)
DK	... 8 (Q. 114A)

113A. Which services were used?

113B. Which services will be used?

	113A Yes	113A No	113A DK		113B Yes	113B No	113B DK
a. Housing for the elderly	1	2	8	....	1	2	8
b. Transportation for the elderly	1	2	8	....	1	2	8
c. Day care for the elderly	1	2	8	....	1	2	8
d. Nursing homes	1	2	8	....	1	2	8
e. Home health services for the elderly	1	2	8	....	1	2	8

ASK RESPONDENT BOTH 114A AND 114B.

114A. Has anyone in your household used services for the disabled like day care, transportation, respite care, or hospice care in the last 3 years?

Yes	... 1 (Q. 115A)
No	... 2 (Q. 114B)
DK	... 8 (Q. 114B)

114B. Will anyone be using these services in the next 3 years?

Yes	.. 1 (Q. 115B)
No	.. 2 (Q. 116A)
DK	.. 8 (Q. 116A)

115A. Which services were used?

115B. Which services will be used?

	115A Yes	115A No	115A DK		115B Yes	115B No	115B DK
a. Day care for a disabled person in the household	1	2	8	....	1	2	8
b. Permanent residential care for a disabled person in the household	1	2	8	....	1	2	8
c. Transportation for the disabled	1	2	8	....	1	2	8
d. Respite care	1	2	8	....	1	2	8
e. Hospice care	1	2	8	....	1	2	8

ASK RESPONDENT BOTH 116A AND 116B.

116A. Has anyone in your household used any services for children in the last 3 years?

Yes	...	1 (Q. 117A)
No	...	2 (Q. 116B)
DK	...	8 (Q. 116B)

116B. Will anyone be using services for children in the next 3 years?

Yes	..	1 (Q. 117B)
No	..	2 (Q. 118A)
DK	..	8 (Q. 118A)

117A. Which services were used?

117B. Which services will be used?

	117A Yes	117A No	117A DK		117B Yes	117B No	117B DK
a. Infant day care	1	2	8	....	1	2	8
b. Day care for pre-school children	1	2	8	....	1	2	8
c. Youth groups	1	2	8	....	1	2	8
d. Youth camps - day only	1	2	8	....	1	2	8
e. Youth camps - overnight	1	2	8	....	1	2	8
f. Programs for youths to visit Israel	1	2	8	....	1	2	8
g. Retreat programs for youths	1	2	8	....	1	2	8

ASK RESPONDENT BOTH 118A AND 118B.

118A. Has anyone used services for singles or single parents in the last 3 years?

Yes . . . 1 (Q. 119A)
No . . . 2 (Q. 118B)
DK . . . 8 (Q. 118B)

118B. Will anyone be using these services in the next 3 years?

Yes . . 1 (Q. 119B)
No . . 2 (Q. 120A)
DK . . 8 (Q. 120A)

119A. Which services were used?

119B. Which services will be used?

	Yes	No	DK		Yes	No	DK
a. Programs for singles	1	2	8	.....	1	2	8
b. Programs for single parents	1	2	8	.....	1	2	8

ASK RESPONDENT <u>BOTH</u> 120A AND 120B.

120A. Has anyone in your household used community services like Jewish or religious schools in the <u>last</u> 3 years?

Yes	...	1 (Q. 121A)
No	...	2 (Q. 120B)
DK	...	8 (Q. 120B)

120B. Will anyone in your household be using these services in the <u>next</u> 3 years?

Yes	..	1 (Q. 121B)
No	..	2 (Q. 122A)
DK	..	8 (Q. 122A)

121A. Which services were used?

121B. Which services will be used?

	Yes	No	DK		Yes	No	DK
a. Pre-school education	1	2	8	.....	1	2	8
b. A Reform day school	1	2	8	.....	1	2	8
c. An Orthodox day school	1	2	8	.....	1	2	8
d. A Conservative day school	1	2	8	.....	1	2	8
e. Jewish community day school - no denomination	1	2	8	.....	1	2	8
f. Transportation for afternoon Hebrew school	1	2	8	.....	1	2	8
g. Transportation for all-day religious school	1	2	8	.....	1	2	8

ASK RESPONDENT BOTH 122A AND 122B.

122A. Has anyone in your household used any of the following services in the last 3 years?

122B. Will anyone be using these services in the next 3 years?

	122A Yes	122A No	122A DK		122B Yes	122B No	122B DK
a. Adult education classes	1	2	8	. . . .	1	2	8
b. Cultural programs	1	2	8	. . . .	1	2	8
c. General recreational facilities	1	2	8	. . . .	1	2	8
d. Child adoption services	1	2	8	. . . .	1	2	8
e. Family, marital, parent-child, or individual counseling and care	1	2	8	. . . .	1	2	8
f. Programs for religiously intermarried couples	1	2	8	. . . .	1	2	8
g. Big brother/ big sister programs	1	2	8	. . . .	1	2	8
h. A loan fund for people to move to Israel	1	2	8	. . . .	1	2	8
i. Assistance for individuals or families with drug or alcohol abuse problems	1	2	8	. . . .	1	2	8

123. Has anyone in the household used vocational or employment services in the last 3 years for aptitude testing, job counseling, or to look for work?

Yes 1
No . . . . 2 (Q. 126)

124. Which member(s) of the household used this service?

HOUSEHOLD MEMBER: ______________________________

125. Specifically, what kind of services did (he/she) use?

____

____

____

126. Will anyone in the household be using vocational or employment services in the next 3 years?

Yes 1
No . . . . 2 (Q. 129)
Maybe 3

127. Which members of the household (will/may) be using this service?

HOUSEHOLD MEMBER: ____________________

128. What kind of service will (he/she) use?

____

____

____

Now I have just a few background questions, and then we'll be through.

**129. A. What is the highest grade or year you completed and got credit for in regular school or college?

B. IF MARRIED: What is the highest grade or year your (husband/wife) completed and got credit for in regular school or college?

	Respondent	Spouse
8th grade or less	01	01
Grades 9 to 11	02	02
High school graduate (12th grade) .	03	03
Some college	04	04
College graduate	05	05
Some graduate or professional school	06	06
Master's degree	07	07
Law degree (LLD, JD)	08	08
Medical degree (MD, DDS, DO) . . .	09	09
Other doctorate (PHD, DHL, DD) . .	10	10

*130. Are you currently working full time, part time, going to school, keeping house, or what? CIRCLE ONE CODE ONLY. IF MORE THAN ONE RESPONSE, GIVE PREFERENCE TO SMALLEST CODE NUMBER THAT APPLIES.

Working full time (35 hours or more)	1
Working part time (1 to 34 hours)	2
With a job, but not at work because of temporary illness, vacation, strike	3
Unemployed, laid off, looking for work	4
Retired	5
In school	6
Keeping house	7
Other	8

131. Do you have a physical, mental, or other health condition which has lasted for 6 months or more and which prevents you from working at a job or limits the kind or amount of work you can do at the job?

Yes	1
No	2

*132. IF WORKING, WITH A JOB, UNEMPLOYED, OR RETIRED:

A. What kind of work (do/did) you (normally) do? That is, what (is/was) your job called?
OCCUPATION:________________

B. What kind of place (do/did) you work for?
INDUSTRY:________________

C. IF NOT ALREADY ANSWERED, ASK: What (do/did) they (make/do)?

____

D. IF ALREADY ANSWERED, CODE WITHOUT ASKING: (Are/Were) you self-employed or (do/did) you work for someone else?

Self-employed	1
Someone else	2

E. What is the zip code of the place where you (work/worked last)? ______

*133. IF MARRIED: Is your (wife/husband) currently working full time, part time, going to school, keeping house, or what? CIRCLE ONE CODE ONLY. IF MORE THAN ONE RESPONSE, GIVE PREFERENCE TO SMALLEST CODE NUMBER THAT APPLIES.

Working full time (35 hours or more)	1
Working part time (1 to 34 hours)	2
With a job, but not at work because of temporary illness, vacation, strike	3
Unemployed, laid off, looking for work	4
Retired	5
In school	6
Keeping house	7
Other	8

134. IF MARRIED: Does your (husband/wife) have a physical, mental, or other health condition which has lasted for 6 months or more, and which prevents (him/her) from working at a job or limits the kind or amount of work (he/she) can do at the job?

Yes	1
No	2

*135. IF SPOUSE IS WORKING, WITH A JOB, UNEMPLOYED, OR RETIRED:

A. What kind of work (does/did) (he/she) (normally) do? That is, what (is/was) (his/her) job called?
OCCUPATION:____________________

B. What kind of place (does/did) (he/she) work for?
INDUSTRY:____________________

C. IF NOT ALREADY ANSWERED, ASK: What (do/did) they (make/do)?

____

D. IF ALREADY ANSWERED, CODE WITHOUT ASKING: (Is/Was) (he/she) self-employed or (does/did) (he/she) work for someone else?

Self-employed	1
Someone else	2

E. Do you happen to know the zip code of the place where (he/she) (works/worked last)? ______

*136. What was your approximate family income from all sources, before taxes in the past year?

Less than $5,000	01
$5,000-$9,999	02
$10,000-$14,999	03
$15,000-$19,999	04
$20,000-24,999	05
$25,000-$29,999	06
$30,000-$39,999	07
$40,000-$59,999	08
$60,000-$79,999	09
$80,000-$99,999	10
$100,000 or more	11

These last two questions are for scientific sampling purposes.

137. How many telephone numbers do you have in your household? I'm referring not to the number of telephone instruments in your home, but to the number of telephone numbers through which I could have reached you today. ___

138. Is your telephone number on which I called you an unlisted number? Is it listed just with information but not in the directory, or is it listed in the directory?

Listed	1
Listed with information only	2
Unlisted	3

Thank you very much, that concludes the interview. My supervisor may want to call you to verify that I conducted this interview, so may I have your name and phone number so that she may do so?

NAME:________________________________

PHONE:________________________________

Appendix

Numbers below refer to question numbers.

1, 2. These items facilitate the estimation of Jewish population (= number of households with Jews X mean number of Jews per household) and of non-Jewish population in Jewish households (= number of people in Jewish households - number of Jews in Jewish households).

3. The household enumeration chart is the simplest, most direct way to obtain:
   household structure and living arrangements;
   age and sex distributions;
   information on mixed marriage and its consequences for Jewish identification.

4-8. The neighborhood satisfaction items, though not absolutely essential, are nonthreatening, noninvasive, and reasonably interesting to the respondent. The measures tend to be correlated and any one instrument may not need all of them. They provide one leading indicator of neighborhood stability and turnover, although neighborhood satisfaction is only one determinant of migration intentions.

9. This measure of neighborhood optimism/pessimism is, interestingly, empirically quite distinctive from current satisfaction measures (Q's 4-8). One finds a fourfold typology (satisfied/dissatisfied versus optimistic/pessimistic) characterizing residents of different neighborhoods with corresponding implications for planning the construction of new community facilities.

10-19. These questions are useful for understanding residential characteristics, migration plans, and history, and who moves and where. They chart recent and prospective population flows. Interestingly, some neighborhoods import residents largely from outside the study area while others export residents to outside the study area. As a result, to obtain as true a picture of population movement as possible, one should ask both about migration history and migration plans. With respect to past and current address, the zip code is a very useful piece of information. It is easy to code and most people know not only their current zip code, but that of their previous address as well.

The question on monthly rent/mortgage costs is useful not only in its own right, but also as a predictor of income (in conjunction with other variables) for those respondents who refuse to answer the income question at the end of the questionnaire. The correlation between income and rent or between income and monthly mortgage costs is at least as strong as that between income and education. Five factors (age, residential neighborhood, education, employment, and housing costs) may explain over 50 percent of the variance in income.

20-26. These questions determine birthplace and generation American-born. They are obviously essential to the study of immigrant populations and of the differences between generations.

27-28. These questions are useful for planning services for the elderly.

29-32. These questions on religious upbringing and current affiliation of respondent and spouse are essential for understanding intermarriage and its consequences for Jewish identity. Not only do intermarriage rates vary dramatically by locale, but so do the patterns of religious resolution of intermarriages.

33-36. Questions on previous marriages are important for assessing the extent and consequences of marital disruption (divorce and widowhood). Current marital status alone yields little understanding of inter-cohort and gender differences in divorce and widowhood.

37-39. Questions on Jewish fertility pertain to a central feature of Jewish population growth or decline. Demographers concerned with projecting future Jewish population size see birthrates as commensurate with if not more important than mortality, migration, intermarriage, and assimilation. The questions here permit comparisons with data on Jews in other locales and on non-Jews in the United States and elsewhere.

40. These questions are useful not only for fertility research, but for planning for services for the elderly as well.

41. The question on denomination is probably the best single indicator of Jewish commitment. Previous research demonstrates substantial differences in several measures of Jewish identification between the denominations. Respondents tend to think of the denominations as shorthand labels for "more Jewish" or "less Jewish," rather than in terms of the institutional or theological concepts often utilized by rabbis, academicians, or communal leaders.

41B. Questions asking for recall information about Jewish identification at age 25 will assist in understanding the dynamics of Jewish identification, especially with respect to the crucial young adult population. Although recall responses are somewhat suspect, nevertheless, they can help us understand the extent to which repeatedly low levels of Jewish active expression among our adults (i.e., ritual performance, charitable giving, institutional affiliation, and in-group association) are a function of family life cycle stage or of birth cohort. If today's middle-aged respondents with relatively high current levels of Jewish participation recall much lower levels at age 25, we can more readily reason that today's young adults' relatively low levels of Jewish activity may not necessarily fall short of those manifest amongst their elders.

42. Self-explanatory.

43, 44. It is a good idea to ask about both respondent and spouse separately wherever there is good reason to expect a difference in Jewish identification between the two. Husbands and wives demonstrate somewhat different levels of synagogue attendance, organizational participation, and, in some cases, ritual performance.

45. This question helps to understand the extent to which Jewish affiliation is a function of affiliation generally. It also might help locate population segments that are generally affiliated, but for one reason or another underaffiliated with the Jewish community.

46. Volunteer services constitute both an untapped and heretofore under-researched resource. The growth in elderly, retired individuals in good health, in particular, suggests that increasing attention should be paid to utilizing volunteers in various capacities both for their well-being and for the contribution they can make to the wider community.

47. Newspaper and periodical reading questions are helpful for learning how to reach different population groups and for assessing the reach and influence of the major Jewish community organs.

48, 49. Those with many Jewish friends are, as one might expect, more active in other spheres of Jewish life than those with few such friends. Moreover, a large number of respondents in several studies reported having many Jewish friends despite low levels of Jewish activity in other areas.

50. Perceptions of the Jewish composition of one's neighborhood are fairly accurate, erring on the side of overestimating the Jewish density of the neighborhood.

51. The question of preference for more Jews in the neighborhood may well demonstrate that Jews living in areas of low Jewish density actually desire more Jewish associational involvement than is commonly believed.

52-60. Since the Six-Day War (1967), American Jewish attachment to and involvement with Israel has increased dramatically. To take one indicator --travel to Israel--the 1970-1971 National Jewish Population Study showed that about 16 percent of American Jews had visited Israel, while by the early 1980s the figure had climbed to between 30 percent and 38 percent on several local Jewish population studies. These questions measure the extent of involvement with Israel in ways which are readily understood by the respondent. Consistent with the model questionnaire's overall preference for behavioral rather than attitudinal measures of Jewish identity, these Israel-related questions emphasize the behavioral dimension of attachment to Israel.

61-65. In the last few years, in particular, the political dimension to Jewish identity has become increasingly important as growing numbers of Jews participate in the American political process out of a sense of Jewish commitment. These questions form the basis for understanding the nature of local Jewish political involvement and, indeed, many more questions in this area could be asked. Such questions are especially important to local community relations councils in their efforts to comprehend Jewish political inclinations and to represent them to local and national policy-makers and officeholders.

66. Religious identification of children is especially important for understanding the impact of religious intermarriage.

67-70. The enrollment of school-age children in various types of Jewish schooling has become a major topic of concern for both planners and researchers concerned with Jewish identity transmission.

71, 72. These questions are obviously quite useful for planners concerned with attendance at Jewish-sponsored camps; moreover, practitioners suggest that overnight camps with Jewish programming have an appreciable impact upon subsequent Jewish identity.

73, 74. Research on the impact of Jewish education demonstrates the importance of both its type and duration.

75. This question helps fill in the picture of the Jewish resources of the home and gives some idea as to the potential for influencing family Jewish identification behaviors.

76-99. The rituals referred to in these questions appear, in one form or another, on almost all Jewish population studies. They are essential for describing the Jewish character of the home. Following the practice of the National Jewish Population Study, the wording of these questions contains a specific time referent ("last Passover...") rather than vague terms ("do you usually"). Such wording should serve to sharpen the results by discouraging borderline practitioners from contributing to an overestimation of these activities.

83, 85, 86. These three items are useful for distinguishing the more traditional Orthodox from their more modern counterparts.

87. The Christmas tree question is especially interesting in light of increasing intermarriage.

88-103. Parents, obviously, constitute a major influence upon the Jewish identity of their children. Asking a full range of questions about the parental home permits two types of analyses. First, we can examine the extent and nature of intergenerational changes overall in the patterns of Jewish identification. Second, we can examine which types of parental activities influence various types of current Jewish identificational behavior on the part of their children, the respondents.

104. Respondents overreport socially approved behavior, such as philanthropic giving. Reports here can be corrected (downward) by asking for actual amounts donated to various types of charitites (Q's 105-110). These questions permit distinctions between actual (or likely) givers, would-be givers, and nongivers of various specific amounts to various types of charitable causes.

105-110. Previous studies' questionnaires, if they asked for amounts donated, asked about donations to concentric categories of charities (all causes, just Jewish, just UJA), a technique which generates difficulties and ambiguities in the analysis. Moreover, by excluding synagogue and school-related costs and contributions, they failed to obtain a complete picture of charitable giving. These questions try to overcome those shortcomings.

111. The mode of solicitation (whether the respondent was asked to give, how he or she was asked, and by whom) has a significant impact upon the incidence of campaign contributions and their amount. This information can assist in campaign planning and in understanding variations in campaign giving.

112-128. Few population studies have asked concise and comprehensive questions on service utilization. Although relatively little experience, let along consensus, obtains in this area, we thought it useful to include these questions drawn from the 1984 Washington, D.C. population study survey instrument, constructed by Gary A. Tobin, Westat Corp., and the Demographic Study Committee of the United Jewish Appeal Federation of Greater Washington, Inc. Some studies have also inquired as to whether respondents have used Jewish-sponsored services and whether, were they to use specific services, they would prefer Jewish sponsorship.

129, 130, 132, 133, 135, 136. These are fairly standard SES (socioeconomic status) questions. As noted earlier, although perhaps a third of the respondents may refuse to answer the income question, the two-thirds who do answer can provide the basis upon which to construct a prediction equation to estimate income for those who did not give their incomes. Earlier work showed that income can be fairly well estimated using education, employment (full-time/part-time; one/two earners), residential neighborhood, monthly rent or mortgage cost, and age.

131, 134. Useful for planning services for the disabled.

132E, 135E. Useful for campaign planning and for understanding residential choices and migration patterns.

137. Important for weighting surveys so as not to overrepresent households with multiple numbers.

138. Useful for understanding the applicability of a Distinctive Jewish Name count of households listed in the telephone directories to estimate the size and distribution of the Jewish population.

Index to Questions

Below are brief descriptions of the questions contained in the annotated inventory of questions. The numbers refer to the numbers of the questions.

1. Total household size
2. Jewish household size
3. Household enumeration (relationship to head, sex, marital status, age, Jewishness)
4. Home satisfaction
5. Neighborhood satisfaction
6. Safety satisfaction
7. Cleanliness satisfaction
8. People satisfaction
9. Neighborhood in 3 years
10. Living in 3 years
    - A. Neighborhood name
    - B. City or country
11. Actively looking to move
12. Plans to move
13. Moves during last 5 years
14. Last residence
    - A. Last zip in city
    - B. Last residence elsewhere
15. Type of home
16. Zip code
17. Duration at residence
18. Duration in neighborhood
19. Own/rent
    - A. Monthly mortgage
    - B. Monthly rent
20. Year first move to city
21. Birthplace
    - A. Year came to U.S.
22. Spouse year first move to city
23. Spouse birthplace

24A. Father's birthplace
24B. Mother's birthplace
25. Spouse's parents' birthplace
    - A. Year came to U.S.

26A. Grandparents U.S. born
26B. Spouse's grandparents U.S. born
27. Both parents living
    - A. Father/mother ages
      Father/mother live in city
      Father/mother in home for aged
      Give them money
      Give them help
28. Spouse's parents living
    - A. Spouse's father/mother ages
      Spouse's father/mother live in city
      Spouse's father/mother in home for aged
      Give them money
      Give them help
29. Both parents Jewish
    - A. Which not
30. Brought up Jewish
    - A. Which religion
    - B. Convert to Judaism
31. Spouse's both parents Jewish
    - A. Spouse which not
32. Spouse brought up Jewish
    - A. Spouse which religion
    - B. Spouse convert to Judaism
    - C. Spouse religion now

33A. Ever widowed
33B. Ever divorced
33C. Number of marriages
34. Former spouse Jewish
35. Age first married

36A. Spouse ever widowed
36B. Spouse ever divorced
36C. Spouse number of marriages
36D. Spouse's former spouse Jewish

36E. Spouse age first married
37. Babies had.
   A. Age at first child
38. Spouse babies had
   A. Spouse age at first child
39. Children expected
40. Children elsewhere
   A. Number
      Live in city
      Receive money
      Receive help
41. Denomination
   A. Spouse's denomination
   B. Age 25 denomination
42. Synagogue member
   A. Synagogue denomination
      Year first joined
   B. Ever synagogue member
      Year last synagogue member
43. Attend services
   Spouse attend services
   A. Age 25 attend services
44. Belong to Jewish organizations
   A. Active member
      Spouse active member
45. Belong to non-Jewish organizations
   Spouse belong to non-Jewish organizations
46. Done volunteer work
   Spouse done volunteer work
   A. Jewish cause volunteered
      Spouse Jewish cause volunteered
47. Newspapers read
48. Proportion friends Jewish
49. Number of friends Jewish out of 3
50. Proportion neighbors Jewish
51. Would like more Jewish neighbors
52. Ever been to Israel
   A. How many times
      When last
53. Intend to visit Israel
54. Ever considered living in Israel
55. Any family in Israel
56. Any friends in Israel
57. Gave money to pro-Israel candidate
58. Written in support of Israel
59. Often talk about Israel
60. Pay attention to Israel articles
61. Registered to vote
62. Voted in last election
63. Party identification
64. Political identification
65. Political contributions
66. Children's religion
67. Children in Jewish school
68. Children's type of Jewish school
69. Children ever in Jewish school
70. Children's last type Jewish school
71. Children in overnight camp
72. Children's camp Jewish
73. Jewish education--type and years
74. Spouse's Jewish education--type and years
75. Ceremonial objects at home
76. Attend Passover Seder
77. Light Chanukah candles
78. Fast Yom Kippur (respondent/spouse)
79. Mezuzah on door
80. Light Friday night candles
81. Separate meat and dairy dishes
82. Buy only from kosher butcher
83. No fish in nonkosher eateries
84. Recite kiddush Friday nights
85. No lights on/off on Sabbath
86. Fast on Fast of Esther (respondent/spouse)
87. Christmas tree
88. Parents attend Passover Seder

89. Parents light Chanukah candles
90. Father fast Yom Kippur
Mother fast Yom Kippur
91. Parents have mezuzah on door
92. Parents light Friday candles
93. Parents use separate dishes
94. Parents buy kosher meat only
95. Parents eat no fish out
96. Parents recite kiddush Friday
97. Parents not use lights Sabbath
98. Parents fast on Fast of Esther
99. Parents have Christmas tree
100. Parents belong to synagogue
A. Parent's synagogue denomination
101. Father/mother Jewish organizations
102. Father/mother buy Israel bonds
103. Father/mother denomination
104. Type of charities
105. Gave UJA/Federation before
106. Money to nonsectarian
107. Money to synagogue
108. Money to tuition
109. Money to UJA/Federation
110. Money to other Jewish
111. Asked to give to Federation
A. How asked
Who asked
112. Used services for elderly
113. Which elderly services
114. Used services for disabled
115. Which disabled services
116. Used services for children
117. Which children's services
118. Used services for singles
119. Which singles' services
120. Used community services
121. Which community services
122. Used miscellaneous services
123. Used vocational services
124. Who used vocational services
125. What kind vocational services
126. Will use vocational services
127. Who will use vocational services
128. What kind vocational services will be used
129. Education
Spouse's education
130. Work status
131. Disability
132A. Occupation
132B. Industry
132C. Employer information
132D. Self-employed
132E. Zip of employment
133. Spouse work status
134. Spouse disability
135A. Spouse occupation
135B. Spouse industry
135C. Employer information
135D. Spouse self-employed
135E. Spouse zip of employment
136. Income
137. Number of telephone numbers
138. Telephone listed

Contributors

STEVEN M. COHEN is Associate Professor of Sociology at Queens College and Senior Research Associate at the Center for Modern Jewish Studies, Brandeis University. He is the principal investigator (with Paul Ritterband) of the Greater New York Population Study sponsored by the Federation of Jewish Philanthropies of New York. For the past several years he has been conducting annual surveys of American Jewish public opinion for the American Jewish Committee. He has published articles on Jewish philanthropy, education, feminism, fertility, family, and intermarriage. Cohen is the author of American Modernity and Jewish Identity (1983).

PETER B. FRIEDMAN, Ph.D. is Assistant Executive Director of the Jewish Federation of Metropolitan Chicago, where he previously served as Director of Research and Planning. He supervised the Federation's Chicago Jewish Population Study, which was conducted in 1981-1982. Friedman has published articles on issues in Jewish community planning and decision-making in the United States.

CALVIN GOLDSCHEIDER is Professor of Demography and Sociology and Chair of the Department of Demography, The Hebrew University of Jerusalem. He is also Adjunct Professor of Sociology and Judaic Studies at Brown University and associated with Brown's Population Studies and Training Center. In recent years his research and publications have focused on the relationship between modernization and demographic changes, sociological and demographic aspects of ethnic minorities, and population issues in Israeli society. Books which he has authored or co-authored include Jewish Americans (with Sidney Goldstein, 1968), Population, Modernization and Social Structure (1971), The Ethnic Factor in Family Structure and Mobility (with Frances Kobrin, 1978), and The Population of Israel (with Dov Friedlander, 1979). A volume based on the analysis of the Boston community surveys will be published under the auspices of the Center for Modern Jewish Studies.

STEVEN HUBERMAN, Ph.D. is Co-Director of the Planning and Budgeting Department, Jewish Federation Council of Greater Los Angeles. He is also Adjunct Assistant Professor of Contemporary Jewish Life at the University of Judaism-Jewish Theological Seminary of America. Huberman has authored a series of reports on Jewish Los Angeles for the

Federation. He formerly served as Research Director of the Intermarriage and Conversion Project, Union of American Hebrew Congregations Northeast Council. The results of the project are summarized in his report entitled New Jews: The Dynamics of Religious Conversion (1979).

LESTER I. LEVIN is Director of Community Planning for the Council of Jewish Federations. He has served on the staff of both Jewish and non-sectarian agencies in the East, South and Midwest. Levin has written on a variety of topics ranging from the problems of low income elderly to social welfare manpower needs in the South. He is currently preparing a paper entitled "Low Income and Unemployed Jews 1980-1983."

JULIE A. LIPSMAN served, while an undergraduate at Washington University, as Research Assistant in the preparation of the "Compendium of Jewish Demographic Studies" that appears in this volume. She is currently a student at the Law School of New York University.

BRUCE A. PHILLIPS is Associate Professor of Jewish Communal Studies at the Hebrew Union College-Jewish Institute of Religion, Los Angeles. He has conducted Jewish population studies in Los Angeles, Denver, Milwaukee, Phoenix, and Las Vegas. His articles include "The Research Needs of the Local Jewish Community," in Marshall Sklare, ed., Understanding American Jewry (1982) and "The Service Delivery Information System: A Tool for Accountability" (with Bernard Dimsdale), Journal of Jewish Communal Service (Spring 1981), and he has presented papers on "Residential and Occupational Mobility Among Boston Jews" and on intermarriage at scholarly conferences.

PAUL RITTERBAND is Professor of Sociology and Jewish Studies at City College and Graduate Center, City University of New York. He has published articles on a variety of topics including ethnicity and education, fertility, migration, Jewish studies in American universities and Jewish philanthropy. He is author of Education, Employment and Migration (1978), a volume dealing with the migration of Israelis to the United States. He is also the editor of Modern Jewish Fertility (1981).

IRA ROSENWAIKE is Research Specialist at the Population Studies Center, University of Pennsylvania. He is author of Population History of New York City (1972) and A Demographic Portrait of American Jewry at the Time of the 1830 Census (forthcoming), as well as numerous demographic studies that have appeared in various journals. Currently he is working on a major study of the aged population, including the problem of differentials in mortality among urban ethnic groups.

MARSHALL SKLARE is Director of the Center for Modern Jewish Studies and Klutznick Family Professor of Contemporary Jewish Studies and Sociology at Brandeis University. He has devoted his scholarly career to the study of Jewish life. He is the author of Conservative Judaism: An American Religious Movement (first published in 1955), Jewish Identity on the Suburban Frontier (with Joseph Greenblum, 1967), and America's Jews (1971). He has edited two recent volumes for the Center for Modern Jewish Studies: Understanding American Jewry (1982) and American Jews: A Reader (1983).

GARY A. TOBIN is Associate Professor of Jewish Community Research and Planning at the Center for Modern Jewish Studies, Brandeis University. He previously was Assistant Professor in the Urban Studies Program, Washington University. He has served as research and planning consultant to Jewish and non-sectarian social welfare agencies, universities and industries throughout the United States. Tobin has published widely on issues in demography, housing, education, transportation, and urban development. He served as editor of The Changing Structure of the City: What Happened to the Urban Crisis (1979), and Social Planning and Human Service Delivery in the Voluntary Sector (forthcoming). His most recent writings of Jewish interest are "Jews on the Edge: A Study of Economically Disadvantaged Jews in the United States" (American Jewish Committee, 1983); and "Developing a Data Utilization System for Jewish Demographic Studies" (with Nancy Boguslaw), Journal of Jewish Communal Service (Winter, 1983).

JACOB B. UKELES is Executive Director for Community Services at the Federation of Jewish Philanthropies of New York. During the fiscal crisis in New York City he served as Executive Director of the Mayor's Management Advisory Board and later as Deputy Director of the Emergency Financial Control Board. From 1971 through 1975 Ukeles served as Professor and Chairman of the Graduate Department of Urban Affairs and Policy Analysis at the New School for Social Research. He previously taught city planning at Columbia University and the University of Pennsylvania. His most recent major publication is Doing More with Less: Turning Public Management Around (1982).

EVE WEINBERG is President of Policy Research Corporation in Chicago. She conducted the sampling, data collection, and data processing for the 1981 Chicago Jewish population study and (with Bruce Phillips) conducted the Milwaukee Jewish population study in 1983. Her publications on survey methodology include Manual of Procedures for Hiring and Training Interviewers (1970); Community Surveys with Local Talent: A Handbook (1971); and "Data Collection: Planning and Management" in Handbook of Survey Research, Peter H. Rossi, James D. Wright and Andy B. Anderson, editors (1983).

JONATHAN S. WOOCHER is Assistant Professor of Jewish Communal Service at Brandeis University. He has written on topics in contemporary Jewish life, Jewish communal affairs, Jewish political studies and modern Jewish thought. His articles include "The Kabbalah, Hasidism, and the Life of Unification," Journal of Psychology and Judaism (Fall, 1978); "The Politics of Scarcity: Jewish Communal Services in an Era of Resource Pressure," Journal of Jewish Communal Service (Spring, 1982); and "The American Jewish Polity in Transition, "Forum (Fall, Winter 1982).